Degrees

of Sight

BY KIMBERLY FLEEK

Dedication

For J and M

May you read this one day as you are older and draw closer to Jesus, then write your own stories as you walk with Him. I see God in you both in beautiful ways. I pray you see Him as well.

Table of Contents

Acknowledgements

It would be impossible to overestimate the contributions of others to the writing of this book. Truly, the words may be mine, but the heart and spirit of what has been written is the result of many who have poured into my life through the years. Deep gratitude is offered to so many individuals who have encouraged me along the way: those who have spiritually led me in teaching and ministry, friends who have encouraged me to pursue the dream God gave to me, and many individuals whom God has placed in my path who have challenged me to draw closer to Jesus. I am indebted to all of you.

I also have deep appreciation for all those who have followed along with me in the path God has led me on through the years, faithfully supporting me in prayers and finances on my many journeys. So many have read my updates from overseas and prayed with me along the way, and I can only hope that the blessings from doing so run as deeply as have mine in having you support me. I am richly blessed to be surrounded by such incredible people.

My thanks go to the many people who have encouraged me to turn these experiences into a book and affirmed to me that my writing may be worth reading. My sincere appreciation is given to my editor, Kim Kimbrell, for slogging through a very long manuscript and offering helpful and encouraging advice, and to my long-time friend Jason Chatraw for his patience and kindness in answering countless questions about navigating the writing and publishing world and helping me to get this in print.

My deepest gratitude goes to my family. Not only did they help me to edit this manuscript, offer suggestions, and proofread along the way, but they have always been amazingly supportive of everything I pursue in my life. They have tolerated me in my shortcomings, encouraged me in my strengths, been patient with my impatience, and loved me unconditionally. Each of you are God's great gifts to me, and I do not deserve you.

My ultimate thanks go to those whose lives have intertwined with mine in Indonesia- those mentioned in this book and the countless more who are not. I pray the Lord continues to reveal to each of you the depths of His love and heights of His glory as He writes your life stories into His.

With love for you all through the
love Jesus has showered upon me,

Kimberly

Preface

Two days ago, the 70-year-old man hobbled into the nondescript building, led by his patient and ever attentive son. The cataracts which completely whited out his eyes had rendered Abu incapable of seeing anything on his own, and 12 years of living in the dark had dampened his once joyful spirit. This previously strong and independent man had spent years working the fields and caring for his family, but his days now consisted of sitting on the floor of his humble wooden hut, watching the images that still played in his mind's eye. He was blind, and any hope of seeing again had long since vanished.

Today the bandage was slowly removed, and the watching crowd held its breath. Abu's head nodded backwards and shook a slight bit, and then he jumped as if startled. He saw the doctor who had performed his surgery standing in front of him. He *saw* her.

Abu turned his head a few degrees to the left, and He jumped again, astounded to see the chairs that sat directly in front of him. He had felt the objects with his hands as he was guided past them many times, but he had forgotten quite what they looked like. Turning the other direction, Abu shifted his gaze out the door of the tiny village clinic to the trees that were blowing in the tropical breeze. He shook his head from side to side then slowly nodded in recognition, almost as if seeing a long lost friend. How green the leaves must look to his long darkened eyes!

Abu looked to his right, and there he came face to face with his son. How different did his child look after twelve years of time had aged him? The eyes were the same; the mouth was the same; those were the same cheeks that Abu had pinched a thousand times. The laugh lines were etched a little more deeply now, though, and the weathering of his skin was more noticeable. A few gray hairs had grown out amongst the dark brown strands that Abu had lovingly stroked so many times. His son smiled. Abu remembered that smile, having seen it every day in his mind and longed for many years to see it again with his eyes. He began to cry.

Abu could see.

CHAPTER ONE:
Praying for Vision

I was blind, and now I see. Actually, that is not true at all, but I wish it was. My vision was about 20/200 the last time I tested it, and were it not for my contact lenses I would fall over anything and everything in my path.

Spiritually, I am pretty blind as well. God opened my eyes to His mercy in Jesus and graciously drew me into a relationship with Him years ago, but I still need a lot of help along the way. There is so much that I still see from a human perspective, and I often stumble over obstacles of distraction, fear, and circumstantial worries. When I look through the eyes of God, though, these giants in my path suddenly seem much easier to avoid and largely insignificant. The prayer of my heart for many years has been that God will give me His eyes: to see Him in His truth, to see myself the way that He sees me, and to see the world the way that He does. Thus far I have seen but a glimpse of these things, but God is opening my eyes more day by day.

I am just a simple woman following an incredible God. There is nothing particularly special about me that led me to write this book, but the God I worship is marvelous. Over the years, as I have prayed to see the world through His eyes, He has quite literally allowed me to see that world. I have been blessed with amazing chances to travel and experience what His love is doing in many countries, and I delight every day to wake up and join the adventure.

My fascination with the world began at an early age. Even from the time I was a very small child, I collected dolls of girls from other nations, perhaps in a foreshadowing of things to come. For as long as I can remember, I have loved everything foreign: foreign foods, foreign films, foreign festivals, and foreign friends. I have always loved seeing God's creativity at work in the diversity of cultures that exist in the world. Soon after my journey with following Jesus began, I was captivated by the thought of all of these cultures worshiping Him. My heart began to beat to see people in every part of the world know about His incredible love, and I have been traveling the world ever since.

On one of my first overseas outreaches, I felt God was speaking to me about getting medical training. I had never wanted to be a doctor, but I did see how the practice of medicine would allow me to show love to people around the world in a tangible way. I am both obedient (sometimes) and somewhat impulsive, so off I went to medical school. Knowing that I was not likely to want to do cardiothoracic surgery and would continually be learning anyway, I chose to follow the abbreviated yet still comprehensive course of becoming a Physician Assistant.

During twenty eight months of training and several years of working, I continually asked God to send me to the poor of the world and to those who knew little about Jesus. I have since learned that you should be careful what you pray for because God just may answer. So one day when a major disaster (one of many that regularly occur) hit the country of Indonesia, I felt that God told me to go. Obedient and semi-impulsive yet again, I was soon on my way to the island nation to use my medical skills to bless the people there with the love of God.

I joined a small team composed of an American doctor and a few other individuals, and the adventure began. I expected that this team would work together for as long as I would be there (which at that point I knew would be at least two years), but within a matter of months they left. Thankfully, on my journey with God through the years, I had already learned to expect the unexpected. So I found myself without a team, and I immersed myself in working with Indonesians. I hired a staff to help in the medical work, and for two years I operated as a medical provider in a clinic that served thousands of people in the villages. After a year a few other foreigners joined my team again, and I became their team leader. God sent me to heal in villages far away, to listen to the hearts of neighbors nearby, and to develop relationships deeper than I ever could have imagined. He allowed me to love the people of Indonesia with passion, and He tested my strength, my character, and my faith to the limit.

I want to honor the people I loved there by writing some of their stories, but mostly I want to honor the God who is so patient and kind to reveal Himself to this selfish and slow to learn creature. I learned volumes in my time in Indonesia, and I think I will continue to learn from the experience for years to come. He used the time in Indonesia to refine my soul, sharpen my mind to His truth, sand the edges off of my rough character, and help me to understand more of who He truly is. It simply astounds me, though, how the more I seem to learn, the less I seem to know. Thankfully God's classroom does not run on our human timelines, and He does not grade me on a pass or fail basis. He is a patient teacher. So my journey of learning continues, and I continue with my longstanding prayer to be able to *see* God clearly and look at the world around me through His eyes. He is answering that prayer daily, but He is only restoring my sight by degrees.

We tend to think of life in absolutes: black and white, stop and go, sighted or blind. Ask any ophthalmologist, however, and he will tell you that vision is a complex process. It involves neurons and blood vessels, brain signals and lenses, liquids and degrees, angles and light--each of which must function correctly in order to allow a person to see clearly. With so many variables at play, calling someone sighted or blind is far too simplistic. Dilate a pupil and increase the amount of light that enters an eye, and an image suddenly looks much sharper and well defined. Change the angle of the lens of an eye or add a corneal wrinkle, and everything will appear farther away than it truly is. A clot in a single blood vessel that feeds the eye can create a distinctive spot of total blindness, while retinal degeneration produces tunnel vision. Cataracts blur vision and create halos of light, and near and farsightedness simply makes things difficult to distinguish.

Spiritually I am vulnerable to similar kinds of interferences in my vision of God. If there is a barrier to or breakdown in my relationship with Him--my source of life--I develop blind spots of distraction that keep me from seeing straight ahead to what is important.

If my mind is bent by other worldly influences, I do not easily recognize when dangers draw near. The deceptive, subtle shades of sin that threaten to veil my eyes may dampen my ability to discern what is destructive versus what is holy. Not actively praying for my "spiritual lenses" to be on every day leaves the world around me appearing dull, passionless and difficult to comprehend. Without the bright lighting and sharpening of His Word and Holy Spirit, I may miss entirely the good things that He wants to show me, or I may not see the obstacles in my path. Many are the times I have stumbled and tripped, looking with my human eyes, because I could not see clearly what was in front of me.

There is an intriguing phenomenon of "double blindness" in which a blinded individual, after receiving his sight through an operation, still cannot understand what he is seeing. He receives a degree of sight physically when the source of his blindness is removed, but his mind cannot process images with which it is unfamiliar. It must then be trained to *understand* what it is actually seeing, and so the complete restoration of his sight comes in very incremental degrees. I think that my own process of seeing God takes a similar course, for each new thing He reveals to me must be processed over a period of time before I can really understand it. He cannot open my eyes immediately to all of His glory, for my mind simply would not be able to comprehend it. Discernment comes little by little as God simultaneously reveals more and more of Himself to me and trains my mind to see what He is doing around me.

Through the years, God has brought His gentle scalpel to the scales on my eyes and allowed me to see, one degree after another, that His glory is indeed all around me--and, if I am following Jesus, *in* me. He is daily answering my prayers to see His glory, but I am slowly coming to understand that it does not just reveal itself in one way. In reality, I think it reveals itself in *every* way. It is my own blindness and inability to comprehend God that limits my seeing the fullness of His revelation. When I left for Indonesia, I had a lovely, romanticized hope that God's glory would be revealed in all kinds of "big, majestic, and marvelous" ways there. I was going overseas, after all, stepping out in faith and expectant to see God working in ways far beyond what I had seen in my life to that point. The traffic, overtime and oatmeal of American life had grown way too mundane.

God definitely did move in hearts, lives, communities, and miracles in Indonesia. I have multitudes of wonderful stories to share about what I thought were "big, majestic and marvelous" moments, and I would not trade those experiences for anything. I loved them. I loved being a part of those moments, and I rejoiced in seeing lives changed in the very undeniable glory of God's presence. The funny thing about it, though, is that those experiences truly were but moments--precious heartbeats in which I felt I captured a piece of heaven. Practically speaking, such moments were rare. My hours, my days, my months and my years were largely filled with very normal daily life activities: cooking, shopping, talking, repairing things, working, communicating, cleaning--all the things that had seemed so mundane to me at home. What did God's glory have to do with that?

Everything.

God showed me His glory in the everyday moments in ways that to me were more miraculous than any healing or deliverance could ever be. I saw His glory in the faces of my patients, in the laughter of the fruit sellers in the market, and in the provision of friends. I saw His glory in the sunrise, but I also saw it in the sewer. I saw His glory when He miraculously started the car, and I saw it on the many days I spent in the repair shop. I saw His glory when I was celebrating the wedding of a friend, and I saw it when I was sitting on a dilapidated wooden floor with a grieving widow. I saw His glory in the radiant face of teammates as they prayed, and, ever so often, I would even sense His glory in myself. Those times came after deep battles in my soul, during which I clearly saw the depth of depravity, selfishness, pride, disbelief, and self-sufficiency that was firmly entrenched in my heart. God would then ever so gently remind me that He sees me as holy, for I am redeemed in Jesus. The deeper the darkness that He revealed in my soul, the more brightly the glory of this redemption working in me shone. Those times were not fun, but they were worth it.

In myriads of ways, God graciously allowed me to see His hand at work in Indonesia. There were also many things I wanted to see, believed in faith I would see, and prayed daily to see, and yet I never did. An example from a journal entry, written five months after my moving there, said: "God, I want to go to the home of my neighbor to share in reading the Book of Truth with her. I want to see a home where the husband chooses to honor his wife and not beat her for disobedience and a city where religious police do not watch every move that is made. I want to see the war weary children in the village laughing again and learning again how to be kids since they know the Kingdom of God belongs to them. I want to see a fellowship of local people who know the truth of Jesus and who are singing with joy to their Redeemer. But I don't see any of these things happening here right now, and I don't realistically see these happening anytime soon. And I get so discouraged."

The threat of discouragement is very real when I look at only what my human eyes can see. Why did God not allow me to see these things happening? For that matter, why does He not allow us to see *everything* in the world as clearly right now as He does? Believe me when I say this may be one of the more perplexing issues in the universe to me. Wouldn't it be easier if we just all saw how things would work out the way God does? What if we all saw how difficult issues would be solved, how trauma would cease, how wounds would be healed and relationships restored and His Kingdom built? Wouldn't it be nice if we saw all of this in an instant and thus would not worry so much? Why on earth does God make us wait, only revealing little bits and pieces of what He is doing while allowing us to walk around looking through lenses clouded by the pressures of the world? Being that I am not a theologian, my best answer is that He does not have to answer questions that begin "Why on earth?" because He is in heaven.

Somewhere along the way, with encouragement and gentle leading from the Holy Spirit on a regular basis, I remembered that I must make a conscious choice to walk by faith and not by sight. God is more than merciful to allow me to see what He does, and I believe He wants to increase my sight each day. It is a slow process, though, and in the meantime, I must actively choose to trust each day that He is working—even when my eyes cannot see that. I must daily pray for increased faith.

At times in Indonesia, I was able to do this. Many more, though, were the times I allowed my limited vision to cloud my belief in what God wanted to do. Yet in His consistent mercy, He patiently continued to answer the prayer of my heart. The entire process of my going, staying, serving, rejoicing and seeing God at work was an answer to that prayer, for it was one of His continually opening my eyes into His world: to see who He really is, to see myself the way He sees me, and to see people as He does. My time overseas has ended, but I am still walking along this path toward seeing Him clearly every day. I am glad to be on the journey.

CHAPTER Two:
Learning Curve

Seeing Through Indonesian Eyes

I will forever say that the fastest route to humility is to enter a culture not knowing anyone, to try to learn the language, and to try simply to survive. When a person cannot so much as buy a banana for herself since she has no idea the word for banana, her sense of self confidence takes a swift nose dive. When she realizes that even if she did know the word for banana, she doesn't know the words for the 5000 rupiah it costs (nor what 5000 rupiah even looks like), that nose dive becomes a solid crash. I have made the grave mistake several times of praying for God to give me humility, and this became lesson number one in Indonesia. It was also lesson number two, three, four, five, and on into the thousands.

Cultural adjustment is a steep learning curve filled with challenges, frustrations, miscommunication, small joys, "aha" moments, desperate moments, and a fair amount of laughter to guide along the way. Even after two years I barely approached the short end of that learning curve: the more I learned, the more I realized how little I knew after all! Who knew, for example, that I would learn that riding an elephant is very difficult and requires a lot of muscle strength not to fall off? Or that it is important to guard your elephant if you get off of it to hike at a waterfall? (Ours, incidentally, ran off).

Basics of everyday living such as shopping, cooking, communicating, and traveling all have to be observed, tried, and put into practice, and I was prepared upon arrival for simple living without a lot of comforts and conveniences. My expressed desire had always been to live as closely to the lifestyle of the Indonesian people as possible: eating local food, shopping in the same markets, taking public transportation, speaking the language, celebrating holidays, and trying to separate myself from my Western ideas as much as I was able. Since I therefore wanted to know absolutely everything, during the first few months of living in Indonesia my eyes were wide open. They were drinking in anything and everything I could see as my mind scrambled to keep up and file things away into my memory. I was praying desperately that I would see what was going on around me through local eyes instead of foreign lenses, and with that in mind, I plunged straight into whatever Indonesian experience I could find. This began, logically, with learning the language.

Knowing that I learn both by reading and by experience, I quickly sought out and found a tutor as well as a family that would host me for a few weeks when I arrived. The purpose of a home-stay was twofold: to learn language by being surrounded by others who spoke no English and to share in the daily life of a local family. The Agus family graciously took me into their home and lives for two weeks, and they patiently withstood all my questioning stares, pointing, and general confusion. They sat with me through my language lessons, tried to converse with me as much as possible, cleared out a room for me in their home, and introduced me to Indonesian food, life, and culture.

It was Bapak (general term of address for a man that also means father) Agus who first brought me "lonton," which later became my favorite Indonesian food. This sweet spirited man was always trying to do something to serve me in a very fatherly way, despite this being notably out of the norm for male culture there. Normally breakfast was leftovers that Ibu (general term of address for a woman that also means mother) had cooked the night before, and after a few days Bapak must have noticed I was having a difficult time choking down spicy fish and rice at six o'clock in the morning. Perhaps it was not the spice that bothered me as much as the eyeballs of the fish that were staring sleepily off the plate straight at me. Regardless of the reason for my troubles, one morning Bapak disappeared and came back with a small package, handily wrapped in a banana leaf, and set it down on the table for me. I said thank you but did not have enough vocabulary to ask what it was.

The pungent curry smell that greeted me when I opened the container was a welcome change from the chili flavored sauce of the normal breakfast. I recognized the hardboiled egg inside, as well as a stray vegetable here and there, and the white chewy chunks appeared to be potatoes. I gobbled this dish down with more vigor and glee than I usually expressed in my morning eating. Later I learned that what I first thought was potato was actually rice that had been steamed for ten hours, rolled into banana leaves, and then cut into bars, and I also learned that this particular dish was eaten more often for celebrations than for daily meals. Months down the road I returned to the Agus home for a holiday and actually learned how to cook it, but on that first day I simply partook and enjoyed while Bapak watched with a smile. The same dish mysteriously appeared on my breakfast plate for the next ten days, and I learned quickly from this experience that guests are to be honored and pleased. In local culture, generosity flowed freely in the homes of friends.

Bapak Agus also introduced me to the mosquito racquet. This handy little contraption, which resembles a badminton racquet, was his weapon of choice when he went in each evening to sweep out my guest room from invasive insect guests. The "snap, crackle, and pop" sounds that ensued while he was sweeping the air with the racquet reminded me of Rice Krispies. After this initial annihilation of a host of mosquitoes, Bapak would spray the repellent that he had specially purchased for me, wait about ten minutes, and then diligently sweep the room again. Doing the cleaning on my own was unheard of, and his simple kindnesses made me feel cared for in a very real way.

Ibu Agus is a quiet soul, rarely speaking unless spoken to, so our first few weeks together were not very conversational. She is full of joy, though, and she was rarely without a smile as she plunked down dish after dish after dish of fiery hot food onto the table each night. As I sat in the living area reviewing my vocabulary, having finished my formal language lesson for the evening, she would shyly beckon me over to the table. As a guest I was to eat first, before the family; there was no use arguing about this despite how awkward it made me feel. Ibu always wore a smile while she watched me eat, and watch she did. She would sit close by and observe every bite that entered my mouth (and my subsequent reaction), and it was initially intimidating to be watched that way. Since I quickly realized the rest of the family would not eat until I was finished, however, I tolerated the audience of one. I dutifully chose a few spoonfuls of various dishes, piled them onto my rice, and silently adjusted my taste buds to the unfamiliar yet flavorful food.

Bapak was always second to eat, after which Ibu, her son, her daughter and son-in-law, and the occasional other relative would sit together and eat in silence. Eating is a social occasion in most cultures, but Indonesians tend to enjoy the food first and socialize afterward. After I finished, I quickly retired to the other room with my dictionary and watched the family from the corner of my eye, learning more in those stolen moments of observation than I could have learned by reading a hundred books about local culture.

Language learning was slower than I would have preferred, but I learned to celebrate small victories. I remember vividly the first time I figured out how to say "I want to bathe" and stood up triumphantly to announce this to the whole family. They were less impressed than I was with my repetition of the simple phrase "Saya mau mandi," but in their graciousness they smiled, answered "silakhan" (as you please), and handed me a towel. They must have sensed my pride in this newfound vocabulary, for both Bapak and Ibu thereafter asked me upon arising, before dinner, after dinner, and before bed if I wanted to bathe, simply because I understood the phrase. It was not important that I had just bathed thirty minutes ago and quite obviously would answer no. The important thing to them was honoring me and my small step towards communication. I later saw this beautiful facet of the culture repeated when I began to test small phrases with neighbors and those in the marketplace, many of them exclaiming praises over my mastery of their language when I could actually only utter a few words.

I was simultaneously fascinated and frustrated by this new language. Some things about it were easy--the absence of much grammar, for example--but the pronunciation was difficult to me. Some of my best moments, commemorated in a letter written home, consisted of telling a woman "you need fake nutrition" instead of "you need dentures," and announcing that I had skin like a pig rather than skin that was pale. At one point I told my language tutor that I needed to be "picked up." I intended to refer to being picked up in a car but actually said I needed to be *physically* picked up--at which he laughed heartily and told me then I would become someone's possession. That was a different cultural problem entirely.

Another way I learned about the culture was by watching the Aguses do their "solat" (prayers) each evening. This was my first glimpse at how the religion of Islam factored into daily life. The 5:00 A.M. wakeup call issued from the mosque's loudspeaker left me no questions about the general directive to pray five times daily, but I first saw this in action in the Agus home. This family was not particularly devout, but the patterned, consistent times of prayer each day were never to be missed. One by one, I watched the family members file off to another room to pray, the women carrying their prayer coverings and the men carrying their mats. Bapak would occasionally kneel down in the room immediately next to the living area, still in my field of vision, and his was the first form I watched making the ritual postures that are prescribed to show reverence to Allah. He never spoke a word when he momentarily left a conversation to go and pray, nor would Ibu or the older children as they followed in turn. This prayer ritual was performed with little to no feeling or emotion as far as I could tell, yet it was an inalterable aspect of daily life that went on as consistently as eating and sleeping. No one ever expected me or asked me to pray, but neither did they excuse themselves when they left me to go and kneel. I always found it a bit odd that they would pay such distinct honor to a guest in other ways and then suddenly and inexplicably leave her alone in the midst of a conversation, but I suppose they did not see the need to explain something as normal to them as breathing.

I often wished the family would ask me to pray, try to discuss prayer, or at least try to explain something about it as they explained so many other things to me. I knew enough about their faith at this point to have a basic grasp of the subject of their prayers, but I wanted to know more. I was also very interested in their knowing it would be possible that I would want to pray with them. The Aguses, who were the first to teach me about local culture, were also the first ones to introduce me to some of the remarkably incorrect perceptions many Indonesians held about Westerners and/or Christians. To many of them these two people groups were synonymous, and in neither case was the connotation particularly positive. The Aguses held to the widespread belief that Christians do not pray; to say they seemed surprised when I tried to communicate to them that I actually did so would be an under-statement. I think Ibu walking into my room and actually seeing me pray was the only thing that helped them to believe this was possible. Of course in their minds, the manner in which I prayed--without set times or form--seemed irreverent and strange, and I could do little in those first few weeks to explain my heart. The presence of prayer in any form in my life, though, taught them something they had not previously known. I had suddenly opened their minds to the possibility that Christians believe we can communicate with God, and I was thankful for this small chance to teach those who were teaching me so much.

After those first few weeks, the Aguses became fixtures in my life. I would visit frequently, always enjoying their company, and as time passed it was delightful to be able to actually communicate with them. We celebrated holidays, enjoyed meals together, discussed local politics, religion, and world events, and shared many moments of laughter. We especially laughed a lot while remembering my confused but well intentioned attempts to communicate during those first few weeks in their home, but I would not have traded those moments for anything. They were priceless days of bonding with a family that adopted me as their own, and they helped me immensely to see the world around me through Indonesian eyes. Those few weeks helped me remove the Western lenses through which I viewed my surroundings, but I still had a long road of learning ahead.

Going Up the Curve

Learning how to adapt to a culture that is very, very foreign from my own was exciting and fun in the beginning, but it was also difficult and exhausting. For months I often found myself wondering why I could possibly be so tired every day. Obviously the 100 degree weather had something to do with it, I thought, especially with power cuts lasting for hours or even days, but there was something more than that. I came to recognize that trying to speak in a non-native language on a regular basis, even as my language skills became more functional, was also very mentally draining. At the end of a long day, even after living there for two years, I would find myself stumbling over words, forgetting things I had long known, and struggling to make a complete sentence! Of course not sleeping much had something to do with the tiredness I felt, at least until I adapted to having the prayer call issuing from the mosque wake me up at 5:00 A.M. every day. As a medical provider, though, I had always seemed to function well on sleep deprivation in the past. So what was making me so tired?

Perhaps it was the feeling of always being hyper-aware of my surroundings and somewhat "on guard." In my home culture, I had refuge in familiar places and people around whom I was totally comfortable. If I chose to, I could go about my daily business without being noticed very much, and understanding most things did not require extensive observation of others. Sometimes I lived in a state of blissful oblivion (perhaps to my detriment), but observation had never been one of my strong points. In Indonesia, however, I was forced into being an observer. I wanted to be in this role, for I strongly desired to understand everything I was seeing and to absorb it so I could fully adapt more quickly. In becoming the observer, however, I lost the ability to feel I that I could ever truly relax. Everywhere that I went, I was actively watching, actively listening, and actively thinking critically about the situation at hand. At the same time, everywhere I went I was actively *being* watched, listened to, and observed in critical ways. Hundreds of sets of wide-open eyes, curious questions, following footsteps, and interrupted personal space make it difficult not to feel a little edgy, or at least highly aware that every word and movement you make is impacting others and defining their opinion about you. In a place where Westerners were not held in high regard, I was eager to correct common misconceptions by being an example of morality and love. I was disturbed to think that any blunder I made could be coloring someone's definition of an entire culture and faith.

I finally came to accept that all of these factors were combining to make me fatigued, and I stopped feeling so guilty about it. It was harder to accept how little I seemed to accomplish in a day compared with in the life which I had lived at home. I have always been a "doer," and not accomplishing multiple things in a day was strange for me. On any given day in the US, I may have awoken at 5:00 A.M. to go for a jog before heading off to work. At lunch time I would run errands at the post office, the bank, and the store, and then I would make a phone call to check in with a family member. After work I may stop and see a friend, go to a church meeting, play on a recreational team, or participate in another social activity, then I often returned home to work on a project of some sort and catch up on emails until 11:00 P.M. In the midst of all of this, my head would always be spinning with thoughts of parties I wanted to plan, ministries I wanted to start, ways to take care of someone in need, people I needed to see, and perpetual dreaming of how and when I could be overseas. A friend often told me I could accomplish more in a given day than any human being he had ever known, and I must admit I felt a certain degree of pride in that.

God loves to humble us on such points of pride.

In order to accomplish things, a person has to be fairly self-sufficient. He or she needs to be able to think clearly, communicate clearly, make decisions that are at least informed (if not necessarily wise), and understand a situation and how to handle the other people involved in that situation. No man is an island, after all. All of these capabilities must work together in order for a human being to function independently, a truth I had never taken much time to analyze until I was suddenly stripped of all of them simultaneously. Here is an example.

One morning I awoke and thought to myself that it would be nice to have a banana that day. This was a simple desire, not asking too much as far as I knew, and it was a task I should easily have been able to handle alone. I could think fairly clearly about the fact that I wanted that banana, but I was a little more confused in thinking about how to actually go get it. To start with, I had no idea where bananas were sold. I would imagine they would be sold somewhere in town at a market (a logical idea), but then again I had no idea where the market was. Moving on, I could surmise the market would be in the middle of the city, but the problem arose that I did not know how to get to the city. Oh, yes, I knew there was a public transportation system called a "labi- labi" that theoretically went towards the center of the city, but I was not quite sure where it stopped so that I could get on board. More importantly I was not sure how to make it stop so I could get *off*. Without language skills, I could not tell the driver or ticket taker where I was going, and he may throw me off too soon if I did not pay enough anyway.

Assuming I could make the vehicle stop, find the market, and even find a banana stand, communication, or lack thereof, continued to be a problem. I did not know the word for banana, but of course the tried and true body language of pointing could work on my behalf, couldn't it? Well, of course, if I knew which banana to point to (aka which one I actually wanted to buy). Here is where the element of informed decision making came in: understanding the eight to ten different types of bananas that were actually in front of me. This was not as easy as just picking the bunch that looked the most yellow like I did in grocery stores at home. No, there were long bananas and short bananas, fat ones and skinny ones, mushy ones and firm ones, and as I later came to understand, each of these bananas had a different texture, taste, and use in cooking. Some of this I learned by unfortunate trial and error, until a kind friend or two guided me into understanding that "chicken bananas," the short ones, are sweet and good for baking, while the long and fat ones are actually bitter and better for frying or mixing with spices.

So my powers of educated decision making had been stripped both by my lack of knowledge about what was in front of me and my inability to ask for that valuable information. Even had I been able to get to the banana stand, understand the bananas, and tell the man selling them that I wanted to buy the banana, one more difficult element would come into play. Nothing is purchased in a market without bargaining, and part of bargaining has to do with the ability to read the person selling the product as well as to know he is reading you. It is about watching more for physical cues such as eye contact and body movements than listening for actual words. To get the banana I wanted and possibly even get a fair price on it, I needed to understand that the merchant had the best corner of the pavement and therefore tended to charge higher prices. I needed to understand that you should never agree to a price in less than three offers, and I needed to understand that when he turned away from me and spat on the ground it was not an indication for me to leave but rather to request a slightly higher price. I needed to understand, with deep and absolute conviction, that no matter how long I lived there I would always be paying a "white skin tax" on every purchase, giving my bananas about a ten percent higher price than any local would ever pay. I may need to understand that the woman fruit seller, as smiley as she was, consistently charged higher prices than the man did and was not interested in talking to me. I also needed to understand that this same man would lower his prices for every word I actually tried to speak to him in his own language. It may be important to understand that it had flooded recently in the villages and the banana crop was not doing very well, thus making the prices legitimately higher than I expected they would be. It was also helpful to understand that buying two kilos of snake fruit and a papaya could actually get me a bunch of bananas for free (I never did figure that out). So, if I indeed figured out where the market was that sold bananas, got on the labi-labi and made it stop in the right place, communicated verbally (or physically) well enough to get the bananas I wanted and know which banana that was, as well as understood the social and economic circumstances surrounding the purchase of that banana, I would have felt self-sufficient. The only remaining problem would be I would have no idea how to get home.

This is a silly and extreme example, but similar circumstances played out in slightly different ways on a very regular basis. These experiences stripped me succinctly of my self-sufficiency and ability to accomplish anything, and that ate at the very core of my identity (and my ego). I tried to comfort myself that at some point in life I would be able to do something on my own again and would not feel like a perpetual imbecile, and maybe I would actually be able to do something for someone else. I realized that it was amazingly difficult for me to be in such a place of dependency, and I always felt instead that I should be the one taking care of things, of people, and of situations. After all, wasn't that why God had brought me there? To take care of people? I often found myself wondering how I could take care of people, much less share the love of Jesus with them, if I could not even buy a banana.

God used those first few months of learning to temper my spirit and shave my ego in some beautiful ways. It was not always easy, nor always fun, but I can say that it was *good*. During those months, as I slowly learned more language, more about how to get around, and more about how to bargain and communicate, I did finally learn what days the bananas were actually better. More importantly, I learned to be quiet and observe. Without being able to take charge, I started to take notice. I stopped to look around, to see the things around me, and to see the people around me. I noticed the trash in the sewer (of course my nose noticed it more than my eyes), but I also started looking at the flowers I passed walking down to the labi-labi stop. Having nothing but time on the labi-labi ride to the market, I watched the faces of the people around me and how they interacted with each other. I watched the separation of men and women in the back of the truck and how the women were always the ones expected to move, and I noticed that a man would give up a seat for a child but not for a grown woman. I noticed that the scenario changed if the woman was elderly, a sign of the deeply rooted respect for age imbedded in the grain of the culture. I noticed the bright array of colors in the market as I trailed behind a friend, asking her everything I could about all the curious herbs and fruits that were unfamiliar to me, and I took note of the little children who were selling things with their parents and unable to attend school for lack of money. I observed how the merchants were generally more cordial and friendly after the evening time prayers, and I noted how they were never in a hurry. Uli, my new friend who had been hired as our team translator and coordinator right when I arrived, became my guide, and I watched everything she did like a hawk. I watched intently how she communicated with people as well as how they responded to her, and I learned quickly what mannerisms, facial expressions and body language could either win you a hearing with someone or turn him away.

Dependence on Others: Uli

Most significantly, I noticed that dependence on other people is not a bad thing. In fact, it can be very, very good, and those few months working with Uli cemented my relationship with her in ways that will last a lifetime. Although she remained, in many ways, my lifeline for the entirety of my time there, I soon became her boss. She always knew more than I did about the culture and how to get things done, but I also became her teacher as our medical work started and life wore on. She came to need me in a lot of ways: to help her understand medicine, to learn how to run the clinic, to learn how to run an organization, and eventually how to take over my job when I left. I needed her just to survive. One of the highest compliments I have ever been paid was Uli telling me upon my departure that she had learned a lot from me, for I always felt it to be quite the opposite. I may have had more head knowledge and training than she did, but never was I tempted to feel myself superior to or more intelligent than her. We needed each other, and without those first few months I could easily have missed that fact.

By allowing myself to be dependent-- almost completely dependent--on Uli, I saw how God had uniquely gifted her to be the anchor I needed, and I developed a deep and lasting respect and love for her. I was able to affirm and encourage so much in her later because I actually took time to look and notice her strong qualities then, and I saw her as God's vessel of provision for my life. I had to admit to her--well to be honest, she saw it in every way--my helplessness, and I found myself curiously pleased that she still seemed to like me anyway. She did not seem bothered at all by the fact that I could not speak, could not find things, and could not understand many situations. Nor did she care that I did not know when the holidays were, why the post office was closed, or that the hospitals had separate wards for rich and poor people. She just loved me anyway, and for some reason I found this surprising. Having been a leader in many aspects of my life, vulnerability with others has never come easily to me. Along with patting myself on the back about my accomplishments, I tend to think other people's opinions of me hinge largely on those accomplishments as well. Uli's love for me in my total ineptness during that season taught me otherwise, and my dependence on her for physical needs quickly swelled over into a deep and true friendship. More than her knowledge and language skills, more than her Indonesian skin and culture, I needed that friendship which was unconditional on my accomplishing anything, for it showed me the face of God. I know that I often speak of this kind of love and tell people I understand it, but to my own detriment I still have a tendency to believe that I am loveable because of what I can do. God, in His mercy, through those months of forced dependency, showed me again how His love is not hindered by my insufficiency. I think this is why He has created us for community with each other.

Continued Humility

If it is not enough to have to be totally dependent on others for living each day to bring humility, falling into sewage will do it. Motorbikes are the most common way to travel in Indonesia, outnumbering cars twenty to one on the streets. Their drivers are not always the most careful or observant people, highlighted by the fact that some of those aforementioned drivers are not more than ten years old. They zip around cars, cows, and other vehicles unconcerned for their surroundings, and despite there being a helmet law in place, it is rarely enforced. Motorbikes are the unfortunate cause of many accidents, disability, and deaths, but admittedly they are fun to drive. Gas for a bike is much cheaper than for a car, and for getting around the city they are practical and cost effective. It is not uncommon to see families of five or more piled onto one bike— perching on the seat, creatively tucking children onto the floorboard, and wearing babies in multiple slings. My agency owned a bike for team use, and after ten days in the country I decided it was time to learn how to drive.

I went out on a Friday afternoon about 12:30, a time when the streets are empty because men are in the mosque and women typically do not drive. My teammate explained the basic use of the vehicle to me--how to change the gears and use the brakes--and I started slowly and jerkily down the neighborhood street. Cautiously I pulled the handlebar toward me, revving the gas to increase speed after I rounded the corner, and within about five minutes I was zipping comfortably along the narrow winding roads. It did not seem all that different than riding a bike, really, I was thinking to myself as I neared the intersection. I was rather enjoying my newfound skill as I braked to look for vehicles which may be coming the other way.

The expansive brick wall across the road ran parallel to a large sewage ditch. When I began pulling out into this road and making a left hand turn, something startled me, and I reacted with my natural instinct to brake. The problem was that I had been riding ten speed bikes for much of my life, and on those bikes the brakes are on the handlebars. I think under stress we naturally revert back to what is known and familiar, so when startled I responded by pulling the handlebars back. My body told me I was braking while my mind, in slow motion, argued that I was actually gunning the gas on this newly learned vehicle. Unfortunately my mind won that argument, and instead of stopping I catapulted across the road and straight into the brick wall. Thankfully, due to our team helmet policy, my head cracking into that wall did less damage than it could have. A helmet does nothing, however, to protect a bruised ego. The bike went down underneath me, sinking into the sewage ditch, and about half of my body followed.

The poor woman who lived in the house behind the wall came out screaming, frantically trying to figure out what had happened. Was I ok? Who was I anyway? All I could do was try to smile at her and wave her away. I had mastered only the art of saying hello, goodbye, and counting to ten at that point, none of which were appropriate for the situation at hand. I was shaken, scratched, and smelly, but not injured, so I pulled myself up and out of the ditch and tried to assure her I was going to live. That moment goes into the record books as one of the greatest humility lessons of all time.

Ten minutes of yanking on the motorbike to try to dislodge it from the drain had no effect, and eventually I was forced to leave it and walk back home. My teammates, once assured that I was not truly injured, graciously used their best efforts to make me feel like this was a normal and everyday mistake. A few of them ran off to retrieve the bike from the ditch while another one tried to clean up my bloody chin. Soon I began to laugh about it and enjoy telling the story, and I started riding bikes again with other people within days. I confess, though, that other modes of local transport suddenly became very attractive as well! The experience was the low point of my learning curve—quite literally--but thankfully did not deter me from pressing onward. The colorful local culture was proving to be a fascinating classroom, and I wanted to explore it in all of its problems and all of its charm.

CHAPTER Three:
Returning to
Medical School

One of my biggest learning curves came in seeing the way the local medical system functioned. Before moving to Indonesia, I had traveled to fourteen different countries, and I had been exposed to third world medicine at its best and its worst. Family members taking care of patients--sleeping on the room floors and providing food and nursing care while the nurses busied themselves with other things--was not new to me. Doctors who had been poorly trained and had sadly little knowledge of some very basic disease processes were not new to me either, and the teacher inside of me hoped that I may be able to share some knowledge with them at some point. Every culture has its own distinctive beliefs about health and healing ingrained in folklore and the medical system itself, though, and these were some of the things I knew I must learn to understand.

"Masuk angin" is my personal favorite. "The wind has entered you," the saying goes, but how that wind actually manages to enter you I am not quite sure. Even before arriving in Indonesia, I had already heard of some form of this infamous wind entering a person and causing colds, fevers, and coughs in multiple worldwide locations. How many kids in the western world, for example, have been told by their mothers not to go outside in the rain because they would catch their death of cold? This is a similar idea. The wind in Indonesia must be a little more powerful than in the rest of the world, though, because it apparently can cause just about any and every symptom in the book.

Headaches are the result of wind entering your head, and of course stomach pain means the wind entered down into your intestinal tract. Coughs arise from that nasty wind in your lungs, and earaches are the obvious result of the wind resting in your ears. I was really fascinated to learn how this Indonesian wind could cause arthritic pain by entering into joints, and it could even cause pain in shoulders or knees that seemed suspiciously more like the result haven fallen off of ladders or other such accidents. The same poor wind was blamed as the culprit that caused high blood pressure, diabetes, cancer, and tuberculosis, not to mention difficulty breathing for chronic smokers. I tried enthusiastically to explain how chain smoking was actually working to knock the wind *out* of my patients, but they never believed me.

The wind was considered capable of causing many different symptoms in the folklore of other cultures, and the Indonesian wind was likewise widely discussed amongst the local people. Yet this community was the first place in which I ever saw the power of the wind also being affirmed by local medical providers. On the day my roommate brought me to see a friend of hers who had been sick for a month, the wind was not in my mind. Maria, this lovely mother of four, had already seen multiple physicians and stayed overnight in three hospitals, none of which had done anything to help her persistent nausea, diarrhea, and fever. She had lost fifteen pounds off of her already thin frame, had no appetite, and was having difficulty taking care of her children in her weakened state. Her diagnosis from not just one, but five doctors, had been that pesky wind, which had apparently decided it wanted to abide permanently in her body. It took me less than five minutes of looking at the lab results from her hospital visits to see that *typhoid causing bacteria* had also entered her body along with that wind, and none of the wind releasing medications she had been given were going to touch it. After a few days of taking the antibiotics I gave her, she was moving around and on her way to recovery, and I had learned a valuable lesson. It was not that doctors there had no medical knowledge at all; rather, if they were in doubt, they would often default to what the general population believed and wanted to hear. So the wind continued to enter people.

Other interesting beliefs I uncovered involved pineapple causing miscarriages, green vegetables making muscles hurt, and my personal favorite--cold water making you fat. Since most of them were harmless, I would tolerate these beliefs to various degrees when dealing with patients, and I would try to educate where necessary. I quickly learned that patients were accustomed to being given very large numbers of different medications, but generally they had no idea what any of them were designed to do. Patients often left a clinic without a diagnosis, yet they carried with them six or seven bags of small, often crushed and unlabeled pills (many of which I eventually surmised to be vitamins). The "less is more" theory did not go over well for most patients I saw, and I found myself fighting an uphill battle convincing them that they would actually get better with a few good medications rather than many that had no real use.

Ibu Karina, whom I now affectionately call my Indonesian grandmother, put me in my place on the very first week of our clinic services. I had just treated her chronic arthritic knee pain with simple Tylenol and Ibuprofen, as well as some vitamin B complex for general dietary deficiency. An hour later when she was still wandering around outside the clinic and excitedly chattering away to waiting patients, I asked Uli to find out why she seemed to be upset. Uli had difficulty controlling her smile when she came back to inform me that I was a stupid doctor, according to Karina, and must not have been at a very good school in America. Why did she think so? Well, I had given her only two medications and a hefty dose of explanation about her arthritis, but at the government clinic she usually received seven types of pills. The fact that she had never gotten any better with those seven medications had done little to diminish her trust in that system. Thankfully time and actual improvement in her condition was able to increase her trust in the way I practiced medicine!

Practically speaking I had to learn more about tropical illnesses not common in the West: malaria, dengue fever, parasites, and skin infections were frequent topics of my nighttime study. I learned to adjust dosing instructions around rice farming schedules and how to explain to patients when to take their medications according to their times of prayer. These were more consistent than meal times, after all, and so such directions produced more consistent results. I had to adjust to patient practices of only taking medication when they felt like it, regardless of whether or not it was needed, and I am not sure I ever crossed the educational hurdle of explaining the difference in chronic and acute disease. Many patients who had chronic diseases such as high blood pressure immediately stopped taking their medication when the numbers dropped, believing themselves to be cured, while just as many patients would request cough medicine to take for months on end for a cough that had long since stopped. Their reasoning? It was such good medicine that they assumed it would just be good to keep taking it so they would never cough again.

I learned about herbal village remedies, some of which seemed to be effective and some of which did not. One of the leaves that grew in the village, for example, was an amazing anticoagulant, and many a day I was greeted by patients who had stopped their own bleeding wounds by wrapping the leaf around their cut in some fashion. On one memorable day, a sweet man burst in the door asking to be seen, and I had difficulty controlling my laughter. He had two very long branches of this tree stuck up his nose, trying to stop a nosebleed, and the twigs hanging down to his chin resembled elephant tusks. Sure enough, the moment we pulled those leaves out he began to bleed again, and we had quite a time trying to get the bleeding to stop. My application of pressure, packing gauze, and even medication did nothing to stop his bleeding, so eventually I went out myself, grabbed some more leaves, and stuffed them back up his nose. The Western medical world still has a lot to learn from such simple, tried and true practices of using the natural resources God has given us for healing.

Some of the local practices were less effective. Mothers trying to burn the fever out their babies by wrapping them up in multiple layers of clothing, for example, could actually greatly slow their healing process. Likewise, the practice of not giving the child liquids because the cold may make him sick contributed frequently to dehydration, and the fear over immunizations causing death was a very real problem as well. Witch doctors and their practices figured heavily into the whole scenario, and patients would often visit the village midwife (who used herbal remedies), the witch doctor (who used a combination of herbs, chants and spirit practices) and the Western medical practitioner in the same week. I had to adjust to seeing many patients with broken bones that needed to be set going instead to the witch doctor to have them massaged, believing their bones would go back together that way. I also saw many patients who had chronic disability as a result.

One such experience disheartened me greatly. I was called to the home of an eighteen year old young man who had recently been in a motorbike accident and was suffering from a broken femur and a broken collarbone. His father had sent someone to the clinic to ask me to come, not to look at his leg but instead to look at his eye which had been red for a few days. The poor young man who lay on the bed in obvious pain told me that the accident had happened ten days ago, and he had been taken to the hospital. The doctor had immediately requested an operation, but his father had denied it and wanted to go to the "duku" (witch doctor) instead. This witch doctor had massaged the patient's broken leg and then tied it down to sand bags for traction, hoping that the weight would succeed in actually pulling the bones back together. The whole process had caused incredible swelling and pain, but his father was uninterested in my concerns that an operation was truly in order. I was asked to just take care of his eye (a simple allergy problem) and assured that the duku could take care of the rest. I never heard any more from the family but assume that the patient's leg would eventually have to be amputated.

The Practice of Medicine

Understanding the thinking of such village practitioners was a challenge for me, and to my surprise, understanding the more traditionally trained physicians sometimes was as well. The lines of authority appeared to be sharply drawn within the local system: several times I watched young doctors at hospitals defer to older doctors, even when the older doctor was obviously in the wrong. Nurses would never question a doctor's order, and patients themselves rarely if ever asked questions about their disease, diagnosis or treatment. It was simply expected that the doctors would know everything. On a few occasions I saw doctors leave patients unattended after surgery, and I saw patients sent home with no diagnosis just because beds were needed. The one city hospital that had been fairly well resourced by donations held onto precious equipment they did not know how to use, and they adamantly insisted that no one else could use it, either. I never understood this. Many of the problems I saw within the system were related to limited resources, in fact, and I empathized with the medical community about their difficult circumstances. What I found most frustrating, however, was how few people showed any motivation to try to make those circumstances better. A pervasive spirit of apathy did not encourage change.

One Friday afternoon I was driving away from the village, hot and tired and ready for a weekend, when my cell phone rang. "Uli, answer it please," I said to my always willing secretary, who was busy peeling the snake fruit she had just been given by a village friend. After listening for a while on my behalf, since I could not talk while driving, she yelled "Turn left! Turn left!"

Left was not the way I wanted to go. Right was the way to the city, a bath, lunch and rest, but I screeched on the brakes anyway. "Why, Uli? Where are we going?" I impatiently asked.

"Go to the puskesmas," she said. "We have to pick up a patient."

I was not eager to go to the puskesmas, the small local government clinic, arguing with her that they had a doctor there on staff. Besides, I had no privileges there and in fact did not like the place anyway. The person who had called was Roger, a Western friend who worked in farming development a half hour away, and he had brought a local woman to the puskesmas that morning. Apparently she was bleeding heavily and had been for several days, but no doctor had attended to her yet. He wanted me to treat her. I was hesitant for two reasons: I did not want to step into a place I did not belong and trample someone's position, and honestly I simply wanted to go home. Thankfully for the woman, the Spirit of God prompting me was powerful enough to override my selfishness, and I begrudgingly turned the car to the left.

The patient had indeed been bleeding for several days and was dangerously anemic. Her blood pressure was low enough to make her pass out as soon as she stood up, and no one had investigated the source of her bleeding. Although she had been lying there on a bed for six hours, she had not yet been seen by a doctor, for the physician on duty was nowhere to be found. Instead, the woman was being monitored by a midwife, which in theory was not a bad situation. It would make sense to me that a midwife would go about investigating the source of female bleeding issues and whether or not something may be done to stop them, but it did not seem logical to that midwife at all. Attending to the patient had involved checking her steadily dropping blood pressure every hour and wondering if the doctor would ever come back, and from her point of view that was all that there was to be done. There was no consideration given to calling for a doctor--any doctor--to come and help, or calling anyone to try to come and take her to another facility. Waiting seemed to be so normal in the community that I think sometimes it stopped people from thinking there was anything to do *but* wait.

Thankfully the midwife was more than happy to have the patient taken off of her hands, so we loaded the grateful woman into the back of the car and transported her to the emergency room at the hospital. It took my telling the story about six times to various people, explaining why I was a foreigner carrying the woman in, and insisting that someone bring her a wheelchair before she fell over, before we eventually got her to the right place. She had an IV started, a gynecology doctor I actually knew and respected on the way, and another friend there to watch her; I left feeling she was in good hands. Later Roger told me that the patient had received multiple transfusions and undergone a hysterectomy, and I was glad she was doing well. I did wonder, though, how long she may have laid there in the clinic had I not chosen to turn the car around that day.

The Worst of Times

How do you reconcile in your heart the goodness of God on days when you see intense suffering? This is a question I have asked myself time and time again through the years and probably will continue to do so as long as some things remain unexplainable to us on this side of heaven. In the midst of learning about this intriguing medical system, I faced head on one of the most difficult experiences I ever had while being in the country.

Just a week after opening our own clinic, my teammate Jason had seen a very sick man in the office. He was unsure at the time whether the patient had pneumonia, malaria, or both, for the man's primary complaint was fever and chills with occasional coughing. At that time we had no diagnostic testing equipment in the clinic to differentiate the diseases, but we did know that the nearest puskesmas had malaria tests. We had also been told they had IV medication, and at this point we considered that they would be our closest referral facility for sick patients.

Jason took this man, Bapak Mustafa, to the puskesmas and asked if he could stay overnight on IV medication. The doctor came out, and after listening to the story, assured him they would place Mustafa on IV antibiotics and do a malaria test. We could consider it out of our hands. Nothing about the facility inspired much confidence, but Jason assumed that with a basic level of IV medication and care, a diagnostic malaria test, and a little bit of attention, this young man would soon be well on his way back to health. This was on a Wednesday.

On Friday, I was the provider at our clinic, and Jason asked me to stop by the puskesmas on the way out and check on the man's condition. I took Suharto (the Indonesian doctor who had just started working with us that week) with me and hoped to find the man sitting up and in good spirits. We edged past the crowds waiting in the front room and found the overnight observation unit, hoping to make a quick visit and not even have to consult with the doctor. Mustafa's labored and erratic breathing--which I heard from outside in the hallway--changed my mind.

He was in terrible condition, his shaking body burning with fever and glazed eyes showing that it had been going on for too long. Mustafa's wife sat by his bed holding his hand, unable to explain anything to us about what had been happening, and I quickly did a visual scan of the room to see what I could surmise. The antibiotic pills Jason had given him lay on the bedside table, untouched other than the one he had taken in our facility, and there were no other medications in sight. He did have an IV in his arm, but from what I could see it only contained fluid. The notes on his chart confirmed that suspicion. It seemed that for the last forty eight hours, Mustafa had received nothing but that fluid and a negative malaria test, and he was in a rapid state of decline.

The nurse who entered the room at that moment became the victim of my agitated state, and she hastily departed to find the doctor whom I demanded to see immediately. While we waited, Suharto and I listened to Mustafa's lungs with our stethoscopes to confirm our suspicions. We really did not need them since the rattling in his chest could be heard fifty feet away. Pneumonia in an aggressive state can wreck a body with amazing speed, and forty eight hours of unchecked illness had done more than sufficient damage to Mustafa. My hopes for his recovery were fading by the minute. However, good antibiotic therapy can also stop pneumonia's progression quite effectively, so I clung to that thought until the physician walked into the room.

We passed the next ten minutes in a surreal, nightmarish conversation in which we were told that the clinic never had IV antibiotics in the first place. Of course they were taking care of him otherwise, the doctor said, but perhaps my teammate had misheard something the day he first came? Mustafa's malaria test was negative, so treating him presumptively had been a bad judgment call on Jason's part, said the doctor. She did not appreciate the patient having been given one malaria pill on such a non-definitive diagnosis. Breathing treatments were not available there, nor was oxygen, and the antibiotic pills were foreign and so she did not want to give them. She stated that she did not think the man had pneumonia, and she seemed quite put out that I was asking so many questions.

I tried to remain calm and polite while raging inside, for I recognized that her lack of understanding was overtaken only by her desire to look intelligent and correct in front of me. Nothing I said was going to make her admit that she was perhaps wrong and the patient was suffering under her care. The worst part of all was that Suharto, who had moments before agreed with me about the whole situation, sat in the corner watching the conversation and refusing to participate because the woman was technically his superior in the medical system. Rather than question her authority, he would allow the patient to die, and it took everything inside me to not start screaming and throwing things at everyone in that room. Instead I tried to play their game, and I suggested to her that it would provide her relief from her busy load of patients if I were allowed to take the man to the city hospital with me. He could get antibiotics, breathing treatments, steroids--all the things I knew he needed--and I would only tell the hospital that it was a referral from the nice puskesmas doctor who was concerned. She would not have to trouble herself any longer. I was trying my best to follow the cultural rules I was learning by respecting her authority rather than placing blame, but I was also trying to keep someone alive.

She would not agree. I asked Mustafa's dazed wife if I could take her husband with me, and her only response was a weak and almost inaudible "whatever the doctor thinks is best." She had no idea what was going on, but in this system patients virtually always took the word of the doctor as gospel truth. Suharto remained silent. I begged and pleaded, but the doctor's stony faced reply was that she had it all under control. Eventually she firmly suggested that I leave and allow her to do her job, and a nurse began to escort me out. Another nurse conveniently distracted Mustafa's wife so that I could not beg her again to follow, and I was forced to turn my back on a dying man.

He did die, about four hours later according to the village leader who told the story the following week. I shook with tears of anger, remorse, sadness, confusion, and doubt the day I left him, and tears stung my eyes again when I heard the end of the story. It eventually came out that the doctor had not even looked at Mustafa for the first twenty four hours he was there, nor did she ever try to make any sense of what was going on. I still don't know if she simply did not really know what was wrong with him, if she had forgotten, if she was too ashamed to say they did not have medicine, or if there was another problem entirely. I only know that a man died unnecessarily, leaving behind a widow and five kids. He died not for lack of money, for we could have paid for his care if needed, and he actually already had access to medication which would have helped tremendously. He died not for lack of knowledge (at least initially), for he had a working diagnosis when he went to the puskesmas which, followed to its normal conclusion, would have been easily treatable for an otherwise healthy young man. He died for lack of concern, lack of courage to question an antiquated system, and lack of willingness to admit a wrong. His life had become the price for another person's pride, and I was furious and desperately depressed over why this had happened.

It was days, actually, before I could stop obsessing so much about the whole thing that I could reasonably function in the rest of life, as I was continually questioning every stage of that week and what could have been done differently. I was furious at Suharto for not helping me, for his only response had been "well she is a senior doctor and I am not." I was furious at myself for not physically picking the man up and bringing him in the car with me. I was angry with God for allowing it all, and I was heartbroken for Mustafa's family.

I never found anything redemptive about that week, and I never received any answers to the fiery questions I shot up to the heavens. In time, though, I was able to shelve them alongside many other unanswered questions which lay peacefully under the banner of trust in God's faithfulness, and I moved on. I wish I could say that I was able to affect great change in that medical system over the next few years, but I cannot say that. I can say that I developed a good relationship with Mustafa's family, frequently visited his wooden house, and tried to help his widow whenever possible. I can also say that I learned my first of many lessons in forgiveness through that experience--forgiveness for those obviously in the wrong, forgiveness for ignorance, and forgiveness for myself.

As the days passed, we developed a tolerant and at times even good relationship with the puskesmas (where I swore I would never go again), and I was actually able to look past all the facades and genuinely care about some of the staff there. It was never easy to do, and many were the days I thought of Mustafa and wanted to scream, cry or run away. Since running was not an option, however, and ignoring the whole system did not seem to be either, I settled instead for trying to invest in small ways into the education of the puskesmas staff. I expressed helpful tidbits of information when asked, brought in speakers to do staff training if I had visitors, and tried to encourage their strengths in whatever way possible. I knew I was not going to be able to overhaul the whole medical system there singlehandedly, much less overhaul a culture of people so desperately afraid of being shamed by their authorities. All I could do was share day by day what God had given me in knowledge, grace, and love, expressing it in a desire to see people reach their full potential. I prayed that in His hands the rest would work itself out for good. If one word that I spoke ever reminded someone to care or one gesture that I made provided education that improved patient care, for Mustafa and me it would be enough.

CHAPTER Four:
A Culture of Being Known

There were a lot of things I truly loved about the Indonesian culture, even more so as time went by. Looking back on it now, I wonder how many of these things are simply elements of life in a smaller town that may still be present in the countryside and smaller communities of the West. At that time, however, they seemed novel to this city girl who was used to hustle and bustle in everyday life.

Soon I came to realize that many of my daily experiences served the purpose of making me feel known--a feeling for which every heart is longing and yet is all too often elusive in modern societies. For example, I loved the routine I developed with the fruit and vegetable vendors, who would wave and smile if I walked or even drove past in our team vehicle because they knew me as the foreigner who came to shop at their stand. Granted, my white skin did wonders to aid in my being known around town, for it was still a bit of a novelty to the local people. Other foreign aid workers lived in the city, but I deliberately placed myself in situations amongst the local people, making any attempt that I could to relate to them and understand their hearts and minds. This often brought me to places that few foreigners would ever go. So rarely when I visited "my banana man" (as I possessively liked to call him), did I ever see another white face in the market, and the ever present stares of the surrounding shoppers reminded me that I was indeed still an anomaly in that area.

For the first few months that banana man, a sweet old soul who sat upright on the same wooden crate and smiled every day, would ask me my name, where I was from, how long I had been there, and if I liked his community. None of these were abnormal questions, and I heard them daily from other local people who were somewhat curious but more often just disinterestedly polite. I was delighted when, after a few months, his questions turned to how long would I stay, would my family miss me if I stayed forever, and what was my clinic in the village like, for I felt like I was making progress in a relationship. I was more delighted still when the conversation turned to what I was cooking, explanations of what kind of bananas were better for cooking sweet versus salty dishes, and how he truly believed I loved local food. My favorite times came a few months down the road when I would arrive, look around, and soon be greeted by eager hands searching for the best bananas for me and good naturedly haggling about price. While this was going on, the man was announcing to anyone that chose to listen that I was the "Ibu doctor" from America who served the village and who liked to make banana bread for her friends out of the small bananas. It was pure delight to my ears and my heart.

"My papaya man," who appeared about sixty years of age but in reality was probably far younger, was a crotchety old soul when I first met him. He sat on a corner, narrowly balanced on an old crate that smelled like musty fruit mingled with the sewage in the ditch nearby, and he seemed to wear a permanent scowl. There was no love lost between us the first few times I visited; he seemed to delight in watching me struggle as he only spoke the local dialect and I only the national language of Indonesian. It wasn't that he did not know the national language, but, like others, he was less than fond of the foreigners who had only recently been allowed to enter his homeland. He enjoyed watching me bluster my way through a purchase as much as he did overcharging me ten times the normal price for a papaya, and I often walked away swearing never to come back. The problem was that no matter how hard I searched, I could not find papayas as good as his anywhere else in the market! That may seem ridiculous, as I know the fruit in many stalls likely came from the same trees. Be that as it may, I loved this man's papayas. I have discovered that certain degrees of stress can be tempered by a few wisely chosen and consistent indulgences, and papayas were mine.

It was probably six months before the papaya man smiled at me, and this glimmer of hope for a congenial relationship came on a day when I defiantly walked up to him and demanded my papaya for a fair price. He was startled at my abruptness, I think, but his grin was unmistakable when he heard me utter the demand in the local dialect. Granted, I had learned how to count to six only that morning, so if he went over that number in haggling over a price I would have lost the battle. I think I shocked him enough, though, that he instantly agreed. Victory! I ate that papaya more gleefully than I should have and eagerly returned a few days later. Now I would be lying to say that we formed a dear and sweet friendship over the next year and he tried to adopt me as his daughter, but I will say that he softened notably towards my presence and even seemed to enjoy my coming at times. He taught me a handful of words in the local dialect, would begin to point me to the better fruit rather than the rotten ones, and at times would stop me to ask why I had not been there in a few days. "I still have papaya at my home," I would say with a smile. "Well, eat faster then," he gruffly responded, "Doctors need their own health." People show love in different ways!

It is common practice when you approach a fruit stand to haggle for price. This bargaining process is not unique to Indonesia, and I had already learned in my years of travel that it is much more of an art than a science. What I loved about fruit shopping in my new homeland, though, was the way that most sellers, before bargaining, would go to great length to help me pick out the best fruit and tell me which one was rotten if I did not know. The woman at the snake fruit stand cracked open one of the nutty flavored fruits for me many times, insisting I try it before I buy it, eagerly wanting to please her willing customer and offer the best goods possible. I was quite shocked the first time I looked out at a sea of mangoes, eyeing them hungrily, and offered up a price only to be told I couldn't buy any of them at all. The man said they were bad and too sour and would not be any good. That day I was hungry and wanted to buy a few, and I didn't particularly care if they were the best fruit I had ever eaten or not. Try as I might, though, he would not sell them to me, insisting that he only sold good fruit and that it would be dishonest and unkind for him to allow me to buy the mangoes. I never did figure out why he left them all out there to begin with, and I walked away that day empty-handed. Yet I held respect for the man in my heart. He wanted to take care of me, was striving to be honest, and was trying to live his simple life well. I could learn from that.

Delivering Mail and Smiles

In the city, I was most well-known at the post office. This cave of bureaucracy would make even the most abysmal government office in the West look stellar, and I would be hard pressed to say how many precious hours of life I actually spent there. Mail was sent in the front of the building, in the order of six separate lines which apparently were designated for different methods of shipping on different days according to the whims of whoever was in charge. Essentially there was local mail, international mail, expedited mail, and returned mail, as well as a different line for government workers to use and another line for mail going to certain mysteriously important people. After some frustrated efforts at figuring out the system, I settled on the fact that I could arrive at most any line, wait an interminably long amount of time while ten people came from behind me and pushed their way directly in front of my outstretched arms, and eventually get the worker to take my mail. When someone announced that I was in the wrong line, I distressingly pleaded my ignorance as a foreigner; ninety percent of the time this produced loud sighs and murmurs among the other workers but an eventual handling of my mail.

After using this trick for about four months, it became obvious to the workers that I was no longer a temporary foreigner. I was indeed going to continue to come often to disturb their peaceful smoking and concentrated efforts at working as slowly as humanly possible. One day a young woman named Nadia asked me what my job was, and suddenly I found myself receiving VIP treatment. I got ushered up to the front of the post office, and in return I answered questions about blood pressure medication, proper diet, if smoking was actually bad for them (not that my answer ever had any evident effect), and was their grandmother really having a stroke every time she was dizzy--or perhaps was it the *jinn* (evil spirit) who had entered her? A little bit of advice moved my mail right along on most days. It worked on those days, that is, when international mail was actually able to be mailed (which seemed to be all days except Wednesday and never after 2:00 P.M.). The same man responsible for taking the mail before 2:00 P.M. was also there at 3:00 P.M., but he dogmatically insisted he would only mail things locally at that point. Some of life's great mysteries are never solved.

The men in the back of the post office, the receiving section, befriended me from the very beginning. Kind family and friends often sent me small packages of letters, candy, or other things I missed from home, and when I received a small note stating I had a package in the P.O. Box, I was filled with anticipation. Rounding the back of the building, I found my way through the mail carts and entered a smoky room filled with a dizzying array of envelopes and packages piled on desk after desk in no visible order. My very first visit drew a crowd of postal workers who were happy to please me by finding my package, and almost immediately they discovered that I was a medical provider. From that first day on, I never failed to enter the room without a friendly cry of "Oh, it's Ibu doctor!" and with that an ambush of postal workers wanting me to attend to their handful of medical ailments. I tried laughingly and somewhat desperately to convince them of their slow and certain deaths from smoking cigarettes, argued that the wind did not enter their lungs nearly as much as the tobacco, and explained patiently that no, their stressful jobs did not indeed cause their asthma and coughs. I enjoyed this lively bunch of men, most of whom had a sparkle in their eyes and many of whom seemed genuinely interested in who I was and why I wanted to care for their people. Over the years I was able to share with many of them that my life was lived in an effort to follow Jesus, and several of them seemed to take that message to heart in a way I hope they will reflect upon later.

Bapak Iskander worked in the final section of the post office, the building farthest in the back where the large packages arrived. I had several deliveries come to this area, primarily medical supplies for which I had begged, pleaded, and bargained from companies or old coworkers, and this delightful man loved to comb through their contents. As did the others, he quickly ascertained my profession and lost no time in presenting to me the complaints of his family and friends. Each of these concerns was summarily offered to me and had to be settled with advice before he would go look for my package.

"How is the news, Ibu doctor?" he greeted me in the local dialect at every visit, inquiring as to how I was. "All the news is good," I would reply, indicating that I was fine. My skills in the local dialect were improving, he noted, and he was proud of me for learning. Amazingly, although the grand total of words I learned in this dialect never surpassed thirty, his pride in me did not waiver. After I miraculously cured him of a strained muscle by suggesting he buy some ibuprofen, I had become his great hero. He would champion my cause to anyone in the office who was giving me difficulty, and I appreciated the advocacy. There was one glorious day when I needed to mail some papers to my headquarters office, but it was past the mysterious 2:00 P.M. deadline for international mailing. I was somewhat desperate, knowing I would be in the village for the next three days, but the postal gatekeeper up front was not in an amiable mood that day. On a whim I went to the back and presented my case to Bapak Iskander, and sure enough he stomped up the front, threw around some papers, shook his fist, and pointed excitedly at me several times. My papers went off in the mail.

He also began watching for deliveries for me and calling me to let me know they were there, trying to save me the time spent in coming to look for an expected package that had not yet arrived. I prayed for Iskander's wife when he told me of her illness, and I rejoiced with him in hearing of her healing. He listened with concern as I told him of my difficulties in getting money for cataract surgeries in the village, and he proclaimed to others in the warehouse all about the success of the surgeries after they happened. He was genuinely concerned when I returned from a three week furlough, not having announced to him my leaving, and he seemed genuinely sad when I later announced I would be moving away permanently. I could blame this kindness, and other similar benevolent acts, on the miracles of modern ibuprofen and the knowledge with which I have been blessed as a medical provider. I prefer, though, to count them as the blessings of relationship given to me by a relational God. He knows that all of us need relationships that involve respect, laughter, service, and mutual concern.

Coming from the busiest culture in the world while having the blessing and curse of a Type A personality does not make fitting into an Eastern island culture easy. For months, maybe even a year after arriving, everything in my nature screamed against the pace of life and seeming unconcern for the clock or value of getting anything accomplished. Even two years into my stay, I found myself occasionally glancing at my watch while visiting in a home that had no clock, and I would sigh as I realized I was still more time bound than I would like to admit. I definitely grew leaps and bounds in patience, though, mostly as a result of relationships like those I just described. How many times have I entered the post office in the US and actually had a conversation with someone there beyond the price of stamps? Sadly, many more are the times I have stood looking at the workers in dismay, tapping my foot, sighing loudly at their slowness, and thinking of the growing list of ridiculously unimportant things I could be doing in that twelve minutes of waiting--instead of wondering what kind of individuals they are. In contrast, once I knew Iskander's name, Nadia's desire to be married, and other snatches of information about the postal workers' lives, the moments of waiting-- in fact many, many more than I would ever wait in the US--became worthwhile since I knew they brought me into conversation with a friend. Time spent is perhaps the biggest price for knowing someone and being known, but it is one well worth paying for a priceless result.

I am so grateful for the small degree of temperance which God cultivated in my spirit through learning how to be patient with the pace of life in Indonesia. I hope that the individuals there, who did their best to make me feel known, know now a different and much more patient woman than the one they first met. Some of the worst aspects of the local culture certainly managed to bring out the some of the worst of my character, but thankfully beautiful parts of the culture--such as this being known--were also able to refine it into something a little bit better.

CHAPTER Five:
Real Relationships

The lighthearted banter of the marketplace and daily business, while making me feel known in a sense that was comfortable and easy, could not fill the deep longing in me that we all have in our hearts for true and real and intimate relationships. God in His goodness, though, is true to His word to "set the lonely in families," (Psalm 68:6) and He provided me with a web of connections and relationships that filled that longing and overflowed with love. As I began to write about some of these people, my eyes filled with tears, for after many months away from them I still found myself grieving the loss of their daily presence in my life. I recently heard a speaker try to make the point that we cannot have deep friendships with people of different faiths. In my dismay I walked right out of the room, indignantly thinking of these precious people God allowed me to dearly love. It is very true that there is a real and deep connection between people who are both seeking to follow Jesus, and points of agreement, vision, and hopes are often very similar. I submit, however, that the core of all humanity—the desire for affirmation, love, belonging, commonality, protection, being known and loved simply for being oneself--is the same across cultures and across all faiths. Different cultures and different faiths may not provide agreement on all issues, but they certainly do not negate deep friendships built on respect, joy, support, encouragement, and the simple sharing of life. Most of the people in Indonesia who filled my soul with joy and days with friendship did not share my love for Jesus. Yet I loved them, deeply and honestly, and I believe they loved me in return. There were many--neighbors, friends, and patients--who were as dear and special to me as friends I have known for many years, and I care deeply about them.

Nirmala

She was my first official friend in Indonesia. I do not know that she knew it, nor do I know when I declared her officially (in my mind) my friend. Nirmala would not care either way. My peer in age, only differing by one year, she was also my peer in singleness, and that alone bonded us since Indonesia is a place where most women are married by the age of twenty two. Nirmala was not a person overflowing with spirit and joy, but there was a simple peace about her. I greatly appreciated how patient she was with my bumbling attempts to build a friendship. She was my neighbor Rahmat's niece, and she had been living with him and his wife Hasmah for several years since leaving her village due to an unidentifiable illness. That being the case, she lived directly across the street, and she was a great companion to me in my first few months in the city.

I do not imagine that being patient with someone who can say absolutely nothing in your language can be very easy, but Nirmala made it seem like second nature. Every morning she was out with her younger sister washing clothing on the concrete, squatting over the half broken buckets and scrubbing heartily before the warmth of the sun caught up with her. When I emerged from our house, Hasmah often caught up with me to drag me over to sit on the porch with her; Nirmala would join in the conversation from her stoop on the ground. Hasmah would disappear after a while to return to her cooking duties inside, and Nirmala would come over and sit with me on the wooden bench right outside the front door.

Initially our time was spent in a lot of silence. We would stare at the sky and swing our legs under the bench, the minutes passing by until I broke the silence by pointing at an object. She would say the word for it in Indonesian, and I would repeat it. This was typically followed by laughter and a repeat of the same word, another attempt on my part and more laughter, and hopefully eventually my mastering some semblance of how the word was supposed to sound. Nirmala would smile widely and nod her head vigorously, and I, encouraged, would move onto another object. We would play this game until I felt I must have been tiring her, and then we fell back into silence.

My mind raced in those times, trying to figure out how to communicate with her and what could be done or said to make things less awkward. I was not comfortable with the silence. I soon began to notice, though, that Nirmala was not bothered at all by the silence, and she seemed as content to sit with me in the quiet for an hour as she was to try to make conversation. Maybe she was just more patient than I was, trusting that eventually this strange foreign woman would catch on a little bit better, or maybe she just did not care. There is a comfort and ease born out of such times that often comes out of years of relationship, at the point in which neither person is trying to impress the other. In our case, I learned from Nirmala that beginning a friendship at this level, simply by enjoying each others' company without having to say anything at all, is a wonderful way to do things.

After a few months I was becoming more competent in speaking, and Nirmala and I started to discuss our lives a little bit more. She was not happy living there in the city, but family obligations made her do so, she said. She began talking about it and sharing parts of her heart with me when we went for evening walks down the street. Around sunset time she would come to knock on the door, asking if I wanted to go see a fish pond or something I cared equally little about--this being her excuse to tell me she wanted to talk. The first night it happened I went begrudgingly, wondering why I cared about small fish, and I grew even more confused when we walked down to the corner and stopped with no fish in sight. She stood, shuffling her feet and making signs in the sandy road, then looked at the sky. I watched her face for a signal of what I was to be doing, and just as I was about to ask her where the fish were, she spoke. She never made eye contact with me as she spoke softly of the difficulties she was feeling with her family, and it was brief. I offered a simple apologetic reply, not knowing what else to do, and then she smiled and looked up. "Ok, let's go back," she said, and headed back the direction we had come. I had not given her any advice, but she had simply needed someone to listen. That was enough.

That scenario was repeated on multiple occasions, and with time I began to be able to respond with something more than one or two sentences. We talked about serious things on our walks and silly things on the porch, and I was delighted to have a friend. It was nothing akin to the relationships I had been blessed with in my friends at home, but I knew we were comfortable with each other and opening up more and more. Then one monumental day she came into my house and sat on the couch; up to that point, about four months into my stay, she had only come to the front door. Crossing the threshold into my house allowed us to cross a threshold into closer friendship, and that day we spent a few hours talking.

Nirmala had a secret boyfriend in another village, and she wanted to tell me about him in confidence. I felt as if I was suddenly transported back to high school, giggling on the couch about things our parents were not supposed to hear. I loved her openness and increasing trust in me, and on that day I began to pray for her marriage. I told her I was going to pray, for I knew that to be her age and single in that culture was horribly traumatic. I offered to her that God would bring her a husband when we prayed. She agreed.

During these talks, Nirmala sometimes told me that she was very sad. She had finished school after year six because her father was sick, but she really desired to learn and be able to work someday. She felt that her potential was being stifled living with Rahmat and Hasmah, doing nothing but cooking, cleaning, and washing dishes, and her heart hurt about it. Months and months into our friendship, she opened up late one night about some traumatic events in her past. It was the first and only time I ever saw her cry, and she wept openly as she related the horror of what she had experienced. I shuddered to listen to her story, and I cried with her that night. Her grief was still very real after several years, for it had been bottled up inside, and she explained to me that she seldom told people she was sad. She could not trust them, she said, but I was different. I saw a precious answered prayer that night, as I had been asking God to help her to trust me!

Nirmala told me clearly that she had decided to trust me, and as a result I was able to begin to speak with her of the God who wanted to heal her heart. I considered trying to get her to study the Bible with me but settled instead for sharing as best I could in prayer and conversation about the God who loved her. I prayed for her on many occasions, about her future husband and her living situation and God being her comfort in sadness, and she was always openly appreciative. On the times I tried to press her a little bit to discuss her beliefs, she was not quick to respond, but I do believe that her heart was open to hearing about the love I was sharing with her as often as possible.

Nirmala was taken out of my life a few months later when she moved back to her village for reasons I never quite understood. We had contact by text message occasionally, but since she rarely had money to send them the news was scattered. I often wondered how she was passing her days in the mountain village. Was she working? Was she walking in the evening? Did she have a porch to sit on? I missed her, and I noticed even more in her absence how she truly had become my friend. Just as she had been sharing more deeply with me, I also felt I could come home from a long and crazy day in the clinic and share with her. She understood nothing of the medical side of things or the administrative nightmares I dealt with daily, but it did not matter. She allowed me to vent all my frustration, patiently listening and nodding when needed, and then we would slip off into that comforting silence. A half hour on the front porch with her like this could calm my frazzled nerves in amazing ways, and I missed those times.

There were a few days in which Nirmala returned to the city, and she would always send me a text message on the way to let me know she was coming. Our visits were unfortunately very brief on those times, but I was always glad to see her. On Idul Fitri, a national holiday, we made a visit to her village, practically swimming through flood waters to reach her humble hut and meet her extended family, and she knew I continued to value her friendship. I also continued to pray for her for a husband, and I especially prayed for her grow into a relationship with God. Then one day I saw my first prayer answered.

Nirmala was getting married, it seemed, to someone she had recently been introduced to by text messaging (the secret boyfriend had disappeared months before). It was far from the typical arranged marriage, but her somewhat strange family situation had allowed her an unusual degree of freedom in choosing her husband. She was absolutely elated. I had not expected her visit the afternoon that she appeared to tell me about her engagement, and I was greatly surprised when I opened the office door to her impatient knock. Smiling broadly with a mischievous twinkle in her eye, she told me she had two surprises for me. The first surprise was her visit; the second was her engagement. I have walked through a lot of engagements with friends through the years, but this may be the happiest one I have celebrated. I knew it meant Nirmala's esteem and respect in the community were secured.

The wedding took place several months later, and it was a joyful day. I trekked out a few hours into the mountains with Hasmah, Rahmat, their family, and Uli, passing monkeys and elephants on the way, until we arrived at the tiny village hut that was arrayed with flowers and hanging bananas to honor the day. I could barely recognize my friend through the heavy makeup and traditional wedding costume she wore, but her smile when she saw me arrive was unmistakable. Of course it was a curiosity for a foreigner to be at a wedding at all, and so a degree of intrigue and increased honor was added to her wedding by my presence. Nirmala was not glad I was there because I was a foreigner, though. She was glad I was there because I was her friend.

As I watched her going through the day long rituals surrounding the wedding celebration, I recalled in my mind our days of sitting on her porch and watching her go through the rituals of daily life there. I remembered the first prayer I had prayed for her, for God to provide a husband, and I was now staring at the answer to that prayer sitting next to her on the brightly adorned floor. It brought me joy to see my friend happy. She called me about a week after the wedding and reminded me of how I had prayed for her husband, and it brought me a greater joy still. It was her first real acknowledgement that she heard and trusted those prayers. Although her wedding day was the last time I saw Nirmala, I still love her. Having last seen her in the midst of a prayer being answered gave me hope for the many more I had prayed for her to be fulfilled. I still pray for her to draw near to the God who loves her, and I must trust Him for that. In the meantime, I can be comfortable in the silence.

Hasmah and Rahmat

My adoptive parents, as I liked to affectionately call them, were a constant and life-giving force in my day to day existence in Indonesia. Our office and home were located across the street from the home of Rahmat and Hasmah, and by the time I arrived to join my small team, they had become accustomed to the strange foreign people living close by. From the first moment I saw her, Hasmah lit up my soul with her smile, and the image of her waving and smiling even through her tears as I left is one etched forever into my memory. When I showed an interest in learning, and learning quickly, their local language, Hasmah made it her responsibility to ensure I had plenty of time to practice each day on her front porch. Even before I knew how to say "thank you," though, she was greeting me at the door each morning with cookies and pastries that she had made freshly made. It was literally impossible to walk out my door and down the street without hearing her yell "Hey! Hey!" to which I would turn and see her merrily waving out the window of their very modest and slightly flood damaged home. Some days she would dash out the door and follow me to try to talk or to put her hand into mine to express her desire to connect. Other days she would just wave from the window, but a day never passed in which I did not see that magnificent smile.

Rahmat, although not quite as radiant as his wife, was a very happy and giving man. He was a government worker, a man of very simple means in comparison to many in the slightly affluent community in which we lived, but he commanded the respect of the neighbors by his humility and concern for others. He was the street's leader, and he was in charge of coordinating local events such as weddings and funerals, organizing donations on religious holidays for the poor amongst the community, and advocating with the government for the needs of the small group of people under his care. On many occasions I noticed him working diligently, late into the night, on some project for the people in the closest surrounding streets. He was always trying to improve his neighbors' situations, even when his own conditions were not as nice in comparison. He was not a man impressive in speech or intellect, but he was a man who earned his position by living a life of character.

Hasmah and he had taken in Nirmala and multiple other family members through the years, expecting nothing in return from their parents or other relatives. They did it, he said, just because "that is what good relatives do." Such generosity was not undertaken with resentment, but with genuine concern. I saw the couple coming and going on a regular basis, heading to a funeral or wedding or some such important event for many in the community, and I knew that each time they did so it cost them income as they were away from the small cooking business that Hasmah had made an amazing success. Again, this time away from their livelihood was not approached with resentment or a sense of duty, but it was done with love. The honest way in which I saw him live his life really drew me to Rahmat. Because of my close relationship with Hasmah, we were also able to connect on a level impossible with most local men.

I spent countless hours and days with these two delightful people. In the beginning our time consisted of the roadside meetings in which Hasmah handed over the daily cookies and donuts, or time in which we sat on the porch and looked at the sky together. Over time we began more conversations, and they would ask about what we were doing and express interest in our clinic and in my life. I, in turn, would ask about their family, their business, and the local community. I soon became a regular squatter on the cement floor in their kitchen, watching Hasmah fry her cookies, stir impossibly large vats of dough, chop vegetables, or make sauces way too complicated for the world's finest chefs. I tried to learn a few things about cooking from her, but I succeeded in learning more about life than I did about her recipes. She, in her forties, had a wealth of wisdom hidden behind her bubbly personality, and I began to love delving into it while chopping chilies under her watchful eye.

My favorite times, those in which I felt I became "part of the family," were times spent sitting in their front room, sinking into the dingy couch with its musty smell and multiple holes, and just talking. During a big holiday celebration the first year, I sat in that front room and listened to Hasmah open up about her childhood. She had the starry eyed look of a child at Christmas as she listened to the distant drums being played in the community parade, and she told me what it was like on the holiday when she was growing up. I cried with her when her family member died and rejoiced when her son got engaged. She tried multiple times to find me a husband and always told me to tell my mother in America that she was taking care of me in Indonesia. It was Hasmah who entertained me on the nights there was no electricity as we'd gaze together at the stars, and she was the one who took me shopping in the market for the first time. On long and hard days, if I was tired and discouraged from clinic, I only had to enter the room and collapse on her couch before I felt her motherly concern taking over. She could not do much practically to help me, of course, but I knew that she cared deeply. That was enough to restore the weariest soul.

There was so much life to be lived with this family. We celebrated holidays, went to the ocean, traveled to weddings, and grieved the deaths of friends. I loved every minute of it, and it was deeply painful to me when I moved away from the street and their continual presence the second year I was there. The loss was only made better by the fact that our office remained in the same location, so essentially I could still see them every day. Hasmah and Rahmat were a force of constancy in my ever changing environment, and I valued that, along with their love for me, immensely.

As deeply as I loved them, I wanted this family to know the God from whom my love for them came. We discussed issues of faith from time to time, beginning I remember with my blubbering attempt to explain Easter when I could barely manage "hello" in their language. So much for deep theology! They were moderately devout in their practice, not discontinuing conversations immediately at the hour of prayer but diligently following the major prescribed rituals and directives of their religion. In words, however, they were one hundred percent adherent to their faith, and conversations along the lines of our beliefs often seemed to fall flat. They were aware I was a follower of Jesus, but they had little interest in learning what that meant. Most attempts I would make to discuss it would be met with polite smiles and an immediate turning of the conversation to another subject, or else the subject would be directed back towards their own faith. I found these conversations frustrating and often wondered in prayer why God did not seem to be breaking through to their hearts. For almost a year and a half (before God worked a miracle to be described later), I even offered to pray for them on several occasions. Each time my offer was met with a smile but politely turned down. I of course went home and prayed for whatever the need happened to be, but I was always saddened that their minds were so indoctrinated into believing my religion was wrong that they would even turn down the offer of prayer. I knew that Hasmah and Rahmat loved me and respected the way in which I lived my life, but the years of false teaching about my faith, now firmly entrenched in their minds, were hard to overcome. In the end, I had to settle on what my mind knew to be true but my heart did not easily believe--that it was only the Holy Spirit who could draw them to God and all I could do was love them. That, at least, was easy for me to do.

CHAPTER Six:
New Birth

Laila

A month after I arrived, with my lessons in survival in full swing, my team started visiting villages to try to find a place for long term work. Sometimes on these initial visits, we would host mobile medical clinics in an effort to get to know the community and determine their level of need. My first venture into the village was on one of these mobile clinic days, and we packed a truck full of medicines and set off into the mountains. I was traveling with two Indonesian female doctors, and I did a lot more observing than I did treating people that day since translators were not readily available. The day provided me a good chance to look around, enjoy the scenery, observe village life in action, and smile at a lot of old women as they chattered away at me, unconcerned that I did not understand a word of what they said. The two physicians worked through the crowd of a hundred or so patients, a long but happy day, and we were packing up the medication to leave as the sun was beginning to cross to the western sky.

About that time I saw an elderly, slightly heavyset woman slowly moving down the road. She was dressed in the traditional village sarong (skirt) and head scarf. As she approached, I noticed that her eyes were a little off center and one was covered over by a traumatic scar, making it difficult to determine if she was ever actually looking at me. She could obviously see me, though, for she hugged me heartily and began stringing together Indonesian words in rapid fire sequence that I found completely unintelligible. She was obviously excited about something going on in the home up the lane, for she alternately pointed at me, at the house, back at me, and then went on with her one sided conversation. My occasional interjections of, "Yes, I am newly here from America and do not understand you," did little to appease her, so eventually I decided to call for backup.

Frisca, one of the Indonesian doctors, determined that the woman wanted us to walk to the house and see her sick daughter. It seemed she was having stomach pain and was unable to come down to the clinic that day, but it was unclear exactly why. So although the remaining staff was waiting and ready to return to the city, we decided to quickly pop in and check on the woman before heading home.

The simple home, sturdier than many of the village huts, had a cement floor, cement walls, and not much else to speak of in the way of furniture or decorations. Thus, we found nothing on the floor that day except a thirty- something year old woman lying on a mat, who was obviously in considerable pain. She was also obviously very pregnant. The stomach pain her mother had described came from the contractions she was having every two to three minutes, indicating her baby's arrival was imminent. Why had her mother not just said that she was in labor? Perhaps she thought we would not come? Certainly, having delivered seven children of her own, she knew what was happening. Farah, the laboring woman, disclosed that this was her fifth delivery, so she was not exactly ignorant of what was causing her pain, either.

Frisca and I listened to Farah's story and checked the baby's heartbeat as best as we could to ensure everyone was in stable condition. Then we asked her to come with us to the city hospital for delivery. She refused, and we were faced with the quandary of whether to stay or go. We did not want to leave Farah laboring alone, but our vehicle was needed to take the other seven staff members back to the city. We could ask them all to wait, but anyone who has ever been around a childbirth knows that what may take fifteen minutes may just as easily take ten hours. So we discussed the situation, determined that Farah was in stable condition medically, and saw that she really seemed quite happy on her own with the village women coming to watch out for her. Eventually we left to return home. It was a strange feeling to me to leave a woman in labor on a cement floor in the middle of the mountains, but to Frisca and the others it seemed fairly normal. Having grown up in a village herself, she pointed out to me the obvious fact that most women there deliver at home and assured me that all would be ok. I knew I would not have been very helpful had I stayed by myself, but it felt strange nonetheless. So that evening and the following day I prayed for Farah for a safe delivery, and I prayed for her new-born child.

Ten days later I returned to that village to teach English (well *try* to teach English anyway) to some very excited and curious elementary age kids. I decided to stop by Farah's house to check and see what had happened, so Uli and I hollered hello and walked into the back room. Sure enough, Farah was sitting there on a mat with a beautiful baby girl sleeping beside her, whom she had delivered with no complications. I realized that life, contrary to our common notions, will go on without--or even in spite of--our medical advances.

I asked Farah what the baby had been named, to which she promptly responded, "You name her!" I laughed at first, fairly certain that I had misunderstood. Either that or she must be joking, I was sure, so I good naturedly repeated the question. She, just as good naturedly, repeated her answer. Uli noted my startled look and assured me that I had in fact heard Farah correctly. This woman, whom I had met ten days ago and known for about seventeen and a half minutes, wanted me to name her child. Talk about a moment of responsibility I had not expected! Only much later did I discover how truly monumental that responsibility was, as naming a child is usually reserved for village leaders, imams from the mosque, other religious leaders, or a family member. In every case it is done by someone in a position of authority who will be expected to retain authority in that child's life. Little did I know that naming this child was a foreshadowing of the authority my team's message of love would carry, not only to her, but to her family and entire community.

I scrambled in my head to come up with a suitable name, running through a list of ones I had heard recently in the country and trying to discard the Western names that were popping into my mind in rapid succession. With the help of Uli's recommendation, I settled on Laila, not for any significant reason other than I had recently heard it and liked it very much. Farah smiled at me and nodded her head, softly repeated "Laila," and smiled again. "Did I really just name your child?" I wanted to ask her. "Why?" Her smile distracted me from my desire to question the moment, so I took Laila in my arms instead and gazed at her innocent little eyes. I whispered a prayer that Baby Laila would grow in the knowledge of God and that her family would as well, quite unsure at that point how it would ever happen or if I would even have any further relationship with them. Over the ensuing months and years, however, I began to see that moment as a prophetic one for the entire village community. Just as God had brought that new life in Laila, at the same time He was (unbeknownst to me) spiritually birthing new life into the whole surrounding community. Just as He allowed me to be intimately involved in Laila's life from the very beginning, He was also going to allow me to take part in the beautiful spiritual growth, which was still in its infancy stages, occurring all around me.

A Vision is Born

Before I arrived in the country, my teammate Jason had spent some time investigating the medical system and what was available. He had seen what the government offered, and he had also been connecting with non-profit agencies and other national and international government projects to see what was being done medically for the province. A lot of aid work was focused on this impoverished region since it had undergone a series of disasters, and in every corner of the city there were buildings with sign and flags stating that they were the results of the efforts of this agency or that. Aid homes were providing housing, many educational and development projects were in the works, and overall a lot of good work was going on. Medically, different agencies had donated equipment to the local city hospitals, and quite a lot of staff training had gone on as well through the last several years. Although the local medical system had a host of problems, at the most basic level care was accessible and affordable to the majority of people in the city. We did not see a lot of reason to build on that foundation.

What Jason had discovered in his investigation, though, was that not much aid work was reaching into the mountain villages a short drive away. These rice farming areas were subsistence communities in which events were dated by seasons of planting and harvest, and the meager living the farming afforded often made life difficult. Most of the families lived on about $3 per day and the crops of their own labor, and little was left over for education, medical care, or other necessities of life. Not only were the people in these mountain regions living in grinding poverty, but they were also suffering the traumatic consequences of frequent civil uprisings. Those involved in the fighting were often farmers by birth who resided in the mountain villages, and the fighting frequently took place in their own backyards. Although the reasons behind these uprisings were many, at the most basic level the men were fighting for the way of life they desired to maintain for their families. The stories I heard of these uprisings made me shudder: people cowering in their huts for fear of armed gunmen and their raids, sniper shootings out in gardens and fields, and bodies being chopped up and left outside relatives' doorsteps. The physical and emotional effects of this instability were long lasting in the hearts and lives of the people, and they were imposed on top of an already impoverished and difficult lifestyle. My team felt we were sent to provide care for people in this kind of situation.

Even had they possessed more money, the individuals in these communities had little access to medical care. From the place we eventually settled, the closest government medical facility was about twenty minutes by motorbike, and the closest hospital was almost an hour away. The vast majority of the people had no transportation other than their feet or occasionally a bicycle, so distances like this were very prohibitive. Most of the sick were cared for by local witch doctors, grandmothers, herbal remedies, or the village midwife, and the results of such care were not always positive. Preventative healthcare was nonexistent, education about the basics of health very limited, and the general health of the community, while not desperate, was certainly not good. Poor nutrition, poor sanitation, a lifestyle of hard labor, and tropical disease all affected these people to some degree.

Historically the entire province had had very little exposure to foreigners until the last several years, and the people in the mountains had far less. They were strongly suspicious of newcomers, so we didn't expect to be welcomed with a great degree of hospitality. Having other Indonesians to work alongside would certainly give us much more credibility, access, and acceptance in the community. Thus, when Jason discovered an Indonesian medical outreach group that desired to go into these mountain regions and begin to work, he went along for the day on a mobile clinic to investigate. He liked what he saw.

Jason had only made that one initial visit before I arrived, but we had been praying (me from across the ocean) that God would guide us as a team to the right location for His work. He felt this area had good potential, for there were no other agencies helping the people there. It was largely uncharted territory. Our team wanted to touch the places where no one else had gone, sharing the heart of the Gospel and the love of God with its people through medicine. This area seemed like a logical fit. So the very week of my arrival, I piled into a truck with Jason and another aid worker who knew the area to go and pray for myself.

There was already a clinic building in this village, placed there by the government years before with the intention of having a midwife or doctor stay and provide care to the area. This was a common situation in the remote regions, but this particular building had been vacant since it was erected. No government medical worker had ever been sent, and an earthquake had since all but destroyed the building. It was in shambles when we discovered it that day, but its basic foundational design would function well as a clinic. It was in a good location, and it could be reasonably easily repaired. It would work.

Most times if I were to say I feel the Holy Spirit communicating with me, it would be in a gentle, quiet, nonspecific kind of way that makes me feel peace, discomfort, joy, warning, or some other vague emotion. That day, though, walking around the crumbled tiles and sagging walls, the sense of the Spirit resonating within me was almost tangible. Something about the place felt real, it felt vibrant, it felt exciting, it felt holy, it felt--well, *right*. It was unexplainable, except somehow in that moment I felt I just knew that God had His hand on this place, and I felt that I was standing on holy ground. I could almost visualize in my mind the patients coming, healings taking place, and souls communing with God, and I said as much to my friend. He agreed.

God was doing something supernatural in this village, although to all outward appearances all He seemed to be doing was watching broken buildings and broken lives sit in disrepair. My eyes and my spirit argued with each other, for I sensed that it was time to rebuild, bring new life, and bring new birth in this community. A lot of that was going to take place in this building. My friend and I prayed together that day while standing under crumbling walls and shattered windows. We prayed not for what our eyes could see, but for what our spirits could sense and our hearts could feel. We prayed that God would inhabit that place, move in His power and might, and begin to restore what had been broken for all too long. We prayed that physical healing would be great, that multitudes would come, and that the clinic would be a beacon of light and hope for the community. We prayed that the physical healings that would take place would highlight the love of Jesus, and we hoped to point many to the Kingdom of God as it was ushered in through individual lives being restored.

Romans 4:17 says Abraham was in the presence of the "God in Whom he believed, who gives life to the dead and calls into existence things that do not exist." In that moment, two people lifted our hearts and voices to that God, believing He was going to call forth something much greater than our eyes told us we should believe. My field of vision that day was limited to dirt, disrepair, poverty, and semi-hostility from people who did not seem to want us there, much less want our help. God, however, was busy calling into existence things that my eyes could not yet see--things that proved far greater than we ever could have imagined.

Moving Forward in Faith

As the following months wore on and we launched into the arduous task of obtaining permissions and permits from the village and government, I held fast to the sense of calling and vision God had given me that day. I had shared it with my teammates, and we prayed that God truly would call into existence something great for the community. We often had to return to that vision and actively place our trust in God, for there were quite a lot of naysayers along the way. Most notably these were other aid agency workers, who noted that perhaps this location was not the wisest choice since the people there were not very friendly and may actually be somewhat dangerous. Another attempted start up clinic close by had been attacked, leaving shattered windows, punched out walls, and damaged plumbing as warning signs that the aid agency in charge was not welcome. Many projects were actually shutting down or moving towards completion in the city, and the status of foreign aid workers in the province as a whole was tenuous at best. We were often questioned as to why we would want to start a new project in a new community when it was uncertain that we could maintain it. We had a string of hassles, irritations, delays, and roadblocks along the way as we tried to get the right paperwork from the government, and there were always a handful of people around the clinic building who looked none too happy that we were there. Some of our friends who came to help build were threatened, or at least interrogated, as to why they were there and what their agenda was, and it was suggested on several occasions that perhaps our work would be better placed in a different location.

We knew, though, agreeing in prayer and spirit, that God wanted us in this site. For all the frustrations along the way, incredible blessings of favor were bestowed on us at every turn. The two village leaders who had to agree to let us operate a clinic in their territory quickly became friends, as did several other key community leaders. Working out the details with the government about how we would use their building, who could work there, and who paid the bills required some negotiation, but the village leaders were advocates with us in this process. They wanted to see their people receive quality care, and the unmerited favor and trust they gave us from the beginning was truly a gift. Minor disagreements arose about who would do the clinic labor, how the well we would install could be utilized, and a few other things, but for the most part we had the complete support and assistance of the community leaders. Had we not had their trust, finding supplies, workers, patients, and eventually friends could have been very difficult. Without a doubt our plans would have failed.

We tried diligently to learn how to best interact with the community, respect their elders and leaders, and allow them to take ownership in the whole clinic process as much as possible. Perhaps it was this concern, prayerfulness, and willingness to adapt that earned us such favor, but more likely it was simply the hand of God. Odds were stacked against us and others told us it was not a good idea, yet God birthed into existence a clinic in just less than four months. In the Western world this would not seem out of the ordinary, but in a place where simply repairing a vehicle tire can require five days, it was astounding. Our international supervisors (who were used to running projects in the less developed nations of the world) were so surprised at the speed with which things happened that they had no time to raise funds for the clinic to actually run. They had assumed such an ambitious building project would require up to a year, but God does not operate according to our timelines.

Not only did we manage to resurrect the clinic building into a useable and quite sufficient facility, but we also erected a brand new wooden house close by. With the clinic located an hour away from the city, we knew that we would be spending a lot of time traveling as we came to treat patients several days per week. In addition, we knew that it would be difficult to have long conversations with people while a busy clinic day was going on, and all of us desired more time in the village simply to *be* with people—to get to know them and become their friends. Friends from another agency, also desiring to show God's love to this region, had plans to teach sewing and cooking to local women and to start English programs for the youth. All of these plans would require a facility that the village did not have. So as we thought about these things, we wondered if the leaders would allow us to build a small house which could be used for community activities. I and some of the other women could stay there as well.

The health department gave us permission for the clinic building since it was actually government property. Permission to build a house in the village would have to come from the village leader, though, and many people thought that we were crazy to ask. After all, we were in a village where they had rarely seen a foreigner (and did not much like the ones they had), and we were already encroaching onto their territory by operating the clinic. Now we were not only asking to visit a few days a week, but to actually *live* there with them, at least part of the time, and this was unheard of. In a true miracle of favor, though, the leader agreed within three days to give us the land, allow us to build a house for the reasons we gave him, and welcomed us to stay there as we desired. Thus, as the clinic was being repaired by hard working local men, some international friends came from neighboring countries and made quick work of putting up a small wooden frame house a short walk away. With no furniture or electricity and a source of water from a well which we dug in the back, the house was simplicity itself.

When I spent my first night in the house a few months later, gazing out the window into the glorious mountains and hazy sunset across the rice fields, I smiled as I thought to myself how God delights to give good gifts to His children. Not only did I love being in the village by that point and love that I could be staying there with my new friends, but it occurred to me that I had desired for a long time to live in a log house in the mountains. In my dreams I never would have imagined that house being placed in the middle of a tropical island, but it was there nonetheless. God is a gift giver.

Making Plans

So those four months were spent in a dizzying array of activity: repairing the clinic, building the house, installing wells and toilets, and trying to get to know the community. There were good days and bad ones, days that seemed productive, and just as many that seemed quite fruitless. There were plenty of problems along with way--problems with getting cheated on the cost of materials, work-ers who wanted exorbitant wages and bribes, jealousy over who got the jobs, and our old dilapidated vehicle that had wheels which liked to fall off. Some days I thought we should open our own auto repair shop with the amount of time we spent having that one fixed. Our builder friends got sick, there was difficulty with the Indonesian agency we wanted to work with, and our first exposure to government paperwork processing was a lesson in patience. We made friends with some local material merchants, former fighters, and rice farming families. The house was built by wonderful visit-ing volunteers, and our activities were a source of great interest to those in the community.

Overall, those few months flew by with relative ease, excitement, and anticipation. As building progressed, we began planning how the clinic would be run once it was actually ready to open. Every few weeks we offered a day of medical care to the community, let-ting them know we were there and would soon be ready for longer term care. These days allowed us to offer simple care for simple problems, but more importantly they allowed us to become famil-iar with some faces, names, and lives of those in the community. We were also able to see what kind of medical needs were most preva-lent and begin to plan accordingly for medication and supplies, as well as try to have an idea of how many people we would be treat-ing on a regular basis. Although we made a few friends during these initial months, the general vibe from the people at the time was not particularly friendly. I had spent some time in mobile clinics in other locations as well, and I was honestly finding the people in our community much more difficult to love. In comparison, they seemed harsh, impatient, hostile, and even bordering on arrogant, and some of them I just considered flat- out rude. They showed lit-tle gratitude for our care, great impatience with our use of transla-tors, and a great disrespect for the building and our property. I knew, though, that God had called us to this place and these peo-ple, so I continued to pray for a changed heart. I also prayed for their hearts to be accepting of us and that I would grow to love each person I saw. This love did come in time, and some of my deepest bonds were later forged with the people I initially found the most irritating and disagreeable. They probably had found me to be the same.

We saw God's hand at work in the favor we received and the speed with which we were able to erect the clinic, and we began to plan for what the daily operations would look like. At this point, our plans were fairly small, for our human vision was clouding our view of the divine plan unfolding around us. We imagined that after the initial rush of curiosity-driven patients subsided, we would operate the clinic a few days each week and see twenty to thirty patients on each of those days. We would enjoy a slower pace of life the remaining days of the week, allowing us to get to know people and invest in their friendship. I imagined I may teach English to students, help my friends with their cooking classes, and spend lots of time chopping chilies, preparing food, learning about gardening, or whatever else women did there on a daily basis. We planned for our budget to be small, covering simple medication orders and minimal supplies since our patient base would likely come from only the two closest villages. Our plans for treatment involved little more than the care of minor illnesses for these small communities, and we hoped to add some health education in as well.

We knew God had called this place into existence, and we believed it would be a light for the small region. We saw a vision of a few hundred people coming from areas around us, so we planned for that as best as we knew how. What God saw, however, was much bigger, While we were planning for small things, He was busy planning to draw over 4000 people to our clinic to be cared for in less than a two year period of time. Never could we have imagined this. We could not envision what God was truly calling forth, the favor that would continue, or the work He would do in hearts and lives of so many people over the next few years. We certainly could not have planned for it, nor do I think He wanted us to. He only wanted us to be faithful in the small things and obedient step by step to His leading. Along the way, He would open our eyes to see His hand at work in magnificent ways.

Left Alone

They were leaving. Walking through the doors of the small security check point in the airport to leave our small little province, they were leaving. Suharto and Sinta were the two Indonesian physicians who had been sent by our partner nonprofit agency to help staff our newly opened clinic, but today they were not reporting for work. They were headed out of town on a plane.

I was leaving, too, headed to another island to attend Uli's wedding, but I was planning on returning in three days. Two days following my return, all of my American teammates-- including the only doctor--would be leaving to move back to the US. So I was relying heavily on the presence of these two Indonesian doctors to help get the clinic off the ground. They had been very friendly when they arrived in the region a week and a half prior, and they were still smiling when they entered the waiting room and saw me that day. There were no hard feelings between us, and their leaving had nothing to do with me personally. However, as I watched them enter the room, I wanted to run and hide as my heart sank down to my toes.

There were problems regarding how our partner agency had promised to compensate Suharto and Sinta, but the larger problem was that they simply did not enjoy being in the small province. They had both been raised in the capital city and preferred the pace of city life, and their decision to return came down to simple math and the ways in which they chose to spend their days. They had never felt the particular burden for the people of our villages that I had, and thus they had nothing to hold them there when their expected compensation did not come through. The crowds of patients that had been coming, numbering into the hundreds, did nothing to deter them. My desperate face and carefully chosen words did nothing to deter them, either, and I was a few minutes away from becoming the only medical provider for a region of fifty two villages.

I struggled that day to be cordial, wanting what was best for them as my friends but wanting much more for them not to leave. I had not come to Indonesia with the idea that I would be without a team, and I certainly had not come with the expectation of running a clinic alone. My independence and self confidence, which often border dangerously on pride, do not come close to covering such a ridiculous task. Had I known in advance what would be taking place that afternoon, I am quite sure I never would have showed up to experience it. God often does not show us things for a reason.

God also does not mind placing us in positions of desperation. I think He may even delight in it when He is dealing with stubborn children such as me, who often need a firm reminder that we are not the ones running the universe. A week after Suharto and Sinta's departure, I saw my teammates off at the airport. Then I sat in the car in the parking lot and cried, hot tears streaming down my face and sobs wracking my body as I suddenly felt very alone. This went on for a while as I yelled and cried and screamed and shouted at God that He must not know what He was doing. At that moment I definitely did not know what I was doing. I did not even want to know what I was doing! What I wanted was help. I wanted companionship, and I wanted another medical provider. I wanted teammates with whom to plan and pray and dream dreams for our small region, so lovingly chosen. I wanted hope. What I had instead was silence, an empty car, and a feeling of loneliness running deeper than I had ever experienced. I was desperate.

Many people encouraged me to leave the area when my teammates announced their decision to return to the US, but I actually never entertained the idea. For all the desperation I felt in those first initial moments, and the many that would follow, I never questioned the calling I felt God had placed on my heart to serve these particular people. It seemed foolish, but I knew God chose the foolish to teach the wise. It seemed overly courageous, but my inwardly cowering spirit knew I was depending solely on the God who could slay a giant with a tiny stone and a sling. It seemed risky and doomed to failure, but I knew that God completes the good works He prepares in advance for us to do. Other countries held no interest for me, nor did other ministry groups. My heart and mind were firmly set on these people for this time, and I had an underlying confidence and hope that could not be shaken. I was so grateful for the deep burden of love for the people that I had developed over my first six months in the area, and I was very grateful for the notations in my journal of all the ways I felt that God had confirmed my calling to this land. I read them often, prayed with whatever shred of faith I had left, and moved through the first few difficult weeks of being alone relatively unscathed.

Small Steps

Everything was new, and every day was different as I sunk my energy into taking the best care possible of whoever came to the clinic. I always believed God was preparing another doctor (or similar medical provider such as myself) to come and help soon, and so I was not bothered by the large number of patients that I was treating daily. Strength and energy can be multiplied and expanded for a season, I knew, and I imagined that after a month or so of pouring myself out to the point of exhaustion I would receive some relief. I also expected that the number of patients coming to the clinic would diminish after the novelty of its existence wore off, so I patiently treated them all with the best care I knew how.

When medications began to run out, I learned how to order them from local pharmacies. The pharmacist our partner agency promised us had never come, so soon Uli was diligently learning how to read my writing, what medications were used for what illness, and how to pack them all into bags with labels that people could actually read. Although patients were unaccustomed to receiving medication instructions from local doctors, I was determined to educate them about its proper use. Our written directions on time soon gave way to hand-drawn pictures of sunrise and sunset, meal times and prayer times, and I found myself explaining to patients how to take their medication when they left for the rice fields in the morning and then before their evening prayers. I had expected the coming pharmacist to be the one ordering the medication and keeping the shelves stocked, for I had no idea of what was really available in the area or how to price it. However, since I did not find the commonly given answer of "habis" (empty) acceptable when trying to obtain blood pressure or other highly necessary medications--and I did not know how long I may be waiting--I learned on my own about local pharmacies. I discovered the alarming array of dangerous drugs that were available for purchase to anyone who asked, the most commonly used medications in the area for certain diseases, and the many kinds of medications I could not find that I really wanted. This learning curve was not the most rigorous I had ever encountered, but it was definitely real.

Uli turned into an excellent pharmacist, and I was swamped with diagnosing and treating patients. Soon I hired a small staff of three Indonesian believers to help operate the clinic, and thus my role expanded into manager as well as medical provider. A poorly trained yet eager nurse, a shy young woman who checked patients in and out, and a boisterous and lively young man who helped with crowd control and maintenance became my employees, and I was grateful for their help and presence. They were all believers in Jesus who had come from other regions of the country, and I enjoyed knowing the Holy Spirit was working in and through all of us each step of the way. They were loving and concerned and for the most part kind, yet they lacked the motivation and knowledge to try to make the clinic a better place.

On my end, day by day I was discovering illnesses that I could not diagnose well, and I began to dream of having more in-clinic testing equipment available. There were simple therapeutic devices such as wrist splints, supplies such as suture kits and scalpels to drain abscesses, and other equipment that I often wanted to have, but none of it was available. Again, our partner agency had promised many things, including money, which had not come through, but more than funding I wanted someone to confer with about these needs. I was well aware that we had not set out to make the clinic a highly equipped, state of the art facility, and I was well aware of the limitations under which we were practicing. Despite this, I had a desire to offer the best care possible with what God had given us, and I did not want to accept mediocre as our standard when there was a potential for something much greater. We had prayed for the clinic to be a beacon of light in the area that expressed the love and majesty of God, and I firmly believed that involved seeking to do things well. God deserves no less from our efforts.

A month passed, and then two, and still no help arrived. I added the search for equipment to my search for quality medications. I had been waiting to confer with someone in this process, talking together through what would make the most impact on the population's health and be most cost effective, but eventually I decided that I just had to begin. Uli and I visited the government clinic to examine their resources and ask advice, only to be disappointed by their lack of equipment, knowledge, and concern. I visited the hospitals in the city with much the same result, and so finally we just sat and prayed that God would guide our desires and our purchases. I added small improvements to the clinic one at a time, which improved our quality of care in incremental ways and made me feel better about what I was doing.

Small beginnings are not to be despised, and over time God reminded me that sometimes we have to prayerfully move out into the unknown in small ways before He will make the path totally clear. The process we went through in improving the clinic was such a slow one that I tended to forget it was happening at times. Sometimes a visitor would remind me, providing encouragement by noticing that I was treating patients with more complicated illnesses than some of the hospitals, and sometimes I was reminded when I began to hold monthly meetings with my small clinic staff. At each of these meetings I would call for reflection, asking what had been better this month and what still needed improvement, and we would evaluate the care we were giving the people and rejoice in what God was doing. It was at one of these meetings, a year after opening, that I recognized how far we had come. I recalled those first days of taking care of people in an essentially empty building, working with only two people and a stethoscope. Now we could treat asthmatic patients with breathing problems, drain abscesses, stop bleeding wounds with sutures, splint broken bones, provide basic therapy for musculoskeletal conditions, test for infections, low blood counts, and malaria, and even offer physical therapy one day each week. We had provided glasses, a short week of dental clinics, and eye surgeries, and we had coordinated with another doctor for over fifty patients to receive surgeries for tumors, hernias, thyroid problems, and gallbladder disease. We could not diagnose heart disease well, run complete lab tests, get x-rays or perform surgeries, but there was rarely a time that someone came through the doors who could not be cared for at some level. We had a filing system, a well stocked pharmacy, patient records, and educational materials, and we had offered health classes to the community and a job to a young village woman in translating Indonesian into the local dialect. I do not know how it had happened, other than step by step and by God's grace, but we had become a fairly well equipped and functional family practice clinic. On one memorable day there had been eye surgeries going on in one room, medical consultations in two other rooms, physical therapy in the back, and prenatal checkups going on in the hallway. I could almost have tricked myself into thinking that simple little place was a hospital!

I never had another long term doctor come to share my thoughts, give me ideas, or discuss these improvements, but God's wisdom had guided every decision. I had moved forward with the principle of Proverbs 16:3 to "commit your work to God and your plans will be established," and He had honored that to a great degree. Several times an individual or organization wanted to come and observe what was happening and try to glean advice about similar projects, and it was at these times that I realized what God had managed to do in a small amount of time. For every day was still a struggle of faith for me, and I often failed to see what was slowly being transformed around me. Many times I felt hopeless, wondering if anything I did made much of a difference, and always desiring for another doctor to come and help me to "make it better." God allows us to be desperate, and I still felt that way almost every day that I unlocked the doors. Yet in that desperation, in a quiet and slow and gentle way, God had moved through my staff and I to already "make it better," for His desire to heal our patients far exceeded my own.

One Day at a Time

When my teammates left me alone, I felt like all I could do was put one foot in front of the other for that day. People would sometimes ask about future plans, and I would just smile and say I needed to focus on that day. All I could think about initially were the 100 patients who were coming through the door that day, not the 4000 who would come later. I could only concentrate at first on yelling for a translator to help the one patient sitting in my room who did not speak Indonesian. I could not think about how to hire someone to help with this on a regular basis, and I did not want to think about beginning to learn the second new and very different language which was the local dialect. I could give pain relievers that would last a month to the arthritic man in front of me, but I could not plan to develop exercise classes that would teach him to prevent further disability. I had to get up each day and focus on getting the car, which had an annoying habit of breaking at the most inopportune times, out to the clinic in time to open. I could not think about how to get it to the repair shop for preventative maintenance or how to consider purchasing a safer vehicle. I was living in daily dependence on God – His provision, wisdom and guidance--and I was doing my best to walk in obedience for *that day*. The funny thing I realized, though, is that eventually a string of "*that days*," lived in obedience to and with a focus on God as the One who sustained me, merged into weeks, which folded into months and on into years. There is great blessing in such daily obedience.

As time wore on and I became more confident in what I was doing, things stabilized. I began to realize that I was likely to be functioning as the sole provider in the clinic for quite a while, and I was able to think more clearly about a bigger picture and the future. Yet I was so grateful to God for those first few weeks and months, made up of vividly individual "*todays*," for they taught me so clearly that God is faithful *every day*. They taught me to look for His hand in the present, reflect on His hand in the past, and trust His hand for the future. If I had imagined the kind of place that the clinic would eventually become- the level of care that would be provided and number of patients seen- I would never have been able to trust Him for it. The task would have seemed too big, the goal too large, and the end result too incredible to believe. Trusting Him for *today*, though, seemed more manageable, since He had clearly shown up yesterday.

They left. Suharto and Sinta left, doctor Jason left, and others came and went through the years. God, however, never left. His presence remained in the midst of my work at the clinic and in my life, constant and not bound by the clock or my own sense of when things should happen. I will always be grateful for those precious days of trial in the beginning--thankful for the way they drove me to my knees to cry out to the God who was constant and the only One who could actually provide. I did not want any of those people to leave, of course, for it is God's heart that we live in community and dependence on each other. For some reason, though, that was not His plan for the time, and I can only trust that His plan is always good. Perhaps if another doctor or more teammates had come, then I would not have been so desperate for God to work in me. Perhaps I would have credited those people with being very intelligent, resourceful, creative, or loving, and I would have assumed that the increase in available treatments and patient healing came from our strong collaboration and cooperative care. Perhaps I would have told people that my wonderful teammates were responsible for the operations of the clinic, or I would have looked first to them for every decision. Perhaps God knows that I can mistakenly offer credit to the human being who is in front of my eyes instead of to the God who is unseen, or perhaps God just wanted to work with me. I will never know.

What I do know is that *God* is very intelligent, resourceful, creative, and loving, and I know that He gives guidance to make decisions down to the most intricate detail of the moment. I know His heart is to heal His people, for His very name is Jehovah Rafah--the Healer. I know that He is patient in working with me, kind when I make mistakes, and encouraging of my strengths. I know that He is faithful, I know that He is able to provide, and I know that He loved those patients more than I or any other teammate ever could have. Most importantly, I know that He did not get on a jet plane and leave me alone that day, nor is He making plans to do so in the future. He will never leave me nor forsake me, and that is a truth on which I can stand day by day.

CHAPTER Seven:
Healing

My American teammates and the other doctors left, but a lot of other people stayed. A *lot* of other people stayed, as in more people than I ever could have imagined. My original team had planned and hoped for a small clinic with about twenty visits per day, thinking this was a reasonable goal and one we could sustain for a while. None of us had experience in running a clinic, and we did not plan to make things too large. Our desire was not to treat massive numbers of people but just to love the ones God brought to us as well as we could. We hoped to treat their illnesses and engage in conversations with them about God--their true Healer--when He allowed.

The first few weeks there were fairly large crowds of people who would gather outside the clinic door before we opened. I knew that much of this was sheer curiosity. After all, most people in the village had never seen a foreigner before, and a white face alone provided a lot of material for conversation. Of course, I could not understand the vast majority of that conversation, my language skills still struggling along, but pointing, nervous laughter, and constant stares let me know I was a great mystery. Many patients would come into the small two meter by two meter room that I called my office and never actually articulate an illness, and a lot of vitamins went out the window that served as a walk-up pharmacy.

After a month or so there was a lull in the patient flow, and daily visits dropped by about half. I took a deep breath and enjoyed this time, needing to evaluate how the first month had gone and still trying to figure out how to hire full time local staff for the pharmacy, nursing, and registration assistance. Mostly I was glad that the patient flow had slowed because I liked spending more time with each patient individually, and I had yet to do that successfully.

In the early days of not understanding the community very well, I was not afforded the luxury of knowing how patient (or impatient) people would be in waiting for me if I was slow in my treatment. What I had experienced thus far had not instilled great confidence in me regarding their patience or kindness, and I was very eager not to let the day go by with people waiting for hours on end if at all possible. It was two months before I was able to convince myself to shut the door between patients and actually try to focus on the one in front of me, for the ever present crowds outside were restless. I felt I needed to keep an eye on them. Every time I opened that door at least five to ten people would try to charge in, declaring vehemently why they should be next in line: the reason may be the severity of their illness or simply how much rice they had to plant that day. Patients did not seem to extend much grace to the foreign woman who was struggling to find the right local words for nose and heart rather than skin and liver, and that made me feel edgy and pushed to move through things in a hurry.

The reason I went into medicine was to be involved in people's lives. I love the moments that God gives to me to share their hearts, listen to their difficulties (which often extend far past their physical symptoms), and try to point them to the hope in Jesus that can heal their souls. In a fifteen to twenty minute office visit, this is somewhat possible. In a five minute visit, even in my native language, it is next to impossible. So every time I sent someone out the door with a hastily jotted note to pick up vitamins and an antibiotic, my heart ached a little bit for not having shared those precious moments of life. I had hoped the better relationships would come with time as the patient flow slowed down, and I was also looking forward to the chance to actually be able to better diagnose what was going on. Both of these things required the luxury of having time with people, but I did not see that as a practicality with fifty people banging on the door outside.

So the second month of the clinic's operations, when the patient flow did actually slow down, was a welcome change. I continued to expect it to decrease further, and I eagerly awaited the time that that would happen. I was waiting for the time when I would recognize most of the patients (the ones who came out of curiosity having disbursed back to their villages), and I expected fully to begin to get to know a small base of people in the immediate communities. I imagined taking care of their very basic concerns--colds, stomach aches, headaches, and the like-- and was even dreaming already of the hours I would have to spend in educating local women about preventative health care. The patients I had treated to that point had fairly straightforward needs, for which I was very glad, and their care did not require a large amount of time. There were a few, however, that troubled me at night when I prayed through their cases, knowing I did not have the proper medication to give them in order to provide for their healing.

Medical Mysteries

Bapak Nasli had a cirrhotic liver. He had come in to see me after having been to city hospitals for a few years, and he even brought lab tests to prove his condition. I did not really need to see the tests, for his swollen stomach told me his story quite well. It was nice to be able to see the results and explain them to him nonetheless. In a perfect world I would have sent him for follow up lab tests to monitor the function of his liver, to diagnose why he initially acquired the disease that was shutting down his system, and to see if anything could be done about it. I certainly would have wanted to drain the fluid from his stomach which was now making it difficult for him to breathe, and I would likely have placed him on several specific enzymes and supplements to augment his nutrition and control other risk factors. I would have ordered an ultrasound to see how badly his liver was decayed and even considered placing him on a transplant list. As it was, I did nothing but provide him with education about his disease.

Bapak Nasli appreciated this education greatly, for in three years of visiting physicians he had never had anyone explain to him what was causing his troubles. The authoritarian nature of most encounters with local doctors did not allow for questions, and he had left each visit with a bag of pills and absolutely no idea what was going on. I was glad to provide him a little bit of information, but I was saddened to tell him that his prognosis, by my best guesses, was for a year or less of life. Our thirty minute conversation did nothing to calm the crowds outside, but I knew this was important. I did not bother to explain to him what could have been done in a different environment (he had no money left to go anywhere else for care anyway), but I told him that I would pray for him. I educated him and gave him some multivitamins, and I did not expect him to come back.

His return a few weeks later surprised me, but I was glad to see him.

"How are you, Bapak?" I asked, waiting to hear a sad answer and watching his breathing for increased difficulty.

"Outstanding!" He smiled at me.

I noticed his breathing seemed to be better and more relaxed than it had been a few weeks prior, and I assumed he must have found a way to get the fluid on his abdomen drained. "Where did you go Bapak?" I asked. "Did someone pay for you to go to the hospital?"

"No Ibu," came the pleasant reply from the elderly gentleman. "I did not do anything since I came to see you. I just came to get some more of that medication you gave me because I feel so much better."

Hmm. I knew I was tired, and I knew I often did not understand what people said with complete clarity. I also knew beyond the shadow of a doubt that I had given him nothing but a multivitamin. "Are you sure you did not go see another doctor, Bapak?" I questioned. "What happened to your swollen stomach?" He did not know, he said, but he was very glad that it seemed to have returned to normal size.

Bapak Nasli came to see me several more times in the next two months or so, each time requesting a refill of the miracle medication I had given him. I was very confused about his improvement, but happy, and I assumed that perhaps I had misdiagnosed his initial illness. I did not know that much about cirrhotic livers, but I did know enough to know they did not heal on their own or with vitamins; naturally I must have made an improper judgment. He delighted me with his visits and his broad toothy grin, and then one day he stopped coming. The thought of the test results I had seen nagged at me, and I began to worry.

It had been at least a month since his last visit when Ibu Nasli came into the room complaining of her knees hurting. I did not recognize her face, or those of her dirt-covered little children who were playing happily in the cobwebs on the bottom of our folding chairs. "How did you know about the clinic Ibu?" I probed. It turned out she was Bapak Nasli's relative by some degree of marriage. He had told her to come and be treated because he was so much better, she said, and I inquired as to his whereabouts.

"He is around," she said. "He just does not come to the clinic because he is so much better." I smiled, knowing that my vitamins had done nothing for him, but curious anyway.

"Yes, Ibu," I said. "But he said he was feeling better because of the medication I gave him. Why does he not come asking for it anymore? Did he finally go to another doctor?"

"Why yes, he did," she said distractedly as a small child pulled at her head scarf and tried to climb the back of the chair. "He received some money and went to the intestinal specialist. He was told that he is completely healed and needs no more medication. He told me to bring you these lab results to see." All the results I quickly scanned, four pages of comprehensive metabolic and liver function tests, were completely normal. "Now, can you make my knees better?" she asked.

I was busy, so I did not have time to think too much about Bapak Nasli and his strange healing. I knew that I had not made him better, and in theory I would have quickly told an inquirer that it was obviously a miracle. I don't think I really believed it, though, or I would have been more excited. This was just at the time I was expecting and hoping for fewer patients to come to the clinic, but the lull was very brief. More and more patients had actually started coming, instead. As they did, I noticed a funny thing happening.

"I came because Ibu Mariana got better," I would be told in response to my question of why a new patient was in my office. "Bapak Samsudin got totally well here," came another reply, and my mind raced to think of who Bapak Samsudin was and what I had treated him for. "Ibu Rohana is cured, her health restored," said the kind man who worked the adjacent rice patty from her, and I recalled with clarity that Rohana had suffered from an illness I was unable to diagnose. It began to happen quite frequently that patients were being referred into the clinic by other patients who were now well, and I began to wonder why. Many of the patients I knew were helped by a simple medication regimen for simple diseases, but others had presented with symptoms that I found unexplainable and almost certainly incurable, even when I had known what was troubling them. I had no lab tests available at this point and only a small arsenal of medications, but I did have a lot of prayer. Often those saying their friends or family had referred them were related to those whom I specifically remembered having difficult conditions, and I was forced to take notice.

The mysterious healing of Bapak Nasli could no longer be ignored, nor could the rash of miraculous healings that were cropping up around me. I did not see most of them first hand, but I heard about multiple cases in which I knew good and well that the patient was not healed by natural means. I tried to take care of people with educated and responsible decisions, but these people I had been seeing had been sent home with vitamins and ibuprofen and little else. Ibuprofen is a good drug, but it certainly does not cure heart failure and liver disease and chronic bone disease and some of the other things that were being reported to me! I was running that simple little clinic while God's mighty hand of healing was swirling all around me.

I have no problem praying for people for healing, and I have been able to do that for many patients throughout the years. I know that all healing comes from God and sometimes in a miraculous way, and indeed that is the message I wanted to carry to this people. Yet I also knew that God can work His healing through modern medicine, and so I assumed that would be the main way He would work in our clinic. I had only seen two obvious miracles first hand in my lifetime, so I was more than a little surprised when they seemed to be occurring all around me on a regular basis. God began to open my eyes to His powerful work as over and over and over I heard stories of His healing power. The more I heard the stories, the more I learned to call it what it was--the supernatural working of a miraculous God.

Hearing of these healings happening in distant villages allowed me some prized opportunities to speak the name of Jesus. We were not allowed to openly proclaim the good news of His gospel in this region, but I was more than eager to tell people *Who* was healing them when I was given the chance. As God showed up, I told many patients that miracles were taking place because the staff prayed in the name of Jesus on the way to clinic each day. During these prayer times in the car, and others, God reminded me that He delights to heal in a variety of ways. He showed me that we had been right in sensing His Holy Spirit at work in this community and that He was moving now even more so through our work and prayers. Most importantly, He reminded me that He is still in the business of doing miracles, being the "same yesterday today and forever" (Hebrews 13:8). Although I did not get to see the majority of the healings--rather heard of them by word of mouth--I was encouraged to pray more frequently and faithfully for healings to continue to happen. On a few precious occasions, God allowed me to actually see those prayers answered.

Hasbah

Hasbah came in to see me with a large abscess on the back of his neck, about the size of a baseball. It was rock-hard the first time I saw it, and this four year old little boy was very uncomfortable. After suggesting his mother apply warm compresses to the abscess and offering antibiotics, I asked her to bring him again in two days. She did bring him back as instructed, but the abscess had actually gotten bigger. Hasbah's mother said that she had not used any compresses on the infection, and it had become red and hot, looking altogether worse than it had before. I was growing quite concerned. I changed his antibiotics to the only other one I had available for children, stressed to his mother again the importance of using compresses to try to soften the lesion, and asked her to return.

Another two days went by. They returned again with the abscess no bigger, but also certainly no smaller. It was possibly a bit softer at that point, but it was also blistered and raw from the hot water his mother had used on his skin. I was not very confident that all was going well.

That day I explained to Hasbah's mother that I had no other better medicine, and on his next visit I would have to cut the abscess open if it did not open on its own. In sterile conditions, with anesthetic and good follow-up, this would be a ten minute procedure and not of much concern. I was not eager to open something on a small child's neck, however, who lived among the goats and chickens and played in the rice fields every day. Besides, I had nothing with which to numb the skin before cutting, for I was still waiting for the anesthetic I had ordered over a month ago to arrive. So I explained this to his mother, telling her that I had no other medicine to offer, and then I offered that I was going to pray to my God in the name of Jesus that he would be healed. She agreed.

Visit number four was three days later. When I opened the door between patients and saw the small boy playing outside, I did not initially take much notice. Had I only seen Hasbah from the back on that day, playing happily in the dirt, I never would have known it was him. Not only was the abscess on his neck gone, but there were no traces of blistering, swelling or any signs he had ever been sick at all! According to his mother, the abscess had "just gone away all of a sudden." She was curious how my medicine had suddenly started to work so well, and so was I! The antibiotic I had given really was not designed to handle that kind of skin infection, and the fluid that fills an abscess must drain in normal healing. She said it never had. What a joy it was to tell Hasbah's happy mother that it was not my medicine at all, but praying to Jesus, that had healed her son. Hasbah received healing, and his mother and friends glimpsed the glory of God. Personally I received a much needed and encouraging reminder that I am merely God's vessel, and amazing things can happen when I allow Him to work through me.

Bapak Hamidi

Bapak Hamidi had suffered a stroke about five years prior to coming to the clinic, and he limped on a handmade cane with one good arm while the other hung lifeless by his side. He was an ornery old soul who was quite upset the first thirty or so times I told him that I could not make him better, and he had no problem telling me so. It took a while for him to stop arguing with me that since other people got better he should as well, but finally he resigned himself to the idea of having a chronic disability. I had explained time and again that all I could do for him was control his blood pressure and try to prevent a second stroke, so he grudgingly returned every few weeks to check in and refill his medications. He was definitely melancholy, and I rarely saw him smile. The few grins I did see were lopsided, the left half of his face being weakened from the stroke, but I grew to like him over time despite all this. His gruff exterior covered a kind heart, and as we grew accustomed to each other, a level of mutual respect grew as well.

After about six months of building a slow relationship with Bapak Hamidi, I was impressed by God to pray for him. I told him so and tried to explain that I prayed in the name of Jesus for his healing, but he ignored me entirely. I prayed anyway, and when he returned a few weeks later I told him again. "I don't believe that," he said shortly, "Just give me my medication." Ok. He received his medication, and I prayed for him again that night. The scenario repeated several times before I saw any indication of his listening to me, but eventually I felt he may actually be paying attention to my words. "Aren't you going to say you'll pray for me?" he asked me one day when I had not told him so.

"Of course!" I answered with delight. "I pray for you every time you come here, Bapak. I told you that. My medicine can keep you from having another stroke, but God through Jesus can heal your lame leg and arm. I will pray tonight." He tried to stifle a half grin on the way out the door. That night I prayed that Jesus, who made the lame to walk in the Bible I believed to be true, would heal him.

It had been perhaps a year since I had begun caring for Bapak Hamidi when things changed. He limped into the clinic one day as usual, and I smiled. If I were to see a smile from him, it usually came at the end of the visit after a lot of complaining about his life, his disability, the state of politics and the state of his crops. This day, though, he was having difficulty suppressing his grin and the twinkle in his eye, and it was noticeable. I asked him what was making him so happy, to which he responded for me to hurry up with his medicine and tapped his finger impatiently on his paper chart. I looked down at his blood pressure readings and was beginning to write a refill order on his visit form, and then out of the corner of my eye I saw his arm shoot above his head. *The paralyzed arm.* Looking up, I stared at him, my eyes darting between his arm and his face, which was full of mischief.

"Look at this, Ibu doctor," he exclaimed before throwing his arm in the air again. "Look what I can do with my arm!"

He threw it up over his head again, and again, and again, making me laugh each time as his exaggerated gestures became larger and larger. I was witnessing a miracle before my eyes as a long-paralyzed limb was being restored, and all I could do was laugh and smile. "I prayed for you Bapak!" I said in between bursts of laughter.

"I know!" he agreed. His arm had been functional for two weeks at that point, according to his report, and he was delighted. I don't know which one of us left happier that day, but I told him again, with clarity and joy, that Jesus had provided that healing for him. He nodded. He still limped out the door, and I still prayed for total restoration. At the time I left the country, Hamidi had not been totally healed in his leg. His heart, however, was on the way to healing, for it had definitely been opened to hearing the truth about a God who loved him enough to breathe life into a lifeless arm.

Nadia

Nadia had been coming to our youth English classes in the village for several months. Some friends of mine, believers in Jesus who worked with another agency, had started these classes along with sewing classes for the village women, and Nadia was establishing a good relationship with some of these friends. She had heard the name of Jesus spoken many times and had asked some questions, and we had all sensed the leading of the Holy Spirit in her life. My friends and I felt great hope that she would someday enter a relationship with Jesus. She was shy and soft spoken but full of grace, and it was just enjoyable to be around her.

I was out of the country on a visa run when I received the text message saying that there had been a bad motorbike wreck. Nadia had dislocated her shoulder and her young cousin had died, and my friends were going to her village hut to pay their condolences. By the time I returned to the village and was able to visit for myself, it was two weeks after the accident and a month since I had last seen her. I hated that grief was what had brought us back together. I offered my sympathy to the small, humble family while drinking tea and hearing the story of the accident, and I prayed silently that God would open the hearts of this family to His healing love. After some time had passed in discussing these concerns, I was able to turn my attention to Nadia and see about her injuries.

I had heard from my friends that she had dislocated her shoulder but gone to the hospital, so I was surprised to see her wearing a homemade sling. "Didn't the doctor give you a sling?" I asked her innocently. "After he relocated your shoulder?"

"I did not let him touch me," she said, averting her eyes and looking between the slats on the hut floor down to the muddy surface beneath. "I was scared."

"You mean your shoulder is still out of joint?" I asked incredulously. "After two weeks?"

It was indeed out of joint, and she would have no part in letting me examine it except from a distance. I tried earnestly to tell the young woman that she would be chronically disabled if that shoulder was not relocated, and I also explained that it would need to be done under anesthesia after such a long time had passed. I knew that this could be done in the city hospital and offered to take her there, but her fear of the pain was clouding her judgment. After well over an hour of unsuccessfully trying to convince her of the gravity of her condition, I eventually left her alone but assured her of my prayers.

For the next few weeks Nadia remained in the village with her family as they grieved, and my friends and I prayed in earnest for her healing. I was praying that she would muster up her courage and go to the hospital, and I offered again several times by text message to take her. My friends, who tended to operate in more faith than I did, were praying for a miracle, and they sent her text messages telling her Jesus was going to heal her. This went on with no answer from Nadia for quite some time, until one day she pulled up to the clinic on a friend's motorbike. There was no sling, and she was walking with both shoulders swinging freely as if she was pain free.

"Nadia, you went to the hospital!" I proclaimed. "Good for you!" I grabbed her arm and lifted it gently over her head, testing her range of motion.

"No, I didn't," she said, brushing right past me to go sit on the bench by the door. I followed.

"What do you mean? How did your shoulder go back into joint?" I asked, sitting down beside her and searching her pale, smooth skinned face for clues to her emotions.

"It just did," she said. And that was all.

There had been no doctor visits, no anesthesia, and no joint replacement. For a joint to spontaneously relocate after a month is unheard of. Typically an unused joint will stiffen, the muscles will tighten and atrophy, and range of motion and function will slowly be lost. Nadia's shoulder, however, was free. It was mobile, and she had no pain. She had been totally restored.

"Did you tell the girls?" I asked her. "They were praying, you know." It was almost a whisper, as if taking her into my confidence about something in which she had not been involved.

"Yes, they said Jesus healed me," she said. "Maybe He did."

With that she arose, smiled her shy smile, and walked away. She hopped onto her bike and rode down the road, offering no further explanation or conversation, and I marveled again at the ways in which God works.

A week later Nadia disappeared. Opposition to the message of hope we brought was becoming increasingly stronger the longer we were in the community, and Nadia had been asking more questions before the wreck than most of the youth with whom we worked. We do not know if it was directly related to such questioning, to her healing, or if it was coincidence, but we soon learned that our young friend had been suddenly enrolled into a strict boarding school for religious studies. Students in the school were allowed minimal contact with their friends and essentially none with those of us following Jesus. It was hard to lose Nadia as a regular part of our class community, and we often found ourselves talking about her and wondering after her welfare. We were able to go and visit on one occasion, but our relationship had changed. All we could do at that point was pray, but in those prayers we could trust in knowing that the God who had healed her body desired to heal her soul as well. If He was willing to relocate her joint, surely He was willing to speak to her heart about His truth. If His hand had been powerfully real in her physical healing, despite being unseen, it must also be at work, although unseen, in her spiritual restoration. Slowly, ever so slowly, I was learning to trust and be immensely grateful for the fact that God's work extends far beyond what my eyes can see.

CHAPTER Eight:
Providential Friendship

One of the longest standing prayers prior to my moving to Indonesia had been for a single woman to be my friend. I knew I would be joining a team with a family and a young college aged man, and I had no idea what other workers may be in the area whom I could befriend. While I was fairly confident I would like my teammates, I also knew that I thrive on good relationships and conversations, many of which would probably be had with a peer. So I prayed, and had many others praying, for a single woman with whom I could just spend time, laugh, go drink coffee apart from work and talk about what was happening around us. I asked God for someone with whom I could share my heart.

I often get disappointed with God when He does not answer my prayers in the timing I feel is adequate or in the ways I think are best. So admittedly after six months when that friend had failed to appear, I was getting pretty discouraged. My teammates were wonderful, and I had met several other believers working in the area with whom I formed quick friendships that supported me emotionally. All of these women were married, though, and not as free as I was at that point for socialization. Even my beloved teammate Uli was on her way to getting married. I suppose had I been more prayerful, wise, patient, or culturally aware, it may have occurred to me more quickly to look for a local person to be the answer to my prayers. At this point, though, I had been searching and waiting for another Christian worker--preferably a foreign one--to be the special connection I so desired.

Thankfully God is much wiser than we are, and He listens to the desires of our hearts. Does it not make more sense, really, to answer several prayers affirmatively at one time, even if they seem unrelated? Of course it does, and I see that now. Hindsight is always 20/20. While I was busy praying for and complaining about the lack of answered prayer for a friend, God was bringing me a friend who not only answered that prayer, but two distinct others as well. On my growing list of recent requests had been a prayer for a local person to help me to truly understand the culture, as well as a prayer—however slightly unbelievable--for someone to disciple.

The first moment I met Ria as a patient, she stunned me with her bright smile, good English, eagerness to befriend me, and general spirit of vitality that contrasted sharply with a heavy apathy in the city that had begun to weigh on my spirit. While many locals seemed to me to be depressed, unmotivated, and fatalistic in their attitudes about their situations and life in general, Ria was bubbling over with excitement and energy. The stream of words and questions she promptly fired at me, the beginning of many, many to come, were lost on me as I distractedly stared at her leg brace, wondering what on earth I was possibly supposed to do to help her miserably broken leg.

My friend Mark brought me to Ria after showing me her x-rays, explaining that she had experienced a motorbike accident several months before and had a surgery that was possibly done incorrectly. A swift glance at her x-rays confirmed his suspicion that indeed the pin had been placed in the wrong part of her knee, but he asked me to see her despite this on the slight chance that I could give her some helpful advice. I was not very eager to go at that point, resigned to the fact that I was not an orthopedist and lost in my own thoughts of my teammates' impending departure. I went anyway, though, following God's leading unknowingly, and walked straight into a friendship with one of the most inspiring people I have ever known.

Ria's leg was propped straight out on the chair, tightly bound in a wrap around brace and pinned from the inside into a locked 180 degree position. A few minutes into her story I realized the gravity of the error committed during her operation, which had been performed in an emergency to repair a fractured femur. In defense of the doctor, her situation had been a true emergency, and mistakes happen in emergency medicine. However, placing a pin in the wrong part of her knee, directly into functional muscle and farther down into cartilage, *and* not requiring any physical therapy for a full six months afterward is inexcusable. It was not until much later down the road that the true horror of the story came to light—that the person who had performed her surgery was not even a licensed physician.

An S3, a third year resident by Western standards, had been on call in the hospital the fateful night her motorbike went skidding. I understand that medical personnel must be trained, and in fact I have had many patients who were kindly, but always knowingly, guinea pigs of sorts for my own education. Education ceases to be such without an instructor, however, and apparently the attending orthopedist decided he did not have time to come to the hospital and assist that night. He expected the residents to cover for his work, and Ria had the misfortune of being the recipient of his poor planning.

So the resident who incorrectly performed her surgery did so for the first time, having never been taught to do that kind of operation. To add insult to injury, it took months for the real physician to confess that he had not been present for the operation at all. His negligence in follow-up and failure to send her to therapy sealed her bad outcome, which could have been rectified if caught in time. Only after months of her own persistence in follow-up, during which the doctor would nonchalantly state that maybe her leg would get better and maybe it would not, did he admit to his absence. He also admitted the possibility that she would never be able to bend her leg again to any real degree, even after the pin was removed.

Had Ria been an older person, perhaps I would have been less angry. Perhaps not, since injustice is injustice at any age. Regardless, it took unbelievable willpower and coaxing from her for me not to go and wring the doctor's neck when I found out what his negligence had cost her. Myriads of possibilities and dreams in this young woman's life were snuffed out by his lack of concern, for Ria was just twenty three when I met her. Her accident took place right at the beginning of her medical residency, displacing--or at least placing on hold--her aspirations to become a great doctor and serve people in the villages. She had spent a month in a coma, from which she had thankfully emerged mentally unscathed. One does not have to have experienced life in residency, though, to imagine how difficult it would be to walk through the halls of a hospital on seventy to eighty hour work weeks while dragging a permanently straightened and useless leg. She was still studying and preparing herself to begin her rotations despite the difficulties, but the fear and sadness behind her broad smile were not completely lost on me.

I met Ria that day as a patient, having been brought in as a last attempt to offer some hope to a seemingly hopeless situation. Hopeless was about all I could feel as I examined her leg, looked at the x-rays again, and promised I would enquire with an orthopedist friend, and I wondered why God had led me into such a ridiculous situation. It did not take many more visits with her to see the reason--that I may not be the answer to Ria's prayers for healing, but indeed she was the answer to my prayers for a friend.

Over the ensuing years Ria became a dear and precious companion. She introduced me to a lot of cultural experiences, always patiently explaining how things worked beyond what I could see and eagerly involving me in local life. We spent hours visiting roadside restaurants, playing at the beach, and drinking tea, and we even tried to have cooking lessons. Unfortunately, the poor girl could only cook rice in a rice cooker and had not mastered the art of cooking a single local dish. I, on the other hand, introduced her to pancakes, scrambled eggs, and good old fashioned mashed potatoes, each of which she loved and insisted I cook for her on a regular basis. I loved to oblige and to have her over for breakfast or dinner, or just to stop by her small rented room close to the hospital and say hello. We celebrated birthdays, both each others' and those of other friends. What did she request for her own birthday? Pancakes. Always easy to please, that was seriously all that she wanted. Pancakes. I loved this simplicity, for it was parts of Ria's personality like this that made it so easy for me to be around her. I did not have to work hard to get to know her, nor did I ever feel I was running the risk of giving her a bad impression or doing something inappropriate culturally when around her. It was an easy friendship and one I quickly came to cherish.

Ria and I were also able to serve together in the practice of medicine. She came on several occasions and translated for me in the village, and we discussed at length the woes of the local medical system and how to fix them. I gave her ideas from my training and experiences, and she shed the cultural light needed on these suggestions to know whether or not they would work. I learned from watching her studies just how deeply flawed the local medical training was, and she eagerly soaked up any knowledge I could give her outside of the minimal information she was being taught. She was amazingly eager to learn, to improve her skills and the world she saw around her, and to serve her people, and I loved that about her.

Once Ria discovered a school for special needs kids in a village, and she promptly set about calling other countries to find out how to bring in trained teachers to assist them. She met a burn victim in the hospital who did not have many visitors, and so she proceeded to visit the young girl herself every day for over three months. She was full of ideas for volunteer hospital programs (which were desperately needed to help direct lost patients through the confusing system), and she took it on as a personal mission to find blood donors for her patients in the hospital who did not have matches. I did not always appreciate the phone calls I received at two in the morning asking me if I could help donate that blood or find someone who could, but I did appreciate her spirit!

In Search of Healing

Back on the medical front, I quickly determined that nothing of any significance was going to happen to help Ria's situation if we remained in Indonesia. I wanted to know if anything could actually be done for her leg or if she must live with that level of disability, and I knew we needed a more qualified opinion. So I set about researching regional hospitals to see what may be done, and I discovered an Adventist hospital in a nearby country which was renowned for its quality of care. Since it was but a few short hours away by plane, we settled on a visit there to seek an opinion. I was eager to see what the physician would say from a medical perspective, but I was also looking forward to the time I could spend with

Ria on the short trip.

Thankfully our clinic budget could provide for her ticket and medical expenses (which were very low at the hospital), and for me the trip was not a big imposition. Ria, however, was astounded by the provision that God was giving in allowing her to seek this opportunity. At that point, although we had only known each other for a few weeks, I had already sensed in my spirit an openness to spiritual things and shared with her that I thought God wanted to heal her. Sitting in our car one night, I told her I wanted to take her out of the country for care, and Ria's tears flowed freely. She could not fully grasp why a virtual stranger would take such an interest in her healing; I was able to state clearly that it was simply the love of Jesus that led me to do so. She did not understand much at that point of what I was saying, but she was certainly grateful for the opportunity to see if he leg could be repaired. So off we went, bound for distant lands and several days of adventure.

Traveling internationally from the local airports was always a bit tricky. You never quite knew if or when the flights would actually go, if there would be difficulties with immigration, or if other random troubles would crop up. It had never been a major problem, though, and I certainly did not imagine that bringing a local person into the mix would make it more difficult. What I failed to consider, however, was the difficulty that may ensue in bringing along someone traveling in a wheelchair. Ria was walking with crutches at that point, but she would not be able to easily cover the long airport distances using them. We planned to get a wheelchair upon entering the airport in order that I could push her through a little quicker, and we succeeded in acquiring one in the first airport-- more than an hour after the request was made. In a few other locations the requested chairs never materialized.

The most amusing moment of the trip came when Ria had to pass the medical "check-ups" before she could get on the plane. At that point, I did not know that a sick person had to be evaluated before being allowed to fly, but I thought in theory it was not a bad idea. Having only thirty minutes before our flight was departing marginalized my acceptance of the practice, however, and it decreased even further after seeing what the check up actually entailed.

"You need a doctor's note," said the man at the counter, straight faced and unsmiling. "She cannot fly without one."

"She is my doctor!" said Ria, pointing to me. "She is taking care of me!"

"You are a doctor?" repeated the man, looking at me suspiciously.

"Um, I am taking care of her medically," I responded, trying not to twist the truth into saying I was an actual MD but knowing my medical degree made no difference to the situation.

"Why don't you have a note?" came the snarling reply.

"I did not know I needed one," I answered, trying to smile and be polite while watching the minutes tick away on the clock. "Can I sign one now?"

"I don't have any of the papers here," he said. This statement should not have surprised me since I had become accustomed to things being out of stock virtually everywhere I went. "You will have to see the doctor here."

Off we went into a closet sized room, where we met two bored looking women who also looked disturbed that we were interrupting their boredom. "What is your sickness?" asked the first one of Ria, looking at her leg and trying hard to ignore the cast encircling it.

"My leg is broken," said Ria, ever smiling. "I am not sick."

"Your leg is broken?" she asked. "Do you have a note? How do you know it is broken?" It was very, very difficult for me to suppress laughter at this point.

This conversation went on for a little while, Ria being much more patient and accommodating than I would have been in her situation. Once the woman was convinced that Ria's leg was indeed broken, not just wrapped up for decoration, we had to convince her that nothing else was wrong. Her primary concern, it turned out, was whether or not Ria was pregnant. I am not sure what relevance this had to her leg being broken, but it seemed to be important. The doctor, the second woman in the room, never looked up from the table, other than to note to the first woman that she needed to check Ria's blood pressure. Finally, being convinced that her leg was actually broken, she was not about to have a baby, and her blood pressure was not at stroke level, they asked us for money for this high quality medical exam and sent us on our way. Right outside the medical room door we were stripped of the wheelchair and told we could not take it through security. Unfortunately, the second floor waiting room was past security, so the poor girl had to hobble up three flights of steps since there were no escalators or elevators to be found.

We eventually arrived at our destination, and the hospital was fantastic. Imagine Ria's surprise when, after being used to basically being ignored in her own hospital, she entered the doors to a warm and friendly welcome by a smiling receptionist who sat her down, empathized with her story, and told her everything would be OK. Surprise is not an adequate word!

The entire experience at the hospital was amazing, from the welcoming receptionist, to the first-class doctor who spent unhurried time answering her (well, more *my*) questions, to the physical therapist who looked as if he had nothing more important to do in the world than help her, no matter how long it took. When we left she kept saying, "How is it that everyone there is so *nice?*" I smiled, believing the sign over the door that said "God heals, we help." The love of Jesus was shining brightly to her, and Ria could not help but notice it.

The orthopedic specialist determined that she needed a month of intensive therapy to regain some motion in her knee, the cartilage and ligaments having calcified due to lack of movement for so long. He could not take out the pins for several more months, but he thought that therapy would greatly increase her chances for future mobility. Over a steaming bowl of fried rice and dumplings, Ria and I discussed this. She was sad, she said, because she had no way to pay for such a luxury, but she was glad we had come for the opinion. When I told her that we (my agency and friends and I) wanted to help her spend this month in therapy and had funds set aside for her, she was speechless.

The three days we spent together were not only wonderful because of the care Ria received, but more so because of the deepening of our friendship and the conversations that took place. I had prayed fervently before leaving that God would allow me to talk about spiritual things, for I knew that long hours spent in hotels and in transit on trips could facilitate such kinds of conversations. God answered my prayers, and I could not have asked for a more open, questioning spirit to be in her heart or imagined the conversations that would actually take place.

We were sitting on the bed in the hotel, and Ria was flipping through a magazine while I was reading my Bible. After a few moments, she glanced over at me and asked what I was reading.

"Oh it is the Injeel (New Testament)," I said.

"Really?" she said. Suddenly I found her face almost in my lap as she quite literally dove across the bed to see the book. "Can I see it?"

I took a second to collect myself from my surprise and handed the book to her. "Of course!" I said, "Have you never seen one before?"

She had not, but she had always been curious to see what the Bible actually said. She had heard things from her religious leaders, mostly negatively slanted, but she had never actually seen a copy of the books (New and Old Testaments) that were considered to be holy books in her faith as well. She had been taught that the books were corrupted and so not worthwhile to read, and she had been taught a lot of false doctrine and information about my faith in general. We spent many, many hours that night discussing false ideas she had about followers of Jesus, what is actually in the Bible and what we believe, what differences exist between Western culture and Christianity, and who Jesus is and how He heals. She admitted that she had had questions for a long time and felt too shy to ask anyone about them, and I was deeply grateful that God opened this time for us to talk about truth.

Ria had a lot of deep questions about my faith and about God in general, and we made plans to study the names of God in the Holy Books after our return. I was elated. After many hours of discussion I mentioned to Ria that I had an Injeel in her language, and she jumped on that information by asking me if she may be able to read it for herself. Before the trip, I had hoped at least to be able to discuss healing in the name of Jesus with Ria (which we did, and she allowed me to pray for her). I had truly never expected such depth of conversation to take place. I saw clearly that it is God who plants seeds in people's hearts, waters them in His time, and causes them to flourish, for obviously Ria's heart had been ready to hear this message for a long time prior to my meeting her. We prayed that Jesus would heal her as He healed so many crippled individuals in the Bible, and I began to pray in my heart that this healing would lead her into a relationship with the True and Living God.

The Search Continues

A few weeks later Ria returned to the hospital for her therapy. I knew the hospital was going to provide for her apartment and transportation, so I was not worried for her in that respect, but I was concerned about her being lonely. God provided companionship for her by allowing her to make friends with one of the young techs in the hospital, and in Ria-like fashion she also picked up volunteering at the hospital around her therapy schedule. She amazed me. The reports from the doctor were very discouraging, unfortunately, for further testing indicated that she had extensive muscle damage in her knee due to the first surgery having been done so poorly. He gave her very little hope for improvement, but I had to continue to trust that there was just enough room there for God to work a miracle. Ria's leg was more functional upon her return, and she was able to walk with a cane rather than full crutches. We continued to hope for the best from the upcoming surgery that would remove the pins many months later. What the therapy failed to achieve in total success was again made up for by her experience at the hospital overall, for Ria returned bubbling over with enthusiasm at how great the facility was. She marveled at how they loved their patients so very well, and I shared with her my belief that it was because of the staff's faith in Jesus. She absorbed that with thoughtfulness.

The following months our friendship deepened further, and I became more frequently and openly verbal about the importance of God in my life. I would mention things about my faith, bring up Bible passages, and pray for her; she said from time to time she was looking at the Injeel I had given to her. The initial impact of interest seemed to have waned, but she was always open and willing to listen to what I said and to receive prayer. Her own faith and religious practice was more devout than that of many of her age, and we had quite a lot of good discussions in which we educated each other about the differences in our viewpoints. I admired her faithfulness to her prayer times, and she admired my spirit of loving service to her people. We talked intellectually about faith, but I prayed that my life and love would have more of an impact than my words. I also prayed for a miracle.

Disappointment and Faith

The time for Ria's pins to be removed had arrived, and I was honestly wondering what we were going to do about that. I knew our clinic budget could not support the cost of surgery and the follow up therapy, but I also knew she needed to go to a place where the surgery would be done well. Having it done locally was simply not an option.

I had been talking to Ria a good bit about God's provision around that time, and He brought a perfect illustration to us through her financial need for the surgery. I was praying about how to help her obtain the needed operation and had asked her to do so as well. Then, from thousands of miles across the ocean, the answer suddenly came. A friend of mine from medical training volunteered, quite out of the blue, to donate the money for her surgery. I had not asked for money for Ria from anyone I knew, nor did I plan to. God did the asking for me. This dear follower of Jesus and her husband had been praying about making a large donation out of the abundance they had been given in their lives, and they had also been praying for Ria for months. The opportunity was perfect in timing and perfect even in the amount they offered to pay, and suddenly the looming problem became a reason to rejoice.

Ria had been surprised at my desire to take her to the hospital the first time and somewhat shocked at my agency's willingness to pay for her second round of therapy. She was absolutely dumbfounded, though, by this new gift being given to her. I could certainly understand her emotion, for it is not often that someone whom you do not know at all, who lives 10,000 miles away, hands you $5000 for a surgery because they love God and have been praying for you. I am not sure she ever got over the shock of it, honestly, but we had a lot of good times talking about it and thanking God for His provision as a result! I prayed with her before her departure, assuring her I still believed that God wanted to heal her in the name of Jesus, and sent her out of the country for the third time. My hopes went with her on the plane, and I pleaded with God to give her the miraculous healing that would reveal His total sufficiency to her once and for all.

The pins did come out, and Ria received further physical therapy. Her range of motion improved, but she did not receive the total healing I desperately wanted for her. She returned from her hospital stay disappointed and tired (emotions I shared with her), and disbelief threatened to take over as I tried to figure out why God was not answering my prayers. Up until the time I left the country, Ria continued to experience incremental degrees of improvement, working with different therapists who would pass through and obtaining new equipment to help her walk. None of these measures offered hope for total restoration and the ability to walk normally again, though-- just improvement and increased functionality. Such a hope in total healing had been dashed by all medical professionals, and my own hope ebbed from time to time as well. Still, I doggedly insisted that there was the possibility of a miracle, and I prayed for God to sustain my belief that it would one day be true.

Spiritually Ria advanced incrementally as well. There were times in our relationship when I thought she was very open to hearing about God, and there were others in which she was much more guarded. I loved her friendship regardless of what she believed, but I definitely became discouraged and saddened at times about her lack of movement towards Jesus. As my hopes for her healing came and went from day to day, so did my hopes for her knowing the truth about the God who loves her. I knew there was a spiritual battle being fought for her soul, and in every great war there are days of victory and days of defeat. I clung to what I read in the Bible and believed what I sensed from the Holy Spirit, though, and tried to trust that in time--His time--God would draw her to Himself.

A few months after her surgery, Ria and I had some really thought provoking and special conversations. Completely out of my control or influence, the spark of passionate interest in studying the Bible that had surfaced a year before on our trip returned. The Holy Spirit *really* is the One who draws people to God, for in the recent past I had been grumpy, tired, irritable and quite far from being interested in sharing much with her at all. It was not that I did not want to talk about Jesus, of course, but I was a little bit weary of trying and very tired physically as I was preparing to make a visit to the US. I invited Ria over for a goodbye dinner the night before I left, secretly hoping to have her leave early, for I was beyond exhaustion and still needed to pack. God had different hopes for her, though, and I think He wanted to teach me a lesson about His sufficiency in my weakness.

That night, Ria initiated a discussion about God (something she had never done before). Four hours later she left my house after an intense conversation filled with questions about who Jesus really is and how He is working in the world today. Not only had she been quietly reading the Injeel for a month on her own, but she agreed to study from it with me when I returned. What an incredible send off to the US that was for me!

The Search Still Continues

We did study together a few times after I returned to Indonesia, combing through the stories of Jesus and discussing what His words meant while trying to filter out our respective cultural beliefs. A few of those times went really well, and I know that Ria honestly and wholeheartedly wanted to know God and what was true about Him. Just as suddenly as the interest in study began, however, it ended. I do not know if someone in her family or one of her friends said something to her, if she saw something she did not like, or if it was just spiritual battle, but one day she simply stopped being interested. Our scheduled meetings to read together were pushed aside for other activities, and her responses to my questioning bordered on annoyance. I continued to share naturally about God in my conversation, and she was never hostile in any way. Her questioning stopped, though, and she became more vocal about her own faith again. Thankfully our friendship never wavered through all these ups and downs of spiritual searching, and I certainly never loved her any less.

By the time I left we had returned to an easy level of friendship in which we just had fun together, and it was a very heartbreaking parting. I still, deep inside, believe God for a miracle for Ria, and I believe it will be similar to the healing of the crippled man in the Book of Acts. In that passage, the lame man, when miraculously healed, goes immediately into the temple and is "walking and leaping and praising God" (Acts 3:8). I believe there will be a day that Ria will walk, and I believe that on that day she will indeed leap and dance in praise of the God who healed her through Jesus.

Before the Beginning

A wise Ghanaian pastor once said to me that my time overseas should be spent trying to "recreate another Kimberly." He told me this just prior to my leaving for Indonesia, and I thought it strange at the time. The seemingly vain advice echoed in my head on many occasions, though, as I came to understand it better. He did not mean that I needed to create someone with my exact personality, and certainly not with my flaws! Rather he was advising that I try to focus on reaching one person for Jesus, discipling that person well and helping her to be as passionate about reaching her people with the love of Jesus as I was. He was recommending I not focus on the big picture of how many people did *not* know God, which provoked discouragement, nor look for "big" results in numbers of people affected by my ministry. Instead he was suggesting the importance of loving one person really well. It was good advice.

I think Ria is that "re-creation" of me to whom he was referring. We are, obviously, very different people, and I would have it no other way. She does not have the same temperament I do, laugh at the same jokes, like the same music, nor respond the same way to all situations. She is shy when I am chatty, and she is respectful when I can be impatient. We both have an intense love for chocolate, but that alone does not make someone into the disciple I was looking for. I would never hope nor intend in any way to make Ria into more of my personality. I love her the way she is.

However, the love of medicine and people and service God has placed in both of us is uncanny. Ria already has the same interest I do in serving the poor, offering dignity and respect to each of them, and she has the same heart to serve those people whom most choose to ignore through the practice of medicine. In a very practical way by profession, she could take over my medical work in the village and run the clinic, and the patients would likely be better off for it. Like me, she loves a challenge and is uninhibited by people who tell her things cannot be done, and she is unconcerned by thoughts that the work may be difficult. Interestingly, many of the things I found most difficult about the medical work itself would be easily bypassed in Ria's care, by virtue of her being a local resident who understands fully the world operating around her.

When I thought of the pastor telling me to create a disciple--a local person who loved Jesus and wanted to share His love other local people--I never considered someone who would fall in line with practicing medicine as well. What better way, however, to share the love of Jesus with people is there than through the practice of healing? How good of God would it be to use this dear one, one of my closest friends, in my very clinic (or at least my profession) to spread the love of Jesus as I so desire to do? With the cultural barriers gone, I cannot fully grasp the influence Ria could have on these communities for Jesus as she loves and cares for them. It gives me chills.

It also gives me hope--great hope actually. I believe that God brought Ria and I together so she could be the one to take my place when I left, not only in medical care but in carrying on the work of sharing Jesus with the local people. I believe that she will be much better suited for the call than I, and I believe that she will bring much glory to Jesus through her life and service. Right now she is missing the integral piece of faith by not yet fully accepting the Truth of Christ and His love, yet I have confident hope that she will in time. I have now left the area, creating a void that needs to be filled, and I honestly believe that God will fill it to overflowing with Ria's life. If my leaving was required to make that happen, then I am happy to be gone. For I believe this plan was in place before I ever met her, and I look forward to seeing it fulfilled. I often pray that what people in Indonesia remember about me is really nothing of me, but all of Jesus. Now I pray that the Jesus they see will come through her.

CHAPTER Nine:
Joyful Celebrations

Part of learning and understanding a culture comes from celebrating the local holidays. Since this country celebrated sixteen official national holidays during the time I was there, I had ample opportunity to learn more about its way of life. Some holidays passed by with few interruptions to daily life other than slight inconveniences such as government workers being unavailable. Since government workers were often unavailable on many days that were not holidays, as well, this was rarely seen as unusual or a problem. Other holidays involved special services in the morning and then spending time with family in the afternoon, and there were some which involved larger community gatherings. Others, such as Independence Day, brought a short lived, carnival like atmosphere to the city, and then there were the days of Idul Fitri, the largest holiday of the year: they were an all out fiesta.

Independence Day was especially entertaining for me. Tradition ensued in a lively activity called "Pajit Pinang," in which a host of young men and boys race to scramble up a pinang tree. (This nut tree closely resembles a coconut tree). The boys' somewhat innate climbing ability, often demonstrated in their own gardens and on coconut trees, was hindered by slick grease that was smeared all over the tree trunk, and one by one they would climb and slide, climb and slide back down. After about ten attempts, enough of the oil may have worn off for a champion climber to reach the top of the tree without slipping and sliding and crashing down upon his teammates, who were trying valiantly to hold him on their shoulders. The team's reward was several small prizes that dangled from the top of the tree, each of which the climber threw down before he slid happily back down to the bottom. All of this took place under the watchful eyes, hoots and hollers of a fun loving crowd. Some members of those crowds enjoyed the real climbing action, but a great number of them just took delight in seeing their friends covered in black slick grease. Young boys down to toddler age circled the bottom of the poles and tried to climb a short way up the side, and I can only imagine the dreams they had in their little heads to one day be big enough to join a climbing team of their own. Worldwide, championship pinang climbing may not be a highly respected aspiration, but for that day the young male climbers were the most important and honored people in their communities.

I shared this traditional holiday fun with Ria and her friend Ika, my gracious hosts and instructors in all things cultural. We spent the first two hours of Independence Day driving around the city trying to find the locations and times of the biggest pinang competitions. For some reason, the details of these festivities were unadvertised and could only be discovered by sheer perseverance and undying curiosity. Finally we stumbled onto a small community event, attracting as much attention with my presence as did the contest itself, and we passed a fun afternoon by joking with other bystanders about the possibilities of the foreign girl climbing the pole. I had a very hard time convincing these people, despite much insistence, that this contest was most definitely not practiced in my home country! My two friends were always so wonderful in trying to draw me into the middle of local life and community, for they were proud of their homeland and delighted in showing me love. They demonstrated incredible patience, taught me well, and tolerated my faults, and I loved simple and fun days like this with them more than just about anything else I can imagine.

Ika in particular seemed eager to draw me as deeply into community as I would allow, and she was full of invitations to attend family affairs and experience cultural activities. Another important holiday in the community was Hari Maulid, a celebration of the birth of Muhammad, and it is traditionally celebrated with food and fellowship in the reveler's home village or neighborhood. I was invited to Ika's sister's house on that day to celebrate, and I discovered that the menu for the day included my favorite local food (a fiery hot mix of greens, jackfruit, coconut milk and loads of aromatic spices). Of course I eagerly accepted the invitation. Upon arrival, I was personally greeted by each and every member of her family as well as many neighbors and friends. She took me around to each visitor in the front room of the house, introducing me and explaining to them all how I came to the area to help their people in the village. I then answered each of them, in turn, in response to their questions about why I could not return to my own home community for this holiday. After their curiosity was satisfied and I had been offered condolences for my tragic plight of being so far away, we moved on.

Ika took me straight into the back room where most of the women of the family were squatting on the ground, chattering and laughing and busily cooking their culinary delights amidst wafting smells of garlic, onion, and lemongrass. We joined in and got right down to business, sitting on the floor in the circle and chopping some unidentified vegetables. What I lacked in language could be made up for in elbow grease, but I was still grateful that the women smashing the coconut shells were on the other side of the room! There was no pretense of my being a guest with Ika, although she did always treat me with great respect. She acted more as if I were a close family member, and although I understood little of what was going on, I felt completely at ease.

I greatly appreciated Ika's ability to include me in life in such a gentle and natural way, and she did so time and time again. She taught me a lot about how to welcome someone into community, and I often reflected about how I would respond were she in my homeland instead. How many times had I taken an international visitor and brought her into my culture? Very rarely. How many times had I taken that same visitor, or even thought of doing so, into my life and family, unconcerned for what she would think, how she would act, or how it may disrupt my current relationships? Sadly, never. I recognized the contrast in Ika's generous love with the boundaries I place on my own relationships, and I was ashamed. I sometimes fancy that I have a spirit of hospitality and love, and I like to imagine that I am good at welcoming people into relationships with love. I realized, though, that I also guard the relationships I already have carefully and jealously, not being willing to completely open them up to new participants. My inclusion of others often depends upon my personal time schedule and desires rather than their needs, whereas Ika's inclusion of me was absolute. Reflecting on this made me wonder what opportunities I may have missed as a result of my incessant desire to make my world and the people in it fit into defined little boxes. Ika's way of fluently moving people *with* her through life with no boundaries, structure, or expectation was a lot more fun.

Aside from including me in holidays, Ika simply showed me how to love a friend well. She obviously enjoyed educating me about her home by exposing me to new food, cultural anomalies, history, and experiences, and she was never unwilling to take me anywhere I may want to go. What most caught my attention after some time, though, was that she really listened to me, noticing the things I liked and did not like very quickly. The patterns of where we would go to spend time together changed accordingly. Several times she showed up on my doorstep in the morning with some food I had mentioned that I really liked and did not know where to buy, and we were engaged in constant battle over who would pay the roadside vendors when we went out to eat. On my birthday she was insistent on throwing me a party, despite my great protests, and it was one of the most enjoyable and memorable nights of my entire time in the country. She made every single local food I had ever said that I enjoyed, some of which I never even remember telling her I liked. Never mind that none of the foods went together: spicy curried vegetables, chocolate cake, fermented rice with sugar, tofu soup, and red chili sauce covered chicken were all laid out on the table and awaiting my salivating taste buds. She cooked for days for the event, invited people she did not know into her home, spent great amounts of money, and did it all with enthusiastic joy. It was not the fact that she threw a nice party that blessed me so richly. Rather, it was that she paid so much attention to detail making everything exactly the way I liked it; I had to question if I had ever paid even half as much attention to her interests and the things she enjoyed.

Ika did not do any of these things to impress me, earn favor, ask for money, or to look important for being friends with a foreigner. She did them naturally because she had made a choice to love me and try to understand me, despite our great differences. I, on the other hand, tend to be far too eager to love only those whom I find most similar to myself, at least in my home culture. I am quite happy to love those I think are already loveable and easy to understand, but I shy away from those whose differences make me uncomfortable or uncertain. What a world of beautiful friendships I might experience if I opened my eyes to see *everyone*, not just those who pass through my filter of what is "normal!" So the Holy Spirit, ever refining me, used Ika as a great tool of conviction and growth, without her ever knowing it. I pray that her example will stay with me far into the future.

Ramadan

Freedom has long been one of the cries of my heart. I love to see God setting people free, be it from an oppressor, an illness, a lie or improper self concept, an addiction, or their own flesh that controls them. For myself, others I had always known, and now especially my new community, I desired to see that freedom take root. I wanted to see people free from the tyranny of religion and rules, and I wanted to see them delighting in and celebrating the freedom Jesus has brought us to relate to God the Almighty.

I knew my local friends understood the concept of freedom well, for Indonesia has suffered its share of civil uprisings and quests for independence through the years. Yet, when it came to their daily lives, the concept of freedom seemed lost within the confines of their religion. The complex set of rules and regulations to which they adhered ordered every part of their daily lives, and the fear of consequences if one strayed from the rules was very real. Never was this bondage as apparent to me as during the month of fasting.

I have been taught through the years that the practice of fasting is supposed to heighten our awareness of, dependence upon, and communion with God, and I have experienced that to varying degrees. I knew moving into the season of Ramadan, the month long fast, that my neighbors professed many of these same reasons for their fast, but I also knew that many of them were only fulfilling it as a duty and one of the critical five pillars of their faith. I had heard that the month could be difficult spiritually and physically for foreigners, and I was bracing myself for adjusting to odd sleeping schedules and the closure of many restaurants and stores. I was also hoping to have some deeper conversations about faith.

I did a lot of observing during that month. I prayed that God would give me very open eyes to see around me, and I was surprised and sometimes saddened by what I saw. Going fourteen hours with no food and water in temperatures easily reaching 100 degrees Fahrenheit is admirable in ways, but it is very disheartening in others. Life was turned upside down as people slept half the day from lack of energy and dehydration. They stayed awake late into the night and arose early in the morning to grab a pre-dawn meal before beginning the fourteen hours of deprivation all over again. Streets were quieter in the morning than usual, and shops, markets, and restaurants stayed closed until about twelve. Then things would begin to come alive again, and shopping would begin.

The focus on food that the "fast" seemed to take was amazing to me, with labor intensive preparations for the evening "buka puasa" (opening fast) beginning early in the day. My experience in fasting (and that which I think is Biblically valid) is that is is to be done with prayer and a focus on God. It should remind us of our utter dependence on Him and His provision and power to bring breakthrough in our lives. Fasting should take our attention away from food, but during Ramadan it seemed there was actually more attention drawn *to* food. Weak and tired people would theoretically be thinking more about the spiritual realm, but it seemed that well over half of their thoughts during the day actually revolved around how to celebrate the evening dinner.

The dinner itself, separated from its religious significance, was a cultural celebration and enjoyable in its own right. I was blessed to attend the opening of the fast with many neighbors and experience it first hand, and I loved the celebratory feel of it all. The fast was first broken with a loud siren from the mosque announcing freedom to eat, after which the people hastily drank "es campor" (an iced sweet drink with small fruits mixed in) before disappearing for evening prayers. For outsiders like me, sitting alone on the floor in front of an open display of food while awaiting a host's return was a slightly awkward moment. Ten minutes or so later, though, the participants would all filter back in and begin the true meal, which consisted of many carefully prepared dishes of local specialties. Fifteen to twenty small dishes covered the floor mat, each filled with mouth watering, flavorful curried meats and fish and chili spiced vegetables. There was laughter and conversation while the dishes were passed around the circle, and each person insisted that the guest eat more and more food every time a plate passed by. Often neighbors joined in the crowd, and in fact it was not uncommon for the feast to rotate nightly from house to house in a neighborhood. Nor was it uncommon to be invited to eat at the last minute if you were walking by an open door when the siren sounded, even if you did not know the owner of the home!

After the meal, the more devout locals got ready to go to the mosque for special prayer and readings which would go late into the night. These individuals were genuinely seeking spiritual truth, and so I knew I needed to pray for them. Sometimes a friend and I went prayer walking past the mosques at night, asking Jesus to reveal Himself as the Truth and as "I AM" (John 8:58) to those who were seeking. We prayed earnestly and sincerely that those who were devoting their nights to seeking the spiritual realm would be rewarded with dreams and revelations of God. We prayed late into the night sometimes, knowing that our friends were doing the same. On a more selfish note, I could often be found praying in my room at about 3:00 AM, when my desperate need for sleep inspired me to ask that God would break the mosque loudspeakers. The chants that blared from them every half hour until dawn were nerve wracking.

I followed the fast most days for several reasons. Primarily, I wanted to understand and relate to my neighbors, and experiencing that part of their culture allowed me to enter into relationships with them on a new level. I received appreciation from those who realized I was standing with them in the discipline, and I appreciated the conversations it afforded me. I was ever cautious, though, for I never wanted to seek conformity to a culture over what I knew to be true about God's grace. For therein lies the freedom I so love: I could choose to fast or not, to drink water or not, to go to fellowship or not, to read the Bible or not--and yet I knew my security in Jesus was always the same.

Fasting and praying that month for my own spiritual growth taught me several things, the first of which was a strong reminder of my inadequacy to make anything happen by my own strength. I prayed some very specific prayers for my neighbors, and it was liberating to see God often answering those prayers very quickly. My faith that He was indeed at work around me soared, and concentrated fasting increased my faith that God was at work in my own heart as well. Most joyfully, again and again I was reminded of my freedom from all guilt and condemnation, and I was reminded that only in Jesus, my Redeemer, am I capable of being in relationship with God. This Almighty God, who is ultimately holy and worthy of my fear, allows me to stand before Him--directly before Him--by the blood of Jesus. This is perfect freedom.

With these revelations, the fasting month was liberating for me. To the community around me, however, this same month seemed to create more bondage in their lives, for the purpose of their fast revolved around its ability to forgive sins. Fasting was a directive; it was a requirement that earned merit points in a spiritual game which keeps people ever guessing about the security of their eternity. I do not doubt that, were I to also believe my eternal destiny rested greatly upon my ability to not drink water for a day, I would gladly follow the prescribed fast for a year! Bondage to such rules and regulations also feeds bondage to pride, and I heard many comments during the month indicating that someone's ability to fast made him more devout and more confident in his own strength to bear up under the difficulties.

Added to all of this was enslavement to fear--not only of eternal separation from God but also of punishment in the here and now. This enforcement of the fast was very disturbing to me. The religious police who strolled the markets and streets had a keen eye for offenders who may be tempted to nibble on a taste of what they wanted to buy. According to the law, someone caught breaking the fast was subject to four years in prison or two lashes, and an individual who provided food or drink to someone fasting was subject to a year in prison, six lashes, and loss of their business license (if it was a restaurant owner, for example). How strictly these stated laws were actually enforced was unclear, but the very thought that people may follow a strict "religious" fast out of fear of human punishment was terrible to me. Fear of any kind is the opposite of freedom.

Although the spiritual atmosphere during the fast was greatly oppressive in some senses, there was a spiritual openness in many people as well. I had more in depth conversations about Christ as a Redeemer in that month than I had in the eight months prior, and it was wonderful when I had chances to explain to my friends the reasons why I was fasting. Many times previously I had tried to begin spiritual conversations with Farah, Laila's mom, but my efforts had always seemed to fall flat. My comments about God, Jesus, or even questions about her own faith were usually met with silence or terse answers, despite the fact that we developed a closer relationship every day. During this fasting month, though, things changed. After apologizing for not having any meals prepared to share with me one afternoon, she discovered I was also fasting. Her initial surprise soon gave way to questions, and I happily answered them on the many afternoons I spent sitting on her concrete floor and playing with Laila. One notable afternoon we talked for a full four hours (a miracle of language in its own right) about the various reasons we were both fasting, and for the first time she actually expressed interest in hearing more about what I believe. We talked about sin and forgiveness, religious rewards and punishment, holiness and redemption. We discussed eternal security, and my heart was broken to see how Farah's heart was laden with fear and uncertainty, however guarded it may have been. She taught me a lot that day about the beliefs behind the fasting month and the eternal rewards and supernatural gifts it can merit, and she helped me to understand at a much greater level why it was followed so closely. She also listened attentively when I spoke of God's complete forgiveness and our inability to earn it, and she said that one day she may be willing to read something about Jesus.

A lot of foreign workers left the city during the fasting month, finding the situation intolerable, and there were days when I was eager to buy a plane ticket out myself. It was an incredibly difficult month of very little sleep, great spiritual warfare, dealing with very irritable people, and general unrest. I grew very tired of seeing people *being* so tired, and I was outraged to watch pregnant ladies depriving their unborn children of food and water in order to show their level of faith. I wanted desperately to disconnect the speakers for the sirens and mosque calls that awoke me all night long, and by the end of the month I was more than ready to be able to give people medication they could actually swallow more than once per day. Yet that month God showed me many of the chains under which my friends labored and provoked me to pray. He also highlighted to me the infinite value of the freedom under which I live in Jesus, and in the end, I was glad to have stayed around. To know better how to pray, to have those precious conversations with friends, and to try to demonstrate the glorious freedom available in Jesus to those I loved more than made up for any physical discomfort I endured.

Idul Fitri

Visitation and eating are the hallmarks of Idul Fitri, the week to month long celebration that follows Ramadan. During this holiday, people ask for forgiveness for offenses they've committed (both known and unintentional) of everyone they have ever known. Upon entering

the door of a household, each person offers "minta mohon maaf lahir batin," meaning, "I offer my apologies for everything done since my birth." This, in theory, is a lovely practice. Would not the world be a happier place if we all were to truly live in such humility and forgiveness? After repeating the phrase 200 times in one day, however, it loses a bit of its sincerity.

On the night before the holiday and the first morning of the event, people spend time with their closest family. I was greatly honored to have the Aguses invite me over to spend the night with them that evening, preparing lonton (that first yummy breakfast food that had fascinated me), cooking all manner of other local dishes, and enjoying their company. This night served as a milestone for me in really feeling I had been adopted into their family as one of their own. I cried myself to sleep that night, tears of joy for such a blessing, and I could not wait to arise the next morning to see what the festivities would hold. On that night, I almost felt like a child again on Christmas Eve, eagerly awaiting the gifts to come when daylight dawns.

The first morning passed in a whirlwind of activity and visitors to the Agus household. Around nine o'clock in the morning, the neighborhood children began to come around with their small envelopes to collect money, a tradition that can quickly empty the pockets of the cheerfully giving adults! The early morning hours had been spent peacefully with just close family, the women chatting and eating and the men making a quick visit to the mosque. Once the visitors began to come though, it was non-stop activity. Extended family came first, then neighbors and others from surrounding communities as the hours wore on. I sat and observed everything with a joyful heart, delighting to hear Bapak and Ibu repeat to their visitors who I was, how they loved me, and how they wanted me to be a part of their family on this special day. That morning was priceless.

By early afternoon the Aguses needed to begin their journey to Bapak's home village, and I needed to go back to my own neighborhood. We parted ways, and I set out with my roommates to make the obligatory visits to our neighbors' homes. Although technically there is a full month allotted for visitation before someone will get offended if a friend does not stop in, close neighbors generally visit in the first two days if they have not returned to their own home towns. So that first day involved visiting the houses of eleven of our neighbors, each of which was serving local "kue," (cookies, pastries, or sweet coconut sticky rice) and sugary syrup. By the end of the day I am certain I had become at least temporarily diabetic, but happily so! The visitations were short: entering, saying the apologetic phrases, agreeing that all the food was wonderful, saying I was glad to enjoy their traditions, and then moving on to the next house. Time does not necessarily equate to value, however, and the effort I made to share one of the most important days in the culture won me deep respect and friendships.

The next day Uli and I set out to see Ibu Aisah, our team house and office helper, in her village. Since a lot of people were traveling on those holiday days, the ride was quite harrowing. Windy mountain roads, too many crazy motorbike drivers, and a wobbly car do not mix well, and by the time we returned that night my knuckles were permanently white and my shoulders in desperate need of a massage. It was worth it, though, for it was a great honor to Ibu that we would cover that distance and come to see the place where she had been raised. The village was nondescript--much like all the villages I had become accustomed to--and I could easily see how it had fostered her gentle but somewhat fearful personality.

Ibu's ancient grandmother sat virtually frozen under the stilt-raised house, seeking shade from the sun and unable to shift her position very far due to crippling arthritic pain. She smiled a crooked smile and croaked some words in the local language, but she did not take much interest in our presence. Others did, though, and it was fantastic to meet Ibu's mother, see her oldest daughter, and experience life in "her world." For that day, I was not her employer, and Uli was not her supervisor. She was not our office and house helper. We were all just friends, and as I watched her nervously and fastidiously serving us and trying to make things exactly right, I felt loved. I knew she felt the same by virtue of our presence. That day, again, was priceless.

The following few days included more visiting: seeing Hasmah and Rahmat, my old neighbors, and of course making the visitation rounds in the clinic village. A few of us set out with no particular destination in mind on the third morning of the holiday, only knowing we needed to be present in our dear village community. It seemed a bit funny to me to be planning to show up uninvited to people's homes, but that was the Western mind in me still worrying. For as soon as we arrived and someone noticed the car, we were bombarded with happy people asking us to enter their huts and eat kue. There was no need for pre-arranged invitations. Open visitation and hospitality were the norm, and on these days in particular people went in and out of each other's homes as if they were one giant family. I stopped counting hut visits somewhere around fifteen, I think, so my trepidation over not knowing who to visit had taken care of itself. Many of the villagers were curious to know why I had not returned to my own home for the holiday, unaware that I did not normally celebrate this time. They also did not understand that my home was thousands of miles away. My explanations fell mostly on deaf ears as they just smiled and welcomed me into their homes, and I welcomed the chance to be sharing this special time in their lives. I asked forgiveness from them for all the many, *many* cultural bloopers I committed on a regular basis, and in my heart I asked forgiveness from God for questioning His ways. For so many times before then I had questioned my adaptation to the culture, questioned my role there, and questioned His sovereignty in it all. On this day, though, as the love we shared was evident in our celebrating together, it was easy to see I had nothing to question--least of all God's leading.

Christmas

One day in mid-December, a new teammate and I headed to the village to eat lunch with a family. Eleanor was a midwife, and she had just delivered this woman's third baby. The family was always very open and warm and truly appreciative of our visits, and so I never minded devoting extra time driving to see them. During the conversation I mentioned that "Hari Natal" (Christmas) would be coming up the following week, and I, on a whim, suggested that they come to my house in the city to celebrate "my" holiday with me. We had celebrated several local holidays with the family, so this would be a nice time to fellowship, as well.

I made the comment in an off-handed manner, not truly expecting a response, so I was quite surprised when Bapak Bustamam perked up and said, "Ibu doctor, I have not been to the city in four years, even to visit my brother. But if you invite me, I will come!" We discussed it briefly, I told him I would be honored, and I let him know my address. Ibu Zuria only smiled, and someone mentioned that of course they normally do not celebrate Christmas. I left with an encouraged spirit that they would even consider making the long journey and overcoming the cultural barriers of Christmas, but I had little real expectation of their coming.

Ten days later, Bapak Bustamam was the first adult guest to arrive at my home on Christmas morning. He trailed only slightly behind the neighborhood kids who came early to eat all the sweets my roommate and I had cooked, and he brought his brother in tow. Ibu Zuria and the kids had stayed home, but I was not at all unaware of the effort Bapak had made to come out to my home. I knew that his curiosity about the life of a city foreigner played a large role in his coming, but he had made a sacrifice nonetheless. His coming, despite the fact that the culture discouraged him from even wishing me a Merry Christmas, spoke volumes in terms of how God's hand had been at work in the peoples' lives in our village.

My current roommate (an American woman) and I had invited many local friends to come and visit on Christmas day, opening our home in the same way they did on their holidays. We baked volumes of cookies and cakes and bread, expecting visitors only to snack, so we were a little surprised when it became obvious most of them expected to "makan nasi" (eat rice)--meaning to eat a full meal. We had to scramble in the kitchen, making noodles and eggs, heating whatever leftover vegetables and old fried fish we could find, and of course making lots of rice. The results was one of the most interesting holiday food displays I can say I have ever seen, and to my heart of hospitality, it was a bit disastrous. Our guests, however, seemed quite happy. I think I need to learn not to worry so much.

The fellowship was the important part of the day. None of our local friends were traditionally allowed, or at least condoned, to wish us well on that day, for doing so may indicate acceptance of our beliefs. So I was more than overjoyed and encouraged when not only Bapak Bustamam came to our home, but also the Agus family, Hasmah and Rahmat, Ria and Ika and several of their friends and family, and many other friends and neighbors. A few close local friends who could not come sent text messages to say Merry Christmas, and a few other village residents even tried to come but got caught in a downpour. We had posted some Bible readings on the walls from the Christmas story, and a few people read one or two of them; of course we prayed fervently that the Holy Spirit would inspire questions and thoughts about who and what we were celebrating that day. We didn't have many extensive conversations about Jesus, but at the very least we were able to clear up the ridiculous idea that we were worshipping the Christmas tree. It was, as a friend often said, an "investment of love" in the lives of our friends, for we wanted them to share with us the joy we experienced in the celebration of Christ.

Around nine o'clock that night, when the last guest had just left, I was reflecting on the day. It struck me how deeply important it was to me to befriend and try to be like the local people, but also how much of a struggle it often was to feel I belonged. Then I thought with awe how much harder still it must have been for a divine being – *Christ* – to feel accepted and "at home" in the human world. I considered my own moments of difficulty in adaptation, when I saw things around me that I did not like or that I thought should be different, and I wondered at how Jesus ever had the patience to deal with humanity at all. Moving from one human culture to another is a trial; moving from heaven to earth is a miracle.

Day by day I was seeing and understanding more clearly what it was to love people enough to want to overlook all those difficulties. I knew what it was to desire the best for them, to want more than anything for them to know they were loved, and to be willing to sacrifice in order to see that happen. Reflectively, I was hushed into silence by the thought of Jesus loving *us* in such a manner. He, the One who sacrificially gave up not just a culture, but heaven's throne itself in order to show us His love, is worthy of our celebration-- with or without a tree and lights and carols. He truly is the world's greatest gift.

CHAPTER Ten:
Ignorance is Not Bliss

The Importance of Knowledge

I have taken my education far too much for granted. I am grateful for my medical training, and I am even grateful for my undergraduate studies as they gave me a basis for this pursuit. High school and below, however, served primarily for enjoyment and social purposes, and I have never taken much time to be thankful for them in the past. Likewise, I have not fully appreciated the wealth of information available to me every day in newspapers, books, the internet, and social networks, and it has not often occurred to me to thank anyone for providing it to me.

Living in a community where education is not easily available and certainly not highly valued changed that. I never ceased to be amazed at how little people in the region could seem to know and still manage to run a business, and I was even further amazed by how little inclination they seemed to have to learn anything more. Take as an example the day I went in search of a pay phone to call home for Mother's Day. I walked into a store (more accurately a small stall) where the entire business consists of running the phone booth. I asked the bored looking attendant how much it would cost to call the US, and was told "Normal price."

"OK, what is normal price? " I politely and patiently asked.

"Not expensive."

"*How much* not expensive?" I said, a little less patiently this time. My experiences thus far had taught me that two people's definitions of what is not expensive varied greatly.

"I don't know. Normal phone prices."

OK, I thought, perhaps he just did not know rates to call the US, so I would ask what a range of normal prices were to call anywhere outside of the country.

"Don't know," repeated the man, who incidentally was sitting next to a big sign that said "Call internationally here." I decided to move on.

The next phone stand I visited had a very eager young man attending to it who knew less than the man I had just left. Having learned from the prior encounter, I decided to ask him not how much, but only *how* do I call outside the country? Do I dial 9, dial 0, etc? He didn't know. He certainly tried hard for me, to his credit, but he had no idea how to make the phone work. This was in a phone store. So he called the neighboring shop owner over to try to help, who again was quite friendly but somewhat useless as far as my phone call was concerned. I realized at that point that I was not going to get far with my phone call, but I had become fascinated with what was unfolding. Deciding to try another route altogether, I asked about the tour to Tawamangung, which was advertised on a large sign right above their heads.

"Where is that?" came the smiling reply.

Not only did he not know how to use his phone, which was supposedly his business, but this man was unaware of the details of the tour he was actually advertising. Time and again I watched similar scenarios when shop attendants did not know what they had in their store, what was available one block away, how to operate things, or how to find anyone who did. Even those working at the information desks in more affluent malls in large cities often failed to have any real information, nor did they seem interested in obtaining it. The complacent ignorance that pervaded much of the culture disturbed me, for I knew that simply having some additional information could greatly benefit the businesses and livelihood of these kind souls. It would also have helped me function better on some very basic levels!

Information is good, but the ability to process that information critically is also required in order to give it value. After witnessing some elementary school teachers deliver lessons in a robotic, rote memory and recitation manner, I began to understand why creativity may be a little stifled amongst the general population. I had often wondered why people did not have any new or unique ideas for businesses instead of aspiring to be one of the hundreds of fried rice vendors already dotting the roadside. Although I knew some very intelligent and even creative college students, I was sad to see how few of them could imagine doing anything else but owning a cell phone store. I started to discern, however, that if children are taught early on that learning means accepting whatever information is given, they never develop the ability to think outside of that or to evaluate a situation from a different perspective. If they are only taught one thing in one way, they never learn to think something through from different angles. The more I observed this method of rote education, the more I began to understand why people also accepted religious teachings with unfailing loyalty and faith and never seemed to question any of it. It also helped to explain why they rarely wanted to discuss religious differences, for in the way they had been trained to think there was simply no room for considering other possibilities. Many times I was frustrated when I'd ask people why they believed something, only to receive a simple smile and be told, "That is just the way it is." They were not necessarily trying to be stubborn; rather, they simply could not imagine that something a teacher or leader had told them may not be true. They had never been exposed to margin for error.

Lack of critical or rational thought made for some interesting and twisted social situations. The ladies in each small community gathered monthly for socializing, cooking, service projects, and religious teaching, and my roommates and I were honored to be invited to this gathering. Although I spent less time in the neighborhood than I would have preferred at that time since clinic life kept me busy, my roommate (another Westerner) had invested considerable effort in becoming known and accepted with the women on the street where we lived. This was not an easy thing to accomplish in a close knit community where no other foreigners had ever lived, but she had worked hard and prayed harder. It was paying off. She had built some good, genuine friendships, many of the women chatted good naturedly to her on the streets, and she was feeling that she had adapted quite well. So she thought.

She returned home one evening heartbroken after attending the women's gathering, which I had missed since it was held during clinic hours. During this meeting a local religious leader came to share a message about faith and its practice, which in and of itself did not bother my kind hearted friend. What did bother her, however, was the angry tone of the message and the disdain it expressed toward outsiders: foreigners in general, and those who believed in Jesus in particular. She endured a full hour and a half of listening to critical, harsh words which described her life and faith, even to the point of calling her "kind" equal to dogs. This entire time she was sitting beside the local women who called her their friend, and not a single one of them seemed sorry for the message, rose to defend her, or even offered recognition that she may be offended. Although they had invited her into their homes and lives and enjoyed her friendship, it did not occur to them that the message that had just been presented about her was inconsistent with the life they knew she led. Having never been allowed to think for themselves, they took without question that such a message coming from their authority figure must be true. It broke both of our hearts to see our local friends walking in such apparent blindness.

Another rung on the ladder of ignorance is the lack of education all together. Of my village patients over fifty years old, probably ninety percent of them had never gone to school; instead they grew up working in the fields and gardens with their families. Perhaps this practice, in and of itself, is not a major problem, for families need support for their trades if they are to survive. The total lack of access to international news and other worldviews that comes as a result of such isolation, though, is the concern. Consider the following example.

I was accustomed to seeing people in the village wearing t-shirts that were obviously donated, and I was often amused by the slogans and logos they were unknowingly advertising. One day, however, I could not keep my eyes off the front of Farah's shirt, and I became so distracted that I was having difficulty making normal conversation.

"Farah, do you know who is on your shirt?" I asked her. She glanced down.

"No, who?" she said innocently.

The bearded face pictured on top of the crossed guns taunted me as I answered her, "Osama Bin Laden."

"Oh," was her only reply, then silence. I stared, trying to see if she was ignoring the relatively significant relationship between him and my nationality. Then she went back to playing with Laila.

"Farah," I said, "Do you know who he IS?"

"No," again came her simple reply.

I tried to remind her about 9/11, but she had absolutely no idea what I was talking about. She had never heard of Osama or the World Trade Center. She did not know that many Americans had been killed or that many people in the world do not like Americans very much. She did not know that an acclaimed terrorist who expressed a desire to kill multitudes more in the name of her religion was on the front of her t-shirt. What's more--she did not care. She did not know that the world was at war against terror, nor did she know that terrorist activity had taken place in her own country several times before. What Farah did know was that Laila needed to be fed every day, as did her four brothers and sisters, and she knew that the garden had not produced much this season. She knew that her rice field had been burned in the war and that her kids could not afford to go to school, and she knew that her aging mother had cataracts that were blinding her by the day. I was amazed that she did not know about the world events of the last few years. She was amazed that I did not know the difference in how to cook with two different colors of chilies.

The Bible instructs us to seek knowledge, and I do truly believe that God uses knowledge to help transform communities. Without knowledge, people do not understand how to prevent nor cure disease. They cannot understand how to supply clean water or improve their crops, and they lack fairly basic improvements such as electricity because they do not know how to install them. Quality of life remains at a substandard level when people do not have the knowledge of how to improve their situations.

That being said, I can understand those who argue that school is not necessary for everyone, and I do understand that a rice farmer may not need to know all that was ever written about philosophy and history. I also think, however, that lack of education denies people the opportunity to see how God is working--to grasp His goodness and creativity and to see His hand at work throughout history. People can still have joy and relative peace while living behind a veil of ignorance, but they will miss the opportunity to understand the tapestry of diversity in which God displays His character. Without being exposed to the capacity for evil in the world displayed through events such as 9/11, the mercy and grace and love of God become harder to grasp. An uneducated person may also lose the ability to relate to a large portion of the world around him and perhaps to comprehend his worth and value as a part of God's plan--aka self-revelation. I do not know for certain that Farah having known about Osama Bin Laden would have made her believe more in herself, but I think somehow there may be a connection. If she knew of such evil--such levels of unmerited hate--she could see how one life has the ability to affect the world around it for good or for bad. Then maybe she would be able to see her own capacity to affect the world, rather than believing as she did that her life was of little worth. Education in the sense of school rooms and books and teaching may not be critical. What it provides in bringing awareness, however, is priceless.

"Seek the Lord," His word says (Jeremiah 29:13), and experiences such as these make me want to seek Him even more. For I see that the less we seek to know about something (and thus the less we actually understand) the more we become oblivious to what is right in front of our eyes. I am convinced that God has great riches in store for us in knowing Him, but I often miss seeing those incredible things because I don't have sufficient understanding to recognize what it is that He is revealing. My heart cries out to grasp all that there is to know of God: all of His character, all of His goodness, all of His love, and all of His glory. My mind just needs to play catch up sometimes, living as it does in various states of unawareness that blind me to the blazing reality of God displayed all around me.

I want to press into learning more each and every day, and I am so thankful for the ability to do so. I am deeply appreciative of those who have greater wisdom than I do and have challenged me to grow, learn, and comprehend the world around me and the God who made it. I am thankful to have grown up with an educational system in which I was taught to evaluate information, process it, and think for myself. Perhaps one of these days I will even go back and thank my elementary school teachers.

Teaching Time

Once we had settled on the idea that we were going to rebuild the clinic and pursue long term work in the village, I wanted to become more involved in the community. Since I am not highly interested in the building side of things, I did not plan to be a lot of help in dealing with the ongoing construction. Even had I known better how to swing a hammer, a woman trying to do so would be far overstepping cultural bounds anyway. Jason and Uli would be overseeing construction, placing them in the village several days per week, but my other teammate and I needed an outlet for getting to know the village and beginning to build relationships.

Matthew, a college student on a yearlong break from school, soon decided to undertake the arduous task of building public toilets for the community. This invention has saved more lives in the last 100 years than any other in the history of civilization, we were told, so it seemed an obvious addition to our health work. The old mantra of an ounce of prevention being worth a pound of cure holds true, and the lack of hygienic restroom facilities creates problems with clean water supplies, waste disposal, and myriads of other issues. So we got permission from the village leader for building locations, and Matthew set out to learn everything he ever wanted to know but was afraid to ask about public toilet construction. Septic tank dimensions, waste water disposal techniques, and more became his subjects of study, and in a short few months he was duly rewarded with two functional, health-promoting septic facilities. The small buildings housed simple but functional ceramic holes in the ground, and we hoped they would be widely used. One was located near the clinic and one farther down into the community for easier access, and our team felt like we had made a good contribution toward promoting community health.

So Jason and Uli were tearing things down, building things up, and instructing a lot of men in what to do and where to do it, and Matthew was deeply absorbed in the study and construction of world sanitation systems. I was still trying to figure out how to spend time in the community, for I certainly did not want to sit around for three months waiting on the clinic to open and then suddenly be the new face in the village. I was ready, eager, and willing to start to observe, interact, and build relationships and trust in the village, and I was also well aware that building that trust would not come easily. So when my friends who were running a ladies' sewing class also began teaching in an elementary school just several rice farms away, I eagerly jumped at the chance to help.

I had taught older students in the past, but I had never seen myself as a particularly good English teacher. However, I did not imagine that teaching some simple English words to a class of eight to ten year old children for two hours, which was what the local teachers were requesting, could be particularly difficult. My imagination is apparently not very good.

Those two hours became some of the most difficult time I would spend in a typical week. My own study of language and the daily cultural bloopers I seemed to make paled in comparison to my trying to manage this class of kids, and there were several days that I actually returned home in tears. I was not alone in my suffering, as several of my friends who were teaching were also having a hard time. Misery may love company, but unfortunately company does not offer solutions to the problem. I quickly began to dread Thursday mornings, when I would awake and know I was headed out for a few hours of "torture by the little people." I had to pray for the love of God to really wash over my soul.

These kids, although beautiful, were absolutely horribly behaved. One could argue it was because of the heat, the lack of materials, or the goats and chickens that would often wander in and out of the classroom, but none of those excuses were adequate to explain the difficulty I was having. The kids would yell, scream, sing, laugh, roam around the room, stand on the chairs, and try to come and go at will from the room, and I felt essentially powerless to stop it. I was there to teach English, and this excited the regular teachers but did little to interest the actual students. Since I still spoke very little Indonesian, I found it basically impossible to try to enforce any kind of discipline. My valiant efforts at loving correction and gentle rebuke soon gave way to desperately harsh words and stern looks, but no amount of wagging my finger seemed to make much difference. The most disconcerting part of the whole experience was knowing that the students behaved like angels for their own teachers, never daring to question their authority, but my white skin erased any authority I may have held. The local teachers were delighted that four young women wanted to come and direct their classrooms for a few hours, and they saw no reason to come and assist us with the chaos. Tea and coffee and social time were valuable to them, and we had given them a free ticket to rest that they couldn't resist.

My friends and I prayed and planned and plotted together for weeks, trying to come up with ideas that would actually interest the kids, better ways to discipline them, and mostly just ways to love them. We prayed each week for the strength to understand their little hearts, for we knew that much of their behavior resulted from their experience. We knew that they were rarely disciplined in their own homes, but more importantly we knew that by and large they had grown up in a warzone of recent civil unrest. It really is no surprise that order and structure were not the default behaviors of children who had been living under curfew for fear of guns and grenades and had seen more death in their young lives than had I. On more than one occasion I had seen very small children playing war in the streets and fields, but they did not play in the way I had seen children play in the past. Their actions, their comments, their facial expressions and their pretend deaths were enacted in a way that was all too real. In a somewhat perverse way they seemed to enjoy themselves as they watched their friends crumple to the ground.

National Independence Day was celebrated with parades, treks to the city, and a carnival like spirit of festivity all day. It took my breath away that day, though, to see several large trucks full of children--teenagers down to virtual toddlers--being driven down the road as they waved toy guns (and even real ones for a few older youth) and shouted about killing anyone who tried to take away their independence. Having seen these things and knowing the country's history, I was not surprised by the children's behavior in my class. My understanding did not help me with classroom management skills, though. Nor did my friends' similar understanding stop the children from throwing spitballs and bubblegum at them on a regular basis.

God did help me to love the kids over time, although I continued to approach the day with a degree of trepidation. I began to learn their names (no easy task in itself since they were so unfamiliar to my ears), and I found that a few of the girls shyly seemed to begin to enjoy my presence. Candy, or the promise thereof, is a miracle of bribery in any language, and some creative games I learned from a friend helped me capture the kids' attention. The boys were much harder to win over, but that came in time as well.

Rajish, a small and wiry boy with endless energy, was the ringleader of the pack and the one who took the most delight in causing me trouble. He directly defied everything I asked him to do, roamed the classroom continually, and even verbally mocked me on multiple occasions. One day I was feeling a bit desperate as he was walking back and forth across the front of the room, singing over top of my attempts to teach the numbers 1-20, and suddenly I just stopped talking. I took the chalk in my hand, sweaty and broken from my tense hands snapping it in two, and walked over and handed it to him. He looked surprised at this action, but not nearly so much as when I went and sat down in his chair. Thankfully I am a small enough person to fit fairly comfortably in a school chair, for in that moment I decided I was going to stay there for a while.

Rajish smiled, sang louder, and ran over to the chalkboard to draw scribbles and letters and graffiti like markings, and then he turned around and shouted his delight at being the teacher. His eyes challenged me, and his words were basic enough for me to understand he was telling the class he could teach much better than this silly white woman. The class laughed, some nervously but most with true interest and fun, while a few began to glance my way. I just stared straight ahead. Rajish turned again and began to write, then swiveled around and said, "What should I teach?" to the class in general. Some more laughter erupted, but no answers came. "Ok, let's sing!" he shouted, looking in the crowd for advocates to join him. "Come on, everyone!" he yelled. I just sat and continued to stare, and interestingly none of the kids moved. "Ok, come on, everyone," he said with more reserve, but by then some of the kids had begun to look at the ground, the ceiling, or out the window into the dust filled sky. This went on for a few more minutes as the awkward silence grew until he finally looked at me and said, "What do I do?"

"Teach," I said.

"Teach what?" he questioned, his eyes becoming less challenging by the minute.

"Just teach. I cannot do it well, so you do it," I said.

From the back of the room came a voice strangled with laughter, "Yes, Rajish, teach!"

"Yes, do it!" came another voice, then another, then another.

Pretty soon the chorus was going up all over the room for Rajish to teach them English words, and the small young boy began to shuffle his feet dejectedly on the ground. His eyes averted to the floor, he whispered, "I can't," just loud enough for a few kids in the front to hear, which only made their mockery increase. After several minutes and a few pleading glances cast in my direction, my heart began to soften and break for this broken little boy, so I walked up to the front with him and stood at his side. His posture said that he expected me to yell, to reprimand, or possibly even to hit him, but instead I placed my hand on his shoulder and gently turned him around to the board.

"Write the numbers," I whispered to him, and then turned back to the class and announced that Rajish and I would be teaching *together* that day. Small victories with small people need to be celebrated, and there was a lot of rejoicing when I later recounted the story to my friends.

I won over Rajish and a few more of the kids, but the teaching times never did become very easy. More than the lack of discipline, what saddened my heart the most were the comments I heard from a few of the students regarding their ideas about foreigners--ideas which had obviously been placed there by older people in their lives. They questioned me about my culture, asked about how many boyfriends I had and the alcohol I drank and the drugs I must have done, and expressed some of the most common misperceptions the community held about people from the West. They asked me about my faith (or, more accurately, stated that I must not have one), and one child declared with more vehemence than I thought possible that I must not pray, did not care about God, and in fact had no morals. He called me "kafir," a word for infidel that has very unpleasant connotations, and he actually articulated that people who did not go to the mosque like he did were idolaters whom God hated. No eight year old says such things without having heard them on a regular basis, and I shuddered to think of the teachings these innocent and moldable minds may be receiving. Later on, I was not at all surprised to hear of a twelve year old girl in the city giving a speech about the depravity of all foreign aid workers and how our presence was wrecking the morality of their society. I began to pray regularly for the children of the area that their ears would be deafened to such hostile and angry thoughts, and I considered how easily kids are molded by what they see and hear. No wonder Jesus says that the Kingdom of God belongs to children, for they take things on faith very simply and literally. They can accept the truths of God without questioning as adults do.

Maybe all that God wanted me to learn from the whole experience of teaching was to notice that children are worthy of being noticed. Perhaps He wanted me to grow in patience and love for people--even little people--whom I found difficult to love. Maybe it was a combination of both. I am fairly certain He did *not* want to show me a life's calling as an elementary school teacher, for I never did excel in that. The kids may not have learned much English, but the in few months I spent teaching, I did accomplish what I had initially set out to do.

Kids and parents began to recognize me when I entered the village. One day as I was passing the coffee stand, averting my eyes from the men's stares and comments as I always did, my heart leapt a little and my spirits lifted. I heard one man say to the others that I was his child's teacher, and he was proud that his boy could say some English words. I kept walking with my eyes still on the ground, but I was smiling inside with the sudden sense of being known. I thanked God for that small encouragement. By that point I had begun to recognize that each day I had there in the village was a gift, knowing that I really had no right to be a part of this culture or these people's lives. Being known, beyond just being present, was an even greater gift, and it was key if I was ever to be able to build any real relationships in the community.

When the clinic opened eventually, quite a few patients came in and asked why I was no longer teaching. They knew who I was, and the familiarity enabled them to trust me more easily as their medical provider. Rajish came in as a patient several times, mostly remaining quiet by his mother's side but always giving me a smile, and I treated the boy who had called me "kafir" as well. He stole a bunch of candy from my desk, ran around outside the window, told his friends I was the pagan doctor, and took delight in destroying things in my room--but I actually think he liked me. For about three weeks he came to the clinic every time it was open to play outside and observe what was happening. He would peer in the back window and shout comments at will as I examined patients, then one day he asked me, very simply, why I was not his teacher anymore. When I explained that as the only medical provider I did not have time to both teach and to run the clinic, he suggested I come to the school on another day. I was on the verge of being flattered, and I thought I even saw a flicker of sadness in his eyes when I declined. I may have been wrong about that, though, for his next comment was something along the lines of, "Well, you are a better doctor than you are teacher anyway." I will try to take that as a compliment.

CHAPTER Eleven:
Loving Through Death

It was not uncommon for people to come to the clinic and ask me to go visit their sick relatives or friends in their huts. Supposedly, the patient was too sick to come to the clinic on his own, and sometimes I would find a patient who was truly ill and needing immediate care. Other times I would find someone who may just be lazy. Regardless, most of the time I enjoyed these visits, for they allowed me to visit with the family, see the way the community cared for those in need, and delve a little deeper into a new layer of local culture. Although I was usually exhausted at the end of the clinic day, these visits would only add an hour or less and brought great relational rewards. Besides, I said that I came to serve where needed, and if those in need would not come to me then I must go to them. However, I also knew that I could not go visit every sick homebound patient in the region, for I was only one person, and I usually limited home visits to the three villages in closest proximity.

When the village leader's wife Fauziah came to me and asked me to go see her relative, I was hesitant. The location she described was well away from our normal community, and the twisted story she was telling lacked a lot of information. The patient sounded quite sick, and it was unlikely I could do anything for him anyway. So I told her as much and suggested that someone bring him to the city hospital. She insisted, unwilling to give up, and pleaded with me by complimenting my great compassion and medical skills. Perhaps flattery goes farther than I thought, or perhaps I just knew that I wanted to help her because she was becoming my friend. So I conceded, and off we went in the rusty old car to find Bapak Ali.

The wasted body of the seventy year old man we met had been

ravaged by advanced prostate cancer. He was lying on the floor of his humble wooden home, weariness in his eyes, and his wife did most of the talking for him. We listened to the story of how he had seen a city doctor who told him the surgery he needed would cost sixteen million rupiah (about $2000 USD), at which point he had returned home hopeless. After all, he had never made more than twenty thousand rupiah ($2) in a day in his life. What frustrated me immensely was that I knew he could have had the surgery virtually for free: he could have applied for a "kartu askeses," a form of government assistance for the poor, which would have covered most of the surgical costs. No one had taken the time, though, to explain this to him. Bapak Ali, an uneducated and humble man, had asked no questions and gone home thinking that all he could do was wait to die. Unfortunately, when I arrived, six more months had passed. The cancer had spread, he had been bleeding, and he had become quite weak.

I struggled with God in my mind as I sat on that floor and watched his gentle wife fight back the tears. I knew I could not help Bapak Ali's cancer significantly, but there were eight people in the room that day looking to me for miraculous intervention. Whatever shred of hope they held onto was that I, the foreign medical provider who had mysteriously shown up at their door, would save their dying relative, and the pressure I felt was immense. I considered momentarily trying to get him to surgery and get it paid for, but I knew we did not have the funds for that in our clinic account. I considered the option of trying to obtain the government card for him, but I knew we did not have that much time. I considered what would happen if God would miraculously heal him, and I hoped against hope that He would choose to do so. Honestly, though, I had no idea what to do in that moment. Yet I somehow knew this was the place where God wanted me to be.

I spent a long time with Bapak Ali and his wife that day talking, crying, and trying gently to explain his prognosis. I told him that I believed Jesus could heal him, and they allowed me to offer a prayer for him right there on the floor. I don't think I prayed with much faith, though, flustered as I was by my tears and blubbering through my limited language skills. Finally I settled on the idea of trying to see if I could offer him palliative care, and I left the suffering family to go investigate some possibilities. I had no privileges to work in the city hospitals, but a surgeon who had recently been helping us did. So I called him and explained the situation, and he agreed to help us in admitting Bapak Ali to a hospital for tests. Two days later I returned to the spartan roadside home, picked him up, and drove him to the city hospital to stay for a week.

Bapak Ali was admitted that day through the ER since he was so weak and anemic from bleeding that he could not sit up on his own. During his stay he received a lot of blood, which made him much more energetic, and some other chemical imbalances were corrected. Our surgeon friend was stellar in helping out, and he ran a lot of tests and gave a lot of advice. Regrettably the cancer had already metastasized and become inoperable, so he suggested placing Bapak Ali on monthly hormone injections which would slow the spread of disease and minimize symptoms. I agreed that was the best option. I wish his family would have helped in making that decision, but each time I went to ask them for an opinion I was met with blank looks and an answer of "Whatever you think is best." They were no more willing to ask me questions than they had been of the local doctors, despite my obvious concern for their loved one; the fear of questioning authority was too deeply ingrained in their minds.

When I took Bapak Ali home for the first time, he was walking again. He had been carried into the hospital by family members, but blood transfusions, fluids, and basic medication had greatly improved his functional status. I had spent a few extra hours that week going back and forth to the hospital, and communication had not always been easy there. Overall, though, I had expended very little effort in order to make a very notable change for this family. We had bought Bapak some time and a better quality of life and hopefully had given him a sense of true love and compassion. Aside from coordinating his medical care, Uli and I had visited daily to provide food, medicine, and companionship to his family, and I felt God was using the situation to reveal His presence. I continued to tell his family I believed Jesus could heal him, and I continued to pray.

The following month I was happy to find Bapak Ali sitting up outside the front door when I arrived, although I was unhappy to see him with a cigarette in his hand. Arguably it was not the best time to wage my personal war against smoking with an already dying man, so I tried to ignore it and drove him to the city for his second injection. The therapy was done on an outpatient basis that time, and although it took all afternoon with the normal aggravations of paperwork and exhaustingly slow employees, we had him back by nighttime. We lingered with the family to enjoy eating the feast his wife had so graciously prepared, although I knew that she was sacrificing much of their waning savings and eldest son's income in order to provide it. Happily, I felt again as if we were making a difference for him, and we left with a promise to return in another month.

A Turn for the Worse

It was only about two weeks later that the nightmare began. I don't know what happened, but Bapak Ali suddenly took a turn for the worse. I don't know a great deal about prostate cancer and its complications, nor did I have diagnostics available to help if I did. What I do know is that I received a call from his son, who was somewhat panicked, saying his father was bleeding heavily, having pain, and waning in strength. It sounded as if he was becoming more gravely ill in a very rapid fashion. I phoned the surgeon, who was not interested in being bothered during the late night hours, and he told me to just bring Bapak in the following day. I called Bapak's son back, then his wife, then his son again, trying to clarify how sick our patient truly was, and eventually Uli and I agreed to go and get him the next day. This was not a menial task, as driving to his home required almost an hour and a half one way, but there did not seem to be another option. I was somewhat reticent to leave him through the night, but my suggestion that the family find a neighbor who could bring him to the city was ignored. I even considered going to get him myself late in the night, but I was finally convinced that it was better to wait until our surgeon friend was back in the hospital in the morning.

The morning came, and by ten o'clock we had Bapak Ali at the hospital. It was midnight before he was admitted. Yes, amazing as that sounds, it took a full fourteen hours that day to get this poor man accepted and settled into the ward, and that was with a native Indonesian and a well educated medical provider trying to jump through all the hoops for him. We went up and down the halls of the giant facility searching for the right people to help; as soon as we found one person, he or she sent us back to where we began to retrieve another form. Even our friend the surgeon, as nice as he often could be, had no interest that day in moving from his clinic chair to go help us find the inane things we needed. Rather, he merely informed us that we needed form A, B, and C for him to sign, asked us to go get them, and went on to his next patient. After finding form A, B, and C and bringing them back to him for signatures, off we went with a folder to the admission desk in the front of the hospital. There we were told that forms A, B, and C were fine, but the doctor needed to sign form G, H, and Z as well, which were included in the folder but which he had ignored. So on and so on this story went, for hours. All the while Bapak Ali sat on the patio weakly propped in a borrowed wheelchair, his strength fading quickly, and his wife watched helplessly as we tried to navigate a nearly impossible system.

After the paperwork was completed, the nursing battle began. When we finally reached the ward nurse's desk after many hours, at that point exhausted but hopeful, the nurse did not want to look at Bapak's papers. He was too busy listening to some kind of music, and so he nonchalantly tossed the folder aside and said, "Go get him."

I only ever saw Uli mad--truly mad--two times, and this was one of them. By late afternoon of that tedious day she seemed ready for all out war.

"*You* go get him," Uli challenged. "It's your job." Then she proceeded to scold the nurse in Indonesian so rapidly that I could not catch anything she was saying. It sounded very threatening to me, but unfortunately it did not have the desired effect.

"I'm busy," the nurse said.

"Busy being the most uncaring soul in the universe," I thought to myself as I went off to wheel Bapak down the hall. I did not mind going to get him as long as we could get the ailing man some help. He really needed fluids and another blood transfusion, and I just wanted something done. My bringing the patient down to the ward was not enough, however. The nurse also could not be bothered to draw Bapak's blood, type it, give him fluids or medicines, or anything else that required movement. We eventually did most of these things ourselves, and when it came time to give Bapak Ali the blood he needed, we discovered that we had to go get it personally. The Red Crescent blood bank, which was a twenty minute drive across the city, told us we had to find family donors on our own before they could help, and that search took another several hours. There were medication mix-ups, empty pharmacy shelves, and multiple other complications, until fourteen hours after we began, we left our quietly suffering friend for the night.

Bapak Ali improved a slight bit this time, although not as much as during his first stay, and we took him home a few days later. The following month's events were deeply difficult for me, for despite my prayers for him, he failed to improve. We had gotten ourselves into the precarious situation of caring for one patient intensively, and I was afraid it was creating jealousy among other clinic patients. In addition, I had been using clinic funds for his care, and I began to question the wisdom of that decision and regretted it over time. Bapak's family did not understand that the money the clinic was using to provide for his care would not stretch to provide for their living expenses as well. All they saw was a rich foreigner who was helping them, so they began to ask for money on a regular basis. Since I knew they had very little income since Bapak had fallen sick, I sincerely wanted to help them. I also knew that many of my other patients likewise lived on the fringes of extreme poverty, and I could not help them all. I was torn.

I started to receive phone calls in the middle of the night saying Bapak Ali was very sick. Would I be able to come to get him? Each call provoked anxiety, for I did not know how sick he really was or if the situation justified driving so far in the middle of the night in a dangerously unreliable vehicle. I knew from a medical standpoint I was in way over my head, but since there was no one else to help,

I could not stop at that point. Subtly, I began to resent that so much of my time was being consumed by just one family, and I recognized that I was partly responsible for creating their strong dependency on me. I was angry with myself for what seemed like poor judgment in getting Uli and I too deeply involved, and I was angry with God for not healing the man. Desperate--beyond desperate--for God to intervene and heal, I cried late into the night on many occasions, asking Him to do so.

People in the nonprofit world will advise you never to give money to one family or individual, for it breeds jealousy and dependency and does not allow people to take ownership of their own situation. Halfway into this experience I noted the wisdom in their advice, and I knew I was learning a valuable lesson for the future. As I prayed about it, though, God led me to Proverbs 3:27: "Do not withhold good from those to whom it is due, when it is in your power to do it." In the most wearying moments, I wanted to withhold good, for I really just wanted to give up and let someone else take over. God urged me on, however, with His kind yet strong leading. I could not see what He was doing in it all, but I knew that I could not give up and would see this through to the end--whatever that may be.

A Different Season

The end came about a month later when Bapak Ali died. I don't know why God did not heal him, but then again I don't know why God does not heal a lot of people. His death was a relief in some ways, removing the burden of responsibility I had felt and the daily anxiety over what might happen next. His death was also a huge disappointment to me, for I had desired his healing so greatly that it had almost become an obsession. Secretly, I believed that after all of my efforts and steadfastness, somehow God owed it to me to step in. I don't know how God puts up with my arrogance.

I was disappointed, and I grieved for Bapak Ali's family and their loss. I was concerned about what they would think about the God I believed in--the God who had not healed their husband and father--and I was concerned for their long term welfare. My ridicu-

lous ego was also concerned with what they would think of my failure to help him in the end, and so it was with trepidation that I
drove out with Uli to offer my condolences. She assured me as we
drove, gentle and loving as always, that the family would have no
anger or disappointment with me, but I did not believe her.
Inwardly I was questioning myself with all the "What if?" thoughts
that plague an unsettled soul.

"What if I had taken Bapak to one more location? Taken him one
more time? Offered one more medication or one more prayer?
Wouldn't he have been saved?" I assumed the family would be asking the same questions.

Surprisingly to me, I did not meet with anger when I entered
their circle of loss. I met with grief, certainly, masked by the interesting custom of actually celebrating for the first three days after a
death, but I did not see anger in anyone's eyes. I did not meet with
disappointment, blame, or condemnation. Rather, I met with
acceptance, humility, and appreciation for the time I had spent and
love I'd poured into the family. The local culture does not fight
death to the same degree as people do in the West, and when it
occurs it is merely accepted as a normal part of life. There is sadness, to be sure, but there is never blame. Blame is not placed on
caregivers, on doctors, or on God. Death is just accepted as
inevitable, and the focus then turns to the living. I found this attitude simultaneously disconcerting and comforting, and I was
immensely humbled that the family was still so willing and glad to
have me as part of their lives.

Uli and I continued to visit Bapak Ali's widow and children
often, but no one ever spoke of his death again. I still questioned
and grieved for quite a long time, wondering what had gone right
or wrong or if I had somehow been disobedient to God. I never
received the answers I wanted, just as Bapak Ali never received the
healing he wanted. The Holy Spirit and time, though, can bring
peace in unsettling circumstances. Once again, I was driven to
appeasing my mind with the knowledge that God's ways are higher than my ways; as difficult as that is to accept, it was all I had to
cling to. I did not enjoy thinking of the distressing circumstances
under which we were introduced, but I was grateful nonetheless for

having been knit together with this special family. My visits to them after Bapak's death felt much less like responsibilities and much more like delights, and their lack of condemnation eventually helped to heal the way in which I was condemning myself.

The final time I visited the family to let them know that I was leaving, God gave me a gift. Although I had mentioned God several times in conversation since Bapak's passing, we had never talked much about Him. We usually talked about the rice harvest, the clinic, the children, and other generic things that were easy to discuss, all the while sitting on the slat board floor of their meager hut and sharing the food they too generously offered. This day, though, I was shocked when Ibu Ali brought up a different subject all together. She told me that a lot of neighbors often asked why the foreign woman and her friend (Uli) came in the car to see their family, and they assumed somehow Ibu Ali must be secretly rich in order for us to want to do so. She just laughed in response, she said, and told them she had no idea why we came to see her. Then she looked at me with honest and questioning eyes and said, "Really, Ibu, I really do not know *why* you come to visit me." After all, there were a lot of sick people around there, I was a busy medical provider, they had never paid me anything, and there was no patient left to treat in their family anyway. My friendship with her was an inexplicable anomaly.

Happily I told her that I did not really understand it all, either, other than that I knew that the God whom I still loved and trusted had led me to their family. I told her I believed it was He who had orchestrated our meeting, and I told her I believed that He loved each member of her family immensely. I loved them, too, of course, but my love was only His love coming through me, and I believed that He wanted them to know that He was real through my presence and friendship. As a follower of Jesus, I said, I was called to love and serve those whom God put in my path. She nodded and listened from the corner of the floor where she was squatting. There was not much discussion after that, only silence, but she had clearly heard what I said.

I doubt anyone can explain why God did not heal Ibu Ali's husband: I know that I certainly cannot. I cannot explain suffering any more than I can explain mercy. Likewise, no one can see the future as God does: I certainly cannot. What I *could* see that day, though, reflected in Ibu's teary eyes when I left, was the result of His love having shone through in our relationship during all the long and difficult days. So now I pray for us both, Ibu Ali and myself, that God will continue to open our eyes to see this love-- His incredible, unexplainable, unrelenting love that will not be thwarted even by death—more clearly in the days He gives us to live.

CHAPTER Twelve:
Trials

Bulek Bodoh

"**The kids were at it** again, writing on the car," I thought, as early one morning I walked down my side street to where our cranky old vehicle was carefully parked in between the sewer and passing dump trucks. From down the street I could see markings on the window, scribbled in the ever present dust and dirt layer that formed from our village trips, and I knew the village children had become quite fond of writing and drawing in the grime. I think one of their favorite pastimes was trying to figure out how to spell my name, and on any given day there were variations of "Kimlee," "Kimbeli," Kiber," and a few other things scrawled alongside drawings of sheep, cows, flowers and the occasional gun or knife. Most days when I left clinic I smiled at the new writing, always curious as to what would appear, although the decorations produced a nagging feeling that I should take the car to the "doorsmeer" (carwash). Rarely was the writing inspiring enough to make that actually happen.

The sun was just rising over the back of the neighbors' houses, as it always did around this time, when I was headed out to another busy clinic day. Golden and amber hues mixed softly in the distance, producing just enough light to be able to walk without falling in the numerous potholes but not yet enough to be squinting because of the brightness. Still, I did squint my eyes a bit to try to read what was written on the back windshield of the car this time, curious since I had not noticed it on the way out from clinic yesterday. Neighbor kids had not yet taken up the game of car art as the village kids had, but there was certainly room and dust enough for them to do so. I just was not sure a lot of them knew my name beyond that of Ibu Doctor.

Suddenly I caught my breath, my curious and half sleepy eyes filling with salty tears. "Bulek Bodoh" read the crudely scrawled sign on our team vehicle, wide, tall and boldly proclaiming for all who passed by its translated meaning--"stupid foreigner." I quickly rounded the car, ducking out of sight of any oncoming cars that may notice the cruel letters and me as their apparent recipient, and jumped into the driver's seat. My eyes scanned the other windows looking for some other writing that would make the statement into a joke, an explanation, or a hint as to who had written the insulting phrase. Mostly my mind and soul were scanning and searching for a reason " *Why?*"

Why would someone write such a terrible thing? I was well aware after having been in the country for more than a year that foreigners were not popular with a certain segment of the population, but I easily became blinded or numbly ignorant of this when I surrounded myself with neighbors, friends and village residents who generally liked me. It seemed that the discontented minority was more concerned with the negative influences of Hollywood, the Western world, and its morals or religion than it was with individual people, and the vast majority of locals with whom I had contact seemed to be fond of me and eager to adopt me into their culture. So why would someone write that on our car? Who did it? Was it the village kids? If so, why did they do it now, after a year? Or was it a neighborhood kid here in the city, or even an adult, whom I may have unintentionally offended by any number of things I did out of cultural ignorance? My mind whirred back over the last few weeks, searching desperately for some scenario that would explain who had suddenly decided I was a less than intelligent outsider and worthy of scathing broadcasts to the general public to that effect. I could come up with none.

The vehicle belonged to our agency, so it was often filled with my clinic staff, team members or visitors, and the occasional patient I picked up on the roadside on the way to clinic. Seventy percent of the time, though, it was in my possession, so I had to assume the writing was likely directed at me. Although I could come up with no logical reason why someone would dislike me, try as I might, my spirit was simultaneously crushed by two thoughts. First of all, pride myself as I might on my amazing efforts at cultural adaptation, I would never, even years down the road, be accepted as a local person. I would always be a "bulek"--foreigner. Secondly, if one person was bold enough to write something like this on the car, how many others had similar thoughts and just did not express them?

My tearstained face revealed my emotional distress to Uli when I picked her up for work, and I simply pointed to the back glass in response to her worried inquiries. Suddenly I felt very weary. Was I doing this all for nothing? Was all the progress I thought I was making in relationships really just something I'd built up in my head to make myself feel better on the days I was sick of the heat and dirt and hard work? Were I and every other worker who were there pouring our lives out for these people secretly the laughing stock of all the kids and the scorn of all the adults in the community? Was our presence merely being tolerated because of the aid we brought? Was I continually doing stupid things that ran counter to the culture and that not only made me seem silly, but were even truly offensive to the people I claimed to love? My mind ran away in its misery while the car sat motionless in the driveway.

"Who did that?" Uli asked quietly, her eyes searching my face. Being quite out of character with her normally boisterous self, I knew she was well aware of how deeply the simple words had cut my spirit. She suggested that the message was just child's play and I should not worry about it, but then she quickly fell silent. We both exited the car after a few minutes and wiped away the words, not feeling the need for anyone else to read them, then started off down the road to pick up the rest of the staff. I requested she not mention it to the others, and she tried her best to affirm me. She reminded me that I did honestly love these people, that most of them knew that and truly appreciated my help and respected me, and that kids will be kids, no matter what culture they are in. She asked me to please try and not feel sad, for she saw the pain etched into my face. I loved every thread of Uli's gently encouraging spirit the entire time I was there, but on this particular day it did little to lift my sagging heart.

Life moves on, and seventy- something clinic patients did wonders to distract me from the message that had so shaken me that morning. The initial sting wore off fairly quickly, and I compartmentalized the feelings into the "think about that later" category where I thought they belonged. I did indeed think about it later, for quite a few days, and I continued wrestling with the message's significance, if any. As I did so, I also soon became consumed with a new revelation. More than the desire to know who wrote the message and more than the desire to know why, my compelling desire became to understand my emotional response to seeing it. I realized I would likely never find out where the writing came from (and I never did), and quite possibly I would be confronted with something similar again, or much worse (and I was). I could rationalize the experience, explain it away with cultural analysis, blame ignorance, or become bitter towards local people because of it, but none of those things would change the circumstance. As with most things in life, I have found that I can do little to control circumstances, but I can do a lot to control my response to them.

So I wrestled in my spirit with why I became so offended with the note on our car. I did not personally believe I was stupid, and quite honestly I did not think anyone else did either. I knew I was trying as hard as I could to respect the culture and love people around me, and I was continually praying for more ways to do so. Those things were not the problem. My musings slowly brought to light the only remaining reason for my sadness: at my core, I felt I deserved something –thanks, affirmation, and love perhaps--in response for what I was giving away in the form of my life.

It is easy to fancy myself a humble human being, boldly and sweetly sacrificing my life for Jesus in foreign lands. Situations like this, however difficult, are graciously used by God to remind me that I, at my very core, am selfish, and only by His grace do I love people at all. *What if* no one ever said thank you or even smiled at me for helping them? *What if* I was called stupid and dumb and invasive and irritating and an outsider every day by my patients and neighbors, simply because I am foreign and also because I follow Jesus? Would I stay there still, and if I stayed would I do it with joy?

Left to my own devices, I think I may persevere temporarily because people were sick and I could help them, but I would likely become bitter and disillusioned with the work, as many humanitarian workers seem to do. When I left home, though, I did not make bold announcements that I was going to help people who would love and adore me and thank me every day for my kindness; I stated I was going to help hurting people and show them the love of Jesus. Did that love truly reside in my soul? By His grace alone it would be so, so I asked God to help me as I brushed away the dust of pride that covered my heart. Then I offered thanks that His love can flow through even a stupid foreigner.

Kissing a Prince

The sweet old man had been into the clinic several times in the past, but it had been a few months since his last visit. As I glanced at his chart, I noted nothing significant in his medical history, his prior visits being for coughs and headaches and other generic illnesses, and I could not easily put my finger on what was so familiar about him. In a day of treating sixty or seventy patients, there were about forty I could usually recognize, twenty whose homes I could locate, and a handful whom I could identify by name, illness, family, or other stories that indicted we had a relationship beyond that of doctor and patient. There was the "chicken lady," who had thrown her blood pressure medication to the chickens when she decided it was too much for her, and there was the "asthma man," who came in every week for his breathing treatments. Ibu Fatima brought three kids in tow every time she came, at least one of whom would be screaming at ultrasonic radio frequencies, and the "laughing lady" spoke every time she came about her husband of whom she was not particularly fond. My "heart failure woman" had family in three countries that sent her news of the outside world, and Bapak Abu's chili harvest was a regular topic of conversation. I breathed a sigh of contentment when a patient like this would enter the exam room, feeling a real thread of a connection that made my work feel more valuable than just giving out antibiotic pills. I loved taking care of anyone who was sick and seeing them get well, but I valued really knowing people and their stories much more.

I recognized this man's weathered but smiling face, but I could not remember anything significant about him as we sat down to talk. Cough and cold symptoms had kept him up for a few nights, he said, and he had tried to wait out the illness. I was happy about this in light of the fact that many of my patients had been sick for an average of about thirty seven seconds before they came in to see me. The elderly gentleman seemed to be a little wiser, or at least more patient than most, so I asked him to tell me if he had bought any medicine at the pharmacy.

Pharmacies are ubiquitous in Indonesia. Next to cell phone credit stores, they are the most prevalent businesses lining the streets of the city and are even found in out of the way places on the way to the villages. Such convenience may be nice, but it can be also be dangerous when patients, carrying with them the normal array of advice and suggestions from family and friends, are able to buy whatever they would like to for their symptoms. So when this man reminded me that his son was a pharmacist and had suggested some medications, I was less than relieved. I was also suddenly aware of why I remembered his prior visits.

People trying to marry me off to a local were a dime a dozen. Sometimes it was a friend, a neighbor or a well known patient insisting I marry someone in his village, but it could just as easily be the labi-labi driver or banana seller on any given day. So it did not surprise me when this man, on several visits I now remembered with clarity, had insisted that I meet his son the pharmacist and marry him. He had given me his street address and cell phone number, and he told me about his personality and hobbies, his intelligence and upbringing, and of course his strong religious faith. The man had then proceeded to discuss with me how many grandchildren he would like to have and how he had always thought that for his children to marry a foreigner would be an accomplishment and a good thing for the family. I remembered his laughter as he envisioned his apparently tall, dark, and handsome son walking the streets with a short and pale skinned foreign woman. I remembered even more clearly discussing faith with him as a result of these suggestions.

In the middle of the mental dating game he was narrating to me, he suggested that I become a Muslim. Mixed faith marriages are unacceptable, so generally it is assumed that the foreign woman (or man) will convert and enter the religion of Islam in order to marry a local person. Naturally, I firmly stated that I would not do that, and he was quite curious as to why. Explaining to him that my faith in Jesus was the most important thing in my life and not negotiable was a giant sized task for the short amount of time a clinic visit usually allowed. Sensing the Holy Spirit on the move, though, I resolved to slow down and savor the conversation. He was a man of higher means than many patients in the surrounding village and thus more educated than most, and I enjoyed the intellectual conversation that ensued. It was a friendly discussion, punctuated by his astonished questions about my truly believing in Jesus, actually praying, thinking religion was more important than just what my parents had taught me ,and why I did not think that his religion was just a more updated and better version of mine. No radical changes took place in either of our hearts in those brief moments of conversation, but I had been happy to present my faith, at least, to someone who seemed to be a man of faith himself who was listening and eager to learn.

So the father of the pharmacist, I remembered, was a kind hearted man of good morals and character, who that day wanted cough medicine along with mixed race grandchildren. I smiled as I talked to him for a few minutes, happy to be in the presence of someone with whom I felt I had a connection, and the conversation soon returned to the topic of the previous visits. I insisted that I had not changed my mind and still wanted to follow Jesus, and he insisted that I was being silly and one day would see the truth. Sometimes I felt the message of hope in Christ would go farther with uneducated people who had little knowledge of the tenets of the faith of their upbringing, but on other days I felt that schooled men like this one were poised and ready to soon receive the truth about Jesus. We talked about faith and family and world issues for a few moments, at which point I was reminded by the bone breaking coughing fits of someone outside the door that large numbers of patients were not going to allow time for extended conversations that day.

He placed his gnarled hand on top of mine and looked at me. Touch between a man and a woman is not normal in this culture, but in the context of someone old enough to be my father I did not find it particularly offensive.

"Come to my house," he said. I smiled, always blessed by my patients' friendly invitations, and suggested one day my staff and I may stop by on the way back to the city.

"No, come on a day you are not working," he said, which I assumed meant he was eager to spend more time with us. I politely stated that we would all try our best, perhaps on a weekend, and tried to remove my hand and start to show him to the door. Evidently he knew that I was misconstruing his meaning, for he held onto my hand and repeated his invitation, this time stating he wanted me to come alone.

"So you can bring your son?" I teased with him. He grinned, his eyes crinkling up as he nodded slyly and agreed that he may possibly do that. Pretty foreign women were not often in his home, he noted with a sigh, and it would be a great joy for him if I were to come. Apparently he often felt lonely after his wife had passed on some years ago.

I was starting to get a bit impatient at this point, knowing the crowds outside were getting restless, but his sudden sadness and seemingly sweet words kept me sitting there. Then before I knew what was happening, I felt the man's other old and wrinkled hand on my cheek, drawing me close enough to his face to smell the breath that held the lingering stench of cigarettes and coffee. A heartbeat before he was able to connect our lips, my startled mind kicked into gear and directed my frozen arm to slap him away. I jumped to my feet, disgust flooding my heart, and announced I was moving on to the next patient. I moved as swiftly as possible to the door to open it, during which time he caught up with me and placed his hand on my shoulder in an attempt to spin me around.

"Please come," I heard his voice insisting as he exited, but I refused to look up at his expression as my eyes stayed firmly fixed on the ground.

The next patient in line had to wait a few minutes while I shut the door and attempted to collect my swirling emotions and thoughts, trying to assuage my ire at what had just taken place. I was shaking as I pondered how ignorant I had to be not to have avoided that situation, and I mentally replayed the visit to see if I had encouraged his actions in any way. Being a foreign woman already made most people think I had questionable morals, and I hated that. I deliberately went out of my way to try to counteract that image with my dress, words, and actions, and while I did make more eye contact with men than most local women, it was only in the context of our provider/patient relationship. I wondered if that alone had been enough to encourage him--or had I smiled too much, or lingered too long? I was irate with the old man, whose description in my mind had just shifted from sweet and kind to dirty and perverted, and I was angry with myself for letting it happen. I was frustrated that I had not yelled at him to bring attention to what he had tried to do, but the suddenness of the whole experience had left me little time to react. I was saddened that someone I thought to be devout in his faith would easily display such questionable morals, and I questioned for the thousandth time how little I seemed to grasp of what was going on around me or what I thought God may be doing in someone's heart.

My anger abated enough to finish out the clinic day, but over the next few days the scenario gave me a good amount of food for thought. Should I have yelled and made a big scene about what had occurred? Perhaps, but in a culture that strongly emphasized honor and shame, this may have done more damage to his reputation than was fairly deserved. Jesus convicted people of their misdeeds, but never in a publicly shameful way that followed a law of retribution. Had I misconstrued what God was doing in those conversations entirely and told someone about Jesus who was just looking at me as an object of lust? Perhaps, but likely not. For that "dirty old man" was indeed an object of God's affection, and nothing he felt, thought nor did in sin would change the fact that God desired to have his heart. All of us, in our sinful nature, are similarly awaiting redemption, and our hearts can be well along in the process of seeking God while our actions are still far from holy. Despite his actions, God could have been pursuing this man's heart, and He used the situation to teach me something about grace.

I had judged the old man to be filthy, offensive, and tricky, defining his entire being from one sinful act I saw him commit. I also counted him as hypocritical for committing this offense while verbally giving praise to the one he worshipped. As I searched my heart that night, though, God gently convicted me that I do much the same, praising His name one minute and acting in rebellion the next. How much more must this be an offense to Him who so freely showers me with His love! I had a choice to make with this man, and it was this: to despise him and identify him as a wretched old man unworthy of my time, or to forgive him and see him as a potential prince in the Kingdom of God. It is the same choice God has to make with me on a continual basis, and I am infinitely grateful that He chooses to forgive, day after day after day after day. Jesus commands us to forgive "seventy times seven" (Matthew 18:22), while He himself forgives a hundred times a thousand. For me to choose the path of un-forgiveness would close off my heart to not only what God may want to do *through* it in relating to the man, but also to what He may want to do *in* it as a work of grace and revelation.

In this moment of clarity, God revealed to me that I had a choice to extend or not extend the grace that He extends to me. Thankfully I chose the former and actually did forgive the man, later referring to him with friends who had prayed with me as the "prince who tried to kiss me." He returned several months later, a few weeks before I was leaving, and I breathed a swift prayer as he entered the room. Happily, I can honestly say that because I had allowed God to change my heart, I was able to welcome him in without anger. We had a good visit, during which I was able one final time to express my love of Jesus, and I was happy to be able to relate to him with an open heart. Only this time I also took care of him with an open door.

Loss of Power, Floods, and Other Small Catastrophes

It is funny how as a person learns to adjust to once unfamiliar things, they can become normal. When I arrived, being a good

Westerner who was quite used to comfort and convenience at every turn, I was a bit appalled by things that later became very commonplace to me. Take lizards, for example. I was none too fond of the small, phenomenally quick little creatures that lived in our kitchen, wardrobes, bedrooms, and baths, and I was particularly not fond of them staring at me with their small beady eyes from the side of the basin where I had to pull out water to bathe. The cute chuckling noises they made were kind of endearing, but I still would have preferred life without them. As time passed, however, I somehow forgot about the lizards--not because they went away but because I could not beat them and had more important things to worry about. I became so used to seeing them dart across the table that I no longer flinched when they scuttled out from their hiding places underneath plates and bowls, and at night I even found myself sometimes saying goodnight to the ones on the walls. "Lizards live in kings' palaces," Proverbs 30:28 tells me, so I tried to pretend I was in a palace as well.

Ants are another example. They are amazing tiny creatures anywhere they live in the world, but the ones living in Indonesia are particularly hearty little fellows. They would party in our kitchen, trailing from the floor to the sink to the table and across the walls, and we would amuse ourselves by trying to draw chalk lines around them with "ant chalk" that was supposed to keep them at bay. It did not work. Ant sprays likewise did not work, but rather brought out their little ant friends, and they even seemed to have adapted to cold enough temperatures to live in the refrigerator. The freezer was the only zone off limit for our ants, but I often wondered at what point they would conquer that terrain as well.

Just as I had adjusted to the lizards, I became so accustomed to seeing the ants after a while that I almost forgot they were there. That is, until one day I opened a drawer in my bedroom and saw piles of them crawling all over my clothes. Someone had just mailed me a care package the day before, including a new tee shirt (which was in the drawer) and some peanut brittle which had not fared too well on the ocean journey. The peanut brittle had evidently melted onto the shirt, and the ants had made quick work of finding it. What would have bothered me when I first arrived by that point only made me laugh, as I thought to myself, "Well I guess I don't have to launder that, since they are handling it for me!" Normal truly is relative.

Bathing was another prime example. Granted, I had never been one to linger for hours on end in hot showers, so the absence of shower heads in my new world was not of great concern to me. I do, however, like to be clean, so upon my arrival I was eager to learn how to use the local system for bathing. "Boks" are large cement tubs in the bathroom which remain filled with water. The bather takes a small bucket, dips it in this water, and pours it over his or her head. Simple. Thankfully I had someone to explain this to me the first time I used one, for it is tempting to gaze at the water filled bok and consider how one might climb inside. The walls are typically about three feet high, however, which makes entry difficult, so I was relieved to learn that it was used for water storage rather than as a tub. (Incidentally, one of our visitors was not so fortunate to receive this explanation and actually climbed inside the closet sized square, later finding it difficult to get out!)

I learned the mechanics of scooping up water in the bucket and dumping it over my head fairly easily, and I also learned that looking into the water first was a wise idea. On more than one occasion I inadvertently disturbed a bathing creature's swim and dumped him over my head along with the water, which produced a fairly disconcerting sensation. After the first such occurrence, which horrified me, I began to search carefully each time I drew a bucket up to make sure I would be bathing with critter-free water. Over time, however, as in all things, I grew more accustomed to intrusive small visitors and virtually did not notice when an occasional bug would flit across my hair or face along with the bathing water. They were not hurting me really, I thought, and after all, they had been there first. An exception to the level of comfort I had developed came when I actually scooped up a bathing mouse. Thankfully the oddly heavy sensation of the bucket stopped me from pouring him over my head!

On a more distressing note, sometime during the heat of the summer a transformer went out in the largest city on our island. Although that city was eight hours away, it was the point of generation for our city's power supply. This transformer issue was a relative disaster. At first we did not realize what was going on, for power cuts of two to four hours per day were fairly routine. We were accustomed to having the lights blink off suddenly, at which point any office work stopped, and we reverted to having meetings or just talking or pretending we did not care. Then a few hours later the lights would return, and we went on our merry ways unharmed and only a little bit sweatier from the experience. This particular month, though, the cuts seemed to be lasting longer than normal and becoming more frequent, and after a week we were up to twelve hours per day with no electricity.

Knowing a language well enough to read a newspaper is a valuable skill but not one that any of us on our team had mastered at the time. If we had, we would have known that the transformer had blown out, and we would have known the power company was forcing a rolling blackout in the city. We would have known that this was going to last for probably over two months, and knowing that we probably would have cried. For it was hot and getting hotter still, and the gentle blowing of a fan made a world of difference in that kind of muggy heat. Even fans cannot run without electricity.

Thankfully, visiting friends had left behind a valuable generator, and within a week we had it wired to power the necessities of the house for a few hours at a time. We could get some computer work done when necessary, have lights in the evening to cook, fill the bucket tubs (the water pump also did not work without electricity), and run a fan for temporary relief. Nighttime use of the generator was out of the question, though, for the noise it made was on par with a freight train and did not merit the good will of our neighbors. When our blackout times were from 8:00 P.M. to 8:00 A.M., we invented all kinds of games: zapping the most number of mosquitoes, playing hide and seek in the dark with flashlights, and telling scary stories about what kind of rodent may be hiding behind the sofa. We certainly could not sleep.

I complained during this season. I complained a lot. After my teammates all left, though (which luckily for them, they managed to do about three weeks into the siege), I did not have anyone to complain to anymore. I could not complain to the local people because they were suffering as well, and they were not complaining. Oh. Perhaps I should learn something from that? I was a spoiled Westerner, accustomed to having comfort and convenience around the clock, but they were much more used to situations like this.

Evening time power outages suddenly became golden opportunities to talk to my neighbors. What else were we to do in the dark besides sit outside on the porch, fan away beads of sweat, and enjoy each other's company? My suffering alongside them, choosing not to go stay in a hotel with generated air conditioning as many Western workers did, significantly deepened our relationships. I was not one of them, but I was at least closer to understanding what it meant to be one of them.

That power issue lasted well over two months, and it taught me a lot of patience. There were a lot more inconveniences to come, but I think I was better equipped to handle each of them as a result of having lived through the first. At least I was in a better mindset to handle the annoyances. For example, at one point about a year later the power company decided that our neighborhood was not worthy of having electricity from about 7:00 P.M. until midnight each night. The problem seemed unique only to a few streets, and there was no explanation on that occasion of transformers being out. There was no explanation given at all, actually, but I knew better this time than to fight and complain about something I could not change. So evenings became an exploration time of what could be done by candlelight. I found myself more often praying and singing and chatting to my roommates, and I tried to learn to slow down and enjoy the moments set before me. I also learned to stargaze more often.

Usually I rarely notice the sky, both because I am focused on where I am going and because stars are not very easy to see past the harsh glow of city lights. During that time, though, having little else to do, I deliberately began stepping out into the dark each night and looking upwards. Each time, I had to catch my breath at the beauty of what I saw. The twinkling glory reminded me that there is much more to reality than what I can or often choose to see, and I was humbled into remembering that God's light will shine through even the strongest darkness.

In the last house in which I lived, I had yet another new experience with the now infamous power company. Who knew that it is possible to have house lights that blink on and off every three to five minutes, creating, free of charge, a personalized strobe light effect? I know it now. I also know that water supplies can suddenly be shut off with no explanation, requiring tanker trucks to come and pipe water into your holding tank through the front bedroom windows. Unfortunately I now know that the pipes coming through those windows do not always get pulled back out without dumping significant amounts of water all over your bed. My neighbors commiserated with me over that woe, and we had some good bonding moments as we shared our limited water supplies with each other that week.

Rainy season came with its unique share of difficulties, and flooding was common throughout the region. It is dangerous to wish for things sometimes, I have learned: take a desire to exercise, for example. I had been lamenting my need for physical activity right about the time the floods in our house began, and that need was more than met when I began to have to bucket out the water from our kitchen floor that rose up to my knees. Almost daily for a few weeks, my roommate and I would find ourselves sweeping, mopping, and bucketing rain and groundwater out the door of the kitchen each morning, sometimes spending up to two hours in this work before we could get to the task of making coffee for breakfast. My complaining spirit often reared its ugly head again during these early morning arm conditioning routines, but I also found myself praying for my neighbors and others in similar situations.

Once life in difficult circumstances like these became more normal, the small inconveniences that used to drive me crazy became much more tolerable. Some of them actually became unnoticeable until visitors who were still accustomed to living in the world of readymade convenience pointed them out to me. I had forgotten what it was like to sleep without squashing a hundred mosquitoes on the wall every night until a guest asked me how to use the mosquito racquet, and I had forgotten what it was like not to have ants covering every shelf in the kitchen until another visitor requested her tea be made with cream but no ants. Conveniences are not a bad thing, and I will never take such blessings for granted. I actually found myself grateful, though, for having lived without them. I discovered that my gratitude flows much more easily when I do not expect so many things, for then I see what I do have as a gift rather than something that is deserved.

On a deeper level, these small trials also made me consider how much I take for granted things like relationships, family, friends, and community. Just as I had with conveniences, I had always expected these things in my life for I had always had them. In actuality, though, they were never things I had earned or been promised to receive. I could learn to live without power and diesel fuel, but I knew it would be much harder to live without such dearly valued people in my life. When I began to recognize these relationships as unmerited gifts rather than assuming they were normal, I moved through each day with a much deeper sense of gratitude in my heart.

All of these experiences helped to ground me in understanding how most of the world lives, and I continue to realize more each day how every single thing in my life is a gift from my Heavenly Father. Back in the Western world, I now breathe a prayer of thanks for the safe vehicle that I drive, and I often offer thanks when I turn on running tap water. I still offer thanks for lights that stay on when I need them to, and I am thankful for restaurants--not to mention my own kitchen—that are not filled with crawling bugs. I say thank you more often to people who try to help me by offering unexpected but appreciated services, and I am thankful for slower periods of time in life to sit and talk to neighbors. I pray often that God will continue to cultivate gratitude in my heart and my actions, and I am even thankful for each of the trials that have brought me this far. In the moment I may not have enjoyed them, but I walked away from each of them as a different person—perhaps a little more patient and a little more gracious. I see God's light in dark situations more easily than I did in the past, and I even still stargaze more often.

CHAPTER Thirteen:
Moments of Happiness

I loved being in Indonesia. For all its difficulties, I truly loved it. There were moments of such joy, perhaps made sweeter because they contrasted with moments of intense frustration and pain. Many days were hard, and there were plenty of days when I cried. Thankfully, though, I think I spent more time laughing. I laughed at the goat riding in the motorcycle sidecar with its feet sticking over the side and knocking the driver on the forehead. I laughed at Ria and Ika when they told jokes and poked fun at my accent, and I laughed at patients who told me I needed to get married in order to be a smarter doctor. I laughed at the restaurants that listed twenty seven items on the menu, only one of which they actually had, and I chuckled at the roadside stands that attempted to join Western culture by having names like "Stars Wars, Burger Queen, and Kentucky Chicken." None of the owners knew what their signs actually meant in English. I laughed a lot when Uli sent me a text message from her hometown saying, "I am eating dog and blood (a local delicacy)--do you want some?" She knew good and well that I didn't and that I had almost gagged on the suggestion the week before, but she also knew it would make me laugh. I love to laugh, and I loved that I could do so on a regular basis. It kept me sane, as did reflecting on moments of real joy. There were many of those.

Ibu Cut

One morning on the way to clinic a patient called and asked me to pick her up by the roadside. Ibu Cut had been coming to visit me for several months, and she, of all my patients, traveled the farthest to our clinic. She had first appeared one day after visiting her son who lived in the area, but her actual home was almost eight hours away by bus. Her family was better off than many I knew, and as a result she had already been obtaining care for her chronic heart failure at the city hospital. Whatever I was able to offer her, though, which I imagined was mostly love and a patient ear, seemed to be more than she had received at the hospital. So I became her "doctor" of choice, and every five weeks or so this very gentle, distinguished woman would travel eight hours to visit me for a checkup. Her wise and restful spirit always impressed me, and something about her persona was calming in an inexplicable way. She was more highly educated than most of my patients, which meant that we could talk on a slightly deeper level. In addition, she was a woman of deep faith, and her conversation was peppered with the statement "In God's will" in virtually every sentence. For many people this phrase was used merely out of habit, but not so with Ibu Cut. She really believed it. I delighted to see her enter the clinic on those monthly visits, and she would always wait to be my final patient so that we could spend more time talking to each other. She also called on me periodically to make home visits to some of her son's neighbors, so on occasion we were able to meet outside the clinic and share a meal.

Ibu Cut's son lived alongside the main road heading into the village, and several times I found her standing outside of his house waiting for me to pick her up on my way in. One morning she surprised me by actually calling me at dawn and asking if I could come and pick her up. In the middle of a week of eye surgeries, I was exhausted, but I still smiled to myself at the thought of seeing her that morning. An hour or so later, I pulled up along the roadside where she was patiently waiting, seemingly oblivious to the dust and grime now soiling her always pristine clothing. Then this sweet, smiling woman told me that she did not actually need treatment that day, but she had wanted to make sure I stopped so that she could invite me to her son's wedding. She eagerly passed me the printed invitation for the festivities, which were the very next day. (Local custom never offered more than a week's notice for wedding invitations!) I would not be able to attend due to the surgeries, but it was acceptable to offer congratulations to the family for several days after the party. So I promised that my staff and I would stop by a few days later after clinic, and then we headed on to a day's work.

I almost forgot my promise four days later, being tired and distracted after having just completed our whirlwind surgical week. This dear lady was not about to let me forget, however, and she began to call me every hour on the hour to find out how close we were to being finished with the day's patients. Around 4:00 P.M. we finally made it over to the house, all secretly hoping for a simple exchange of pleasantries and a quick visit. I even told her upon arriving that we were tired and could only stay for a few minutes, and I imagined we could eat a cookie or two and then head on our way. Surprise quickly altered this expectation when we saw the elaborate spread of delicious food she had prepared just for us.

Ibu Cut had basically recreated the entire wedding meal in an effort that certainly took hours of extensive preparation, and she had done it entirely for us. Greatly humbled, I realized that she was essentially calling us her family, for no other post-wedding visitors would have received such lavish treatment. So we sat on the decorative floor mat she had unrolled, wrapping ourselves in a semi-circle around the brightly colored and aromatic food, and set aside our plans for leaving anytime soon. Instead, we inquired about the wedding day itself, which she said had gone off quite well. Yet I could see fatigue etched into the lines of her aging skin, so I asked, "Ibu, when will you return to your home? You must need some rest."

"Yes, "she replied. "I would have gone back yesterday, but I wanted to have you come and celebrate with me, so I waited." Again, a sense of humbling gratitude washed over me, and I realized that I truly loved this woman. The mysterious closeness in our relationship must have come from God, for our experiences and lifestyles were worlds apart. Yet she considered me her family, and I suddenly realized I considered her mine as well. I did not feel the hurry to leave her home that I often felt when making visits from obligation. Rather, I wanted to be there celebrating with her, enjoying her company, and reveling in the moments God had given us to share as friends. So I reclined onto her floor, unhurried, sighed a contented sigh, and ate another coconut cookie.

My Little Log Cabin

The first night I spent in the village house goes down in my mind as one of the truly "sacred moments" given to me by God. I left for the village early Wednesday morning as usual to drive to the clinic, but this time I carried six Filipino friends with me who would be staying there as well. These friends had been teaching and working on income generation projects in the same village, and I was delighted to be working alongside them.

We shared a common vision for the people in that region to know Jesus, so we had a sweet time of prayer together as we drove. When we arrived, I went off to attend to the busy clinic as usual, and the other women spent the morning cleaning the house and chatting with the neighbors. I was eager to join them once my patients were gone and I had everything set for the next day. Once I did, I sat and played with Laila and talked to Farah for a very long time. I loved being able to do this without feeling rushed to return to the city as I normally did, and I knew immediately that extended days here in the village would become highlights in my week.

My friends had planned a children and youth program at the house later that day, but at the appointed time it was pouring down rain. No one appeared to be coming. Many young people had told us they would be attending, but I did not blame them for not wanting to slosh through muddy village waters. Not to be discouraged, though, I decided to go pick up the kids in our car. So I prayed a quick prayer (knowing I would again be testing my still questionable driving skills) and grabbed a nearby teenager as a guide to help me navigate the village lanes and find our young friends.

Passing many cows, chickens, and potholes, we ventured farther into the housing area of the village. We narrowly escaped being stuck in the mud several times, but we were determined not to be deterred from our quest. When we finally did pull up amongst the stilted huts, a lot of the village women were standing around laughing and pointing at me driving, especially when I got out of the car and several recognized me as the "doctor girl." My heart jumped with happiness to be recognized with such brilliant smiles. I knew perfectly well that the smiles most likely stemmed from watching me slip and slide over the roads, but I decided to consider them instead as an indication of my growing acceptance in the community.

So the "doctor driver" returned to the house with a carload of curious kids. It had stopped raining at this point, so the younger ones went into the house while the teenagers went outside for their English lessons. I stood and watched a good part of this with Farah (who incidentally had turned out to be our next door neighbor), and I marveled to see life coming into this house that had not existed even in our minds four months prior. I delighted in seeing smiles on the faces of the young people who were starting to see us care for them, in seeing the beauty of God's glory reflected in the surroundings, and in feeling at home.

After the programs were over and the kids returned home, curious neighbors wandered in and out of our new house to visit. Sri and Aisah, two young ladies who had been helping us in the clinic, sat on the floor making bracelets and talking for about three hours. A sweet little grandmother came and sat on the floor and watched us quite closely for a while, and I watched her as well as she laughed at my language blunders and all we were attempting to do. We spent the evening by candlelight since there was no electricity in the house (or in fact in most of the village). Silently, while watching the flickering glow, I pondered how a life that God ordains, no matter how simple in nature, can feel nothing short of amazing. Then before retiring in a happy state of fatigue, my friends and I prayed that others who entered our new home would feel the same sort of amazement and somehow sense God's presence. I proceeded to fight a valiant battle with the resident mosquitoes throughout the night, but the red marks on my body the next day told me I had lost.

Early the following morning, I found myself alongside two village women drawing pails of water from the fourteen foot well behind our house. Coming from a suburban Western background, I had always found it difficult to relate to Biblical accounts of women congregating at a local well. Suddenly those passages came alive to me, though, for on that day (and many to follow) I began to understand the importance of the community well in daily life and relationships. My biceps got bigger while my worldview expanded, although it was several months before I could pull up a full bucket of water with the same speed as my neighbors. I even tried diligently to master the skill of carrying the water bucket back to the house on my head as they did, but I never met with success. Thankfully my happiness was not dependent on such skills! The simple village life I had experienced that night was a joyful one, and it was but the first of many more to come.

Clinic Stories

Every month at our clinic staff meetings, I would ask what we were doing well and what needed improvement. Most of the time my questions were met with silent stares, for meetings in which anyone other than the leader is expected to speak were rare in the culture. One staff member, though, was always eager to give his opinion, and I usually loved what he had to say. Leo was responsible for maintenance of the building, occasional car maintenance, and various other odd jobs, but many days he was left with nothing to do but sit outside and talk to those who were waiting. He thus was able to monitor the spirit of the patients--their level of satisfaction with the care being offered--and keep a finger on the pulse of the community. Since I rarely saw past my closed office door, I appreciated this greatly. Virtually every month Leo had a different short story or random tidbit of information to present, but he also consistently commented that everyone loved coming to our clinic because they felt well taken care of.

Obviously this was our desire--to offer quality care to people in a way that made them feel valued, respected, and loved by our staff and by God. I wanted to take excellent medical care of the patients, and I was glad to know they thought I was doing so. Leo said that most patients emerged from the building saying that I took the best, most thorough care of them imaginable, and they were awed by the completeness of the physical exam I had given them. No matter how many times he said this, I could not contain my laughter, for what I was offering was in reality far from complete. I sometimes affectionately referred to my standard of care as "garbage can medicine," for I spent about as much time with many of them as it took to light the incinerator outside. An average visit lasted three to five minutes, and my only non negotiable part of a physical exam was listening to make sure the patient's heart was still beating. I checked very little on each of them, never beyond what their complaints warranted, for I simply did not have enough time. Many times I even worried that may be missing things, and yet the patients felt they were receiving amazing care.

As I thought about all of this, I realized maybe it was just God's hand of grace over the whole operation. People were exiting the clinic feeling something more than well examined: they were feeling well loved. It does not always take a lot of time to make someone feel this way. It only takes concern. As a staff we would pray on the way to clinic each day that God would love people through us, and I think that was happening. Offering a simple smile, stating a name, asking about a family member, looking in someone's eyes-- all of these were easy gestures that made the patients feel worth as individuals. That sense of value made them leave with a satisfied heart. Since I honestly never believed we were offering outstanding medical care, I was much appeased to know we were at least offering genuine love. We prayed for the Holy Spirit to touch each person entering the building, and I joyfully believe that thousands of people had moments of interaction with God through our care.

Clinic life was busy, and some days it was stressful. Some days it was sad, and other days it was a lot of fun. Regardless of the emotion that pervaded the day, though, it was always good. I often remarked to Uli that I loved my job, and I wondered why God allowed me to be a part of these peoples' lives. I loved taking care of the community, and I loved just being with them. The once foreign faces soon became people with names and stories and emotions and families, and I loved interacting with them in myriads of ways. I loved the women who came in the morning to stretch before going to the rice fields, and I loved the men who insisted their cough had nothing to do with the four packs of cigarettes they smoked each day. I loved the sweet old demented man who came every day for two months asking if we could remove his facial tumor, forgetting each time that we had offered him direction on how to get it done. I loved the patients who thought they had malaria if they were hot for more than five minutes, and I loved educating them that their self diagnosis was not necessarily correct. Perhaps most of all, I loved the patients who made me laugh, and thankfully there were many of them.

Curing the Chicken's Blood Pressure

An elderly woman from the village came to see me one week, brought by her son whom I called the "noodle man." He owned the only place in the village to buy food--a fried noodle stand that kept the staff well fed. The woman hobbled along slowly, hunched over from arthritis, and she came to complain of her joint pain. She was probably in her upper sixties, although it is difficult to predict the age of someone who does not know her own birthday and has years of hard work and sun etched into her skin. Speaking not a word of Indonesian, she emphatically chattered away at me in local dialect, insisting that I give her new medication for her pain.

"OK," I agreed, "I see that your arthritis medication has probably run out. I am concerned about your blood pressure, though, Ibu," I said, then waited for her son to translate to her. "Why is it so high today? Did you take your medicine?"

She told me it was finished.

"No," I argued, "That is not possible. Seven days ago I gave you thirty pills. What happened to them all?"

Still smiling, as she always was, she giggled and insisted it was all gone. I checked again through her son, asking him to please make sure she understood and asking did her son happen to know where the medicine may be. This went on for several minutes with all of us getting progressively more confused, until all of a sudden she remembered.

"Oh that little pill you gave me?" she asked. "I thought it did not help my back pain." (I was not surprised by this since blood pressure medication is not designed to help back pain).

"The other one did help, though," she said, "so I threw that little one outside. I think the chickens ate them."

I choked back my laughter and tried to move on with the visit. With the mystery solved at last, I spent some time explaining her different medications again and asked that she return in a week. As she shuffled out the door, I breathed a quick prayer for this sweet woman's soul, and I smiled at the thought of the chickens that now had very good blood pressure.

Looking at Faces

As much as I loved working in the clinic, there were times in which I grew weary. At one such point, when we were quickly outgrowing our staff, medication supply, and space in the building, I was growing tired of being ever rushed and crowded. I loved the patients that I knew well, but I was feeling little empathy for the large number who were unfamiliar to me. I was not enjoying treating what seemed to be just an endless sea of faces, and I was bordering on downright irritability. Then, by God's grace and guidance, I began to notice something in my daily Bible reading. It was not a deeply theological revelation, rather just something to which I had not paid much attention in the past. The Bible, I noticed, often mentions Jesus *looking* at an individual. He of course saw the masses of people who were pressing in to Him for healing and teaching and a touch of His robe, but often it is clearly stated that he *looked* intently at one person (Mark 10:21). So I decided one day that even amidst the chaos, I should stop and look at—really *look* at-- people's faces. As a result, I began to marvel at the beauty that God had etched into each one. For example, "patient number 52" one day was a grubby faced boy with a toothless grin, sparkling eyes of mischief, and a slightly crooked nose. "Patient number 14" was a gray haired grandmother of twelve with droopy eyes, freckles all over her face, sari juice running down her chin, and anxiety written deeply into the lines in her skin. "Patient 76" was a man with a face full of expectation--wide eyes, a slightly raised forehead sagging with wrinkly weathered skin, and a wide open smile that made me want to dance and laugh. Looking at people in this way made such a difference in how I approached the day, and in my mind I created a guessing game of what marvelous creation of God would next walk through my door. It was one lesson I truly enjoyed learning.

Hiking for Smelly Fruit

Hasmah was raised in a small village on the side of a mountain about ten kilometers away from the city street where we both lived. I had grown up doing chores for my family from time to time, and so had she. I had worked on files and cards for my parents' business, and she had worked in her family business, too. Our jobs were quite different, though. While I sat inside doing mostly paperwork, she was hauling fruit down the side of a mountain to be sold in the city markets. It was not just any fruit, either: she was carrying the infamous queen of the fruit world--the durian.

Few people in the world probably ever wake up with a craving to go eat something that smells like dirty gym socks, has the texture of slimy custard, and can violently wound you if its shell is dropped on your foot. People in Southeast Asia, though, consider this fruit a delicacy and a local favorite. A durian can range in size from that of a small football to a large watermelon, and its shell is peppered with giant spikes which are more than capable of puncturing skin on contact. The white, creamy and stringy edible portion of the fruit surrounds individual seeds, each of which is sucked clean by eager eaters as they sit by the roadside stands where the fruit is sold. A person new to the region cannot help but take notice of the curious looking piles of fruit on the corners, and it is difficult not to stare with fascination at the manner in which it must be consumed. A durians's most distinguishing feature, though, which even a visually unobservant person cannot ignore, is its smell. I have heard this odor variably described as smelly gym socks, formaldehyde, mold, and rotten cheese, but each seems inadequate to describe the pungent smell that can be detected up to a mile away. The scent of the durian is so strong and lingers so long that it has even been banned in hotels, malls, and other public locations in larger cities in Thailand, Malaysia, and Singapore. All this being said, my local friends absolutely loved this strange creation. Its short growing season and the difficulty of transporting it down from the mountains where it grew made it a delicacy. Thus, it sold for a fairly high price, making it worth the efforts of Hasmah's family to transport it down the mountainside to be sold at the market.

Hasmah and Rahmat had become much like my own family, and

I loved my daily chats with them in their home. Still, completely unhurried, unscheduled time with them was rare, so I was delighted when Hasmah asked me to drive them to her former village and spend the day with her relatives. She told me she wanted to visit family and "take out fruit," for it was durian season, and the queen of fruits was in abundance in her former home. My first experience in eating durian had been tolerable, although not particularly enjoyable, but I was not eager to wander off into a land thick with the scent that would cling to my clothes for days. However, I saw it as a wonderful opportunity to spend time with these dear friends, and I knew it would bless them as well to have my company--and our team car.

Early one morning we set off for an hour's drive to the beachside village where Hasmah's sister ran a small coffee stand. We passed the expected time sitting with her and exchanging pleasantries, and as we did, my eyes happily drank in the scenic mountains starkly jutting out of the sandy shore nearby. No matter how many times I came to the local beach, I was always enraptured by the glory of God's creation. A few small cups of coffee later we were on our way again, stopping briefly to pick up some distant relatives who would join the hike as well. All during the drive, Rahmat had been marveling at the seatbelts in the car and how they worked, commenting on my scary driving skills, and giving directions twenty seconds after I passed the place at which I needed to turn, and we had already been laughing a good bit on this happy day.

Finally we parked the car at the base of a small mountain and began to hike up through the woods. We took our time and walked at the local pace, which was about ten times slower than I would have gone on my own. It did not matter to me that day, though, for I knew I was there simply to enjoy my friends and experience a place that was important to them. The day was as much about the journey as it was the destination, and I was happy to go along with whatever was to come.

We passed mangosteen plants sprouting from the ground and mango trees abundant, and I took a botanical lesson about the many beautiful and unfamiliar flowers, leaves, and herbs that lined the side of the trail. After a few hours we arrived at a rundown, makeshift lean-to, which I found out was our destination. I had noticed the scent of durian wafting on the air, but I had been too busy looking at all the other curious things around me to really notice that we had begun passing their shells on the ground. When I sat for a moment and looked around, though, they were everywhere. I looked up, astonished at how many were hanging in the trees above, and I wondered from what height a durian must fall before it would kill an unsuspecting bystander below. Not high, I decided. Durians and their shells covered the ground all around the lean-to, some whole and fresh, others cracked and old, and still others hollowed out and eaten. Hasmah, Rahmat, and their cousins lost no time in gathering as many as they could safely hold in their arms and piling them onto the wooden slats serving as a floor, and in a flash we were all sitting with the edible seeds in hand, ready to dig into the feast.

I was absolutely astonished at how many fruits could be consumed by so few people in such a short period of time, as one by one by one Rahmat cracked open fruit after fruit to be devoured. Some were eaten alone by chewing the flesh straight off of the seed and swallowing it with a satisfied smile, while other times the creamy flesh was spread onto bread Hasmah had brought along in her bag. Within half an hour I think at least twenty fruit were consumed, a marvel in that normally two people will share one fruit between them when bought in the city. Since the normally expensive fruits were free for the taking, though, my friends were taking advantage of it. I personally found these fresher fruits much more palatable than the one I had tasted a few months prior, and over the course of the day I probably polished off two or three entire fruits on my own. My cultural adaptation skills were at their finest.

After passing an hour or so in gluttonous delight, the eating slowed down and the storytelling began. Hasmah explained a lot about life in her village growing up, how she had worked to bring this fruit down (on her head) to raise money for her family, and how close she was to relatives who had since passed. Rahmat told stories of his childhood as well, and I listened with rapt attention as they shared their hearts about parts of their lives of which I had never heard. I learned the story of how they had met each other and convinced their parents that their marriage would be good (during a time when almost all marriages were still arranged), and I smiled because I had seen the consistent love they still showed toward each other after twenty years together. They told sad stories of deaths and happy stories of children's births, and they laughed a lot while sharing memories from the past. Moments like those in that lean- to can only be described as divine, for they are moments of honesty, heart-felt sharing, and emotional connection that do not come easily amidst the everyday busyness of life. I was experiencing a few blessed moments of feeling truly included and knowing I was loved, and I silently offered joyful thanks to the God who had brought me there.

We passed a very long and lazy morning sitting in the lean- to, munching on durian slowly in between napping and chatting, and sometime along the way one of Hasmah's extended family members came by. He was a wiry, energetic old man and someone whom I think could be called a durian trafficker, for his duty was to sit in the shack and order young boys to carry durians down to sell in the city. He took up his corner of the dilapidated floorboards and rapidly fired questions at the family in the local dialect about who I was and why I was there. I did not understand a bit of the conversation, but I knew it was about me because there was a lot of pointing and laughing going on. He seemed happy enough to have me around, though, so I did not worry about it very much.

Sometime later, when the sun had risen a little higher, Hasmah stirred up a fire on gathered sticks, produced rusted iron cookware from somewhere behind the structure, and began to cook rice and vegetables for everyone to eat. Durian fills your stomach not only with its substance but also with a remarkable amount of gas, so I was unsure how my friends were able to add any more food to their already overflowing bellies. As the locals say, though, "If you have not eaten rice, you have not eaten," so eat they did, before stretching out for another afternoon nap. More durians were consumed in small portions in the remaining afternoon hours, and then eventually the time came to head back down the mountain toward home. The young man accompanying us packed up twenty or more fruit to take home, placing them into a basket which he balanced with great dexterity on his head. Regrettably, at that time our trusty old vehicle did not have functioning windows, and in 100 degree heat smells are greatly exaggerated. So it was a good two months before the lingering smell of durians finally cleared from the car, but I did not mind too much. Each time I entered the car I was reminded of that glorious day, when I understood in my heart that I had been adopted into Hasmah and Rahmat's family as one of their own. This kind of relationship was what I had prayed for and hoped for before I even arrived, and God brought it to pass. To know that kind of love, I would bear the smell of musty old feet in my car any day.

Rainbows of Faithfulness

The ocean always reminds me of the majesty of God, and I love solitary early morning and late afternoon strolls on the sand when I can get lost in reflection and praise. God, in His goodness, had placed me in the midst of an amazingly beautiful tropical island where the small rolling mountains jutted down into the sea, and I always appreciated taking visits to the local beach. Since it was a half hour away from our home, however, and there was no such thing as privacy in this area as a foreigner, I had to give up my isolated, contemplative strolls and resign myself to the beach being just for fun. I threw myself into this newfound use of God's creation with delight, and I always looked forward to filling the car with people and heading out for an afternoon or sunset visit. I knew that God was always present in those fun group times, but I must admit that I was rarely actively looking to see His presence as I did when I was walking alone.

One special evening, my teammates and I traveled with Ria, Ika, and a few others to the beach in hopes of frolicking in the waves and watching the sunset. It was misting rain, but we decided to make the half hour drive anyway in the hopes that it would stop. The gigantic waves that greeted us had been stirred by a recent storm and made swimming impossible, and the sunset was hidden behind the clouds. Still, as we all sat there munching on watermelon and local snacks, I was content, feeling at home and enjoying the presence of friends. We laughed a lot, and these friends became possibly the first Indonesians to ever take part in a watermelon seed spitting contest. My southern heritage had to be spread from time to time, after all.

As if the simple joy of being with these friends was not enough, my good and gracious God then reminded me of His faithfulness, presence and covenant. Quite suddenly, through the clouds broke a glorious rainbow, appearing brighter moment by moment as it stretched through the chilly gray and lit up the sky. Only once in the past had I ever seen a full rainbow, and I was dazzled to watch this one unfold. Yet there was more to come, for soon there appeared not just one, but *two* full rainbows side by side. Entranced, I became lost in the thought of how creatively beautiful God truly is, and I stood awestruck for quite some time, as did the others.

When someone finally broke the silence, we took turns photographing each other under the splendid display of color and light. The rainbows--symbols of God's promise to save His children and reminders of His faithfulness--arched over Ria as she smiled, and I could not help but smile as well. I had recently been feeling very frustrated with not being able to discuss many spiritual matters with her and wondering if God was no longer doing anything in her heart. Yet as He shined His light through the rainbows that day, I felt my tension ease away.

"*I am* working," it was almost as if I could hear Him say, "Just look at how I created this stunning beauty out of a place in which you saw nothing. I can do that in her heart."

Impatience often floods my own heart, and dark clouds of doubt often threaten my mind. God's faithfulness, though, can brilliantly shine through them all.

CHAPTER Fourteen:
Selfless Love

She was my first observer. She was not the first person that I observed, but my first *observer*--meaning the one who watched *me*. Ibu Aisah, a shy and demure soul until she was comfortable in a situation, had been hired to clean the team house and office around the time I arrived. As such, she was to spend seven hours each day in the house with our team, and that gave her a lot of time for observation. Initially, none of us could speak Indonesian, and she didn't speak a word of English. So Uli became our translator, telling Ibu what her job was to entail and even communicating the smallest pleasantries on our behalf. Ibu Aisah, like my neighbors, was very patient in watching me struggle to learn her language, but I think she secretly laughed a lot at me after she went home.

I deeply desired relationships with local people in those first few months, so naturally Ibu Aisah became my friend. That is, she was my friend to the extent that a friendship can consist of smiles, quiet moments together, and shared laughter when trying to get a point across to someone who obviously has no idea what you are trying to say. When she seemed at a loss for housework to do, she would often sit on the couch and just watch us all. If Uli was not around at the time and no communication could take place, we had no choice but to allow her to sit there and watch--or else to try and sit and talk to her. Having someone watching me constantly and having no idea what she was thinking unnerved me, so I chose to try to talk.

Ibu Aisah and I would sit on the couch together, and I would throw out a few words I had learned in my language lesson while eagerly watching for recognition on her face. Nine of ten times she just looked at me with a curious smile, but on a rare occasion her eyes would light up with understanding. She would laugh a bubbly, joyful laugh and then proceed to answer me for a few minutes with a string of words which had no meaning to me. It was not initially the deepest of relationships.

Since hers was the most consistent relationship I had with a local person, however, I really felt burdened to pray for Ibu Aisah. I knew little about her other than that she had three children, one of whom lived with her mother, and I knew that she had been very emotionally traumatized in the past. Her demeanor, timid almost to the point of being wary, masked the beauty in her young thirty five year old face and made her appear older than she was. When she smiled, though, joy radiated from her eyes, her body would shake with laughter, and I saw a glimmer of what I imagine was once a soul filled with vitality. I suspected she was relatively religious, for she would disappear for a short time each afternoon around prayer time, but of course I was not capable of asking her about it. I knew she had come from a small village years ago when she married and that she loved her kids deeply (information courtesy of Uli's translation), but I knew little else of who she truly was.

I love getting to know people. I love asking them questions about their past, their interests, their stories, and their dreams, and I found it difficult to be spending a lot of time around this woman yet having no real way to get to know her. Since I had recognized that on my own I was fairly useless at this point, dependent entirely upon God's Spirit, I decided the best thing I could do was really pray for her. So pray I did. Ibu Aisah's name went onto my daily morning prayer list, and I often found myself praying for her several times throughout the day as well. Not knowing anything specific to pray, I simply asked God to reveal Himself to her, to knit her family together, and to create a friendship between us that exceeded our level of language comprehension.

God is so good to answer our prayers for relationship, and it was not long at all before I felt Ibu and I really did have a unique bond. I tried to talk to her on a more consistent basis, or at least to sit with her every day, and I quickly grew to really care for her. I loved praying for her and longed for the day I could tell her so, and I asked God to use me to love her with His love. I was still unnerved by the way she was always watching us, for I realized that her being in our house and office was allowing her to see me at my worst moments. Outside the walls of the house I could put on a happy face and make myself appear very selfless and holy. That façade could not be maintained twenty four hours a day in our home, however, or at moments of heavy pressure at work, so she saw me (and my teammates) at our most base and honest selves. Ibu Aisah saw the worst of my character during moments of stress and disappointment, but thankfully she also saw me celebrating moments of joy and delight when I saw God moving all around me. In short, she saw me as I am—an inherently selfish, sinful human who is continually grateful for the filling and changing power of the Holy Spirit in me. I prayed God would help her to understand that as He helped me to grow more into His image.

I had lived in Indonesia for two months when Ibu Aisah caught me praying one day in my room. Not realizing I was there, she entered my room to clean without knocking and found me face down on the floor; her shock was apparent. It took me a few moments to convince her I was not injured or upset (natural conclusions one would make seeing me on the ground with tears in my eyes), but she was not so easily convinced that what I was doing was actually praying. Ibu Aisah, like many others, had believed that people in the West did not pray. She was shocked at the *manner* in which I was praying, to be sure, for in her faith prayers are rote in form and unemotional. I, in contrast, had been crying out to God from my heart. Aside from the method, though, she was simply shocked to hear me say I was praying at all. She had believed that "our religion" was fairly insignificant to us and not a meaningful part of our daily lives. In her own religion, well prescribed daily rituals were followed, none of which she had observed us doing in the home. So her conclusions were logical. Her eyes grew large as I explained that the way I practiced my religion was simply very different, and not only did I pray daily, but often many times throughout the day.

"What do you pray for?" she asked (or at least I think that was what she asked), and I told her I prayed for the local people. At that point she almost fell off the bed on which she had just perched. I told her I prayed that the people there would all know God loved them, and that was in fact why I had come to help her people. She had already recognized that we were volunteering in service and was touched by that, and she knew we desired to help her people without expecting anything in return. She did not have any idea why we did that, though, and so she chose that moment to ask me.

"Because I am a follower of Jesus," I said, delighted I had just learned how to communicate that idea a day or so before. We muddled our way through talking a few more moments, and then my eyes fell upon my Bible, which was lying open on my bed. I grabbed it and pointed and said something about Jesus stories being in this Book, and she nodded with faint recognition. The discussion did not progress much further that day, but my heart swelled in knowing she had seen that I loved God in a very real way. I prayed for more opportunities to talk with her.

Happily, over time I was able to ask Ibu the questions I had wanted to from the beginning and to get to know the person behind her shy veneer. As our relationship grew, I learned about her children and her husband, her life growing up in the village, and her hilarious story of running away after her wedding. I cried when she told me about some great traumas she had experienced in life, and I grieved with her for the many family and friends she had lost. I tried to introduce her to American foods that would arrive in care packages from home and laughed when she reacted by crumpling up her nose in disgust. She taught me a few basics about local cooking, and we eventually came to the understanding that she could cook fish for our team in the evenings as long as she would eat the fish heads that she left on in the process.

Prayer was a topic of conversation on many other occasions, and I began to pray for Ibu about specific things going on in her life. The first time I was able to actually pray with her, she had come to work with a headache. She often had headaches, and she would walk in carrying a small bag of unlabeled and unidentifiable pills from a local clinic. We never understood why she did not just ask us for medical help, knowing we were in the process of setting up a clinic; perhaps she thought that was unacceptable since she worked for us. So she visited local clinics in the evenings instead, where she was usually told that she had low blood counts and given some useless medication. Then she would come to work on the following day still in pain, until one day I tired of this routine and offered to pray for her. She was surprised, but said, "Ok" and walked out of the room. I followed her.

"I want to pray now, Ibu," I offered, "Can we do that?"

Slightly confused, she followed my lead in sitting on the couch and opening her hands, and then she giggled the way she always did when she was nervous. I offered a very simple prayer to God to heal her headache, asking in the name of Jesus, and He answered. Her headache was gone within an hour, and it did not return.

Many more times I was able to pray with her after that--for illnesses, for family, and for financial situations--and in time she became more open to it as she saw these prayers being answered. She knew *I* cared for her by the fact that I would pray with her, but she began to see that *God* cared when He answered our prayers. It took over a year before she would articulate that fact, for she was still hesitant to give recognition to a God whom she thought was different than the one she had been taught to honor. Eventually she did agree that perhaps God cared for her, and we had long conversations about faith over time. She taught me more about the way she was schooled in her religion, and I shared with her how I believed God was constantly teaching me, as well. As I worked to dissemble many of the false ideas she had been taught about my faith, I prayed that what she saw in our lifestyle and service would match the words coming from my mouth. I asked her questions about the religious laws which enveloped and defined the local culture, and her explanations shed a lot of light on behaviors and attitudes I saw in the community.

Encouraging Moments

God does indeed know when we need encouragement. He had used the first conversation about prayer with Ibu Aisah to encourage me to persevere through the mundane and seemingly fruitless first months, and He had reminded me that day to pray with patience. Later that year, God used a conversation with Ibu Aisah again to remind me that He was working beyond what my eyes could see. My team had all just left, and I was feeling the significant strain of being alone with the clinic opening. The power had been out, the water broken, the car in disrepair, and my heart a bit broken as well, and I found myself wondering what on earth I was really doing there in such a crazy place after all. I knew the clinic was going to be a good thing, but I seriously doubted that God was doing much otherwise to show Himself through me. I was in poor spirits, sitting by myself at the kitchen table and half heartedly thumbing through my Bible, when Ibu came in and sat down.

I honestly was not in the mood to talk to her. I was feeling more inclined to be by myself and sulk, but thankfully God knocks me out of such selfishness when I will not do it otherwise. So Ibu came in and sat down across from me, and she obviously *was* in the mood to talk. There didn't seem to be any work for her since my teammates had left and she had little to clean, so she had a lot of free time in the day. I swallowed my self-pity so we could begin to talk, and it was not long before she began to question me about the Bible I was reading. This was the first time she had ever voluntarily asked questions about God without my initiating the conversation, and I perked up to see the interest in her eyes.

We talked for over an hour that afternoon about the Bible, and I one by one dissembled myths she believed about its contents being corrupted and containing stories that were not true. Eventually we came to an understanding that she could read the Bible for herself, since its components are actually some of the Holy Books of her religion, and she said that she wanted to do so. I flipped through various passages and showed her stories about Jesus, and I highlighted Scriptures I had prayed for her for healing and provision. I told her to come read my Bible anytime--the one I had in her language in my room--and then I sent her off with a small New Testament of her own to take home. I was not certain that she would read it, but I was certain that she had been listening that afternoon. When the Holy Spirit is at work in drawing someone's heart close to God, there is eagerness and genuineness to her questioning that enlivens a conversation. Such was the case that day with Ibu Aisah, and it brought a breath of fresh air and spiritual revival to my weary soul.

Time constraints and a busy workload eventually took over, and unfortunately I found myself spending significantly less time with Ibu Aisah. I was often in the village, in the clinic, in staff meetings, or running around town doing endless and seemingly fruitless administrative tasks, and conversations with her fell behind these duties on my priority list. In addition, my no longer living in the team house limited the time I spent there, and I sorely missed our conversations. I never stopped loving her as much, though. I wonder now if God was simply preparing my heart for separation, for somewhere in the midst of that busy second year Ibu's contract came up for renewal. Her decision to leave, as difficult as it was, was not a surprise, for she wanted to go and start a roadside store with her husband. We all shed a lot of tears on the last day she worked in the office, but I knew it meant a shift in, rather than an end to, our relationship. For that matter, I was relieved to no longer be the one writing her paycheck. Now I could focus on being her friend instead of her boss, and I preferred that role immensely.

Ibu Aisah's home and store were located about fifteen minutes away by car, and of course I no longer saw her every day. However, the times when I did make the effort to go and visit were more enjoyable than the rushed and distracted conversations in the office had often been, and I think she valued these times as well. Discussing her kids and business and local gossip was certainly more fun than telling her the bathroom needed to be cleaned or a guest was coming for a lunch meeting and she needed to cook. If she had not known how much I cared about her already, my efforts to go visit and check on her and her family would have left no doubt. She herself did not often come to our side of town to visit since it was difficult to get away from the store and her children, but on occasion she was able to stop by. On one such day, she paid me an enormous compliment which I will never forget.

We had been sitting at the kitchen table for a while talking, catching up on what had been going on in each other's lives and in the village work. She was always interested, especially in the details of our difficulties in obtaining visas and registrations for our agency to work. At this point, we were in the process of trying to obtain national registration to guarantee that we could stay in the community on a long term basis, and it was not going very well. I expressed my concern that we may soon lose our ability to get visas to stay there, and her eyed welled up with tears.

"You have to stay forever!" she exclaimed with an unusual level of emotion. "You cannot leave from here! Why would they not want you to stay?" I wondered the same thing, so I had no answer for her.

"I do not understand it," she said. "You are here volunteering, serving our people, and you do it with love. You do more than our own people do for each other sometimes, and you do it without expecting anything in return."

I quickly turned the conversation. "Ibu, I have told you so many times before that the reason I serve and love people here the way I do is simply because of Jesus. I try to follow His example, but I have no goodness in myself. I am only what God allows me to be as a follower of Jesus."

Her tears were now spilling over and her head nodding as she wiped them away. "I know that," she said softly. "I know that, and sometimes I now ask God if He will make me like you."

I was stunned. Ibu Aisah saw me on the days I was screaming in frustration at the government bureaucracy, stomping my feet at the unfairness in the medical system, and just feeling downright mean. She saw me on the days I talked to Uli about people that drove me crazy with their refusal to help with things, on the days I was crying, and on the days I just wanted to hibernate and not leave my room. Only one time had she actually seen our clinic-- the tangible "work" of what I was doing in serving the people--but she had listened to stories day after day with genuine and unfailing interest. In theory I agreed that perhaps what I was doing was nice; in actuality I felt that I spent more days operating in my own flesh than I did filled with the love of Christ. Despite praying daily that His love would flow through me and be all that people would see in my life, I felt woefully far from living out such an existence. Yet here was Ibu Aisah saying exactly what my heart longed to hear--that she was seeing in my life past the *me* to the *Jesus in me*. I was stunned, and I was grateful.

Tears filled my eyes as well as I thanked her, and I told her that she *would be* just like me if she asked Jesus to change and fill her as I did every day. "I may ask Him to do that," she said, ever so softly and with only a slight degree of hesitation. "I would like to live like you, with such love."

That was the end of the conversation for the day, and we never returned to it. I prayed with more intensity, though, that those moments--whatever times she remembered in which God was able to shine through my darkness--would be the things Ibu would remember long after I was gone. I prayed that she would, indeed, one day have a heart like mine--one that had been changed by God as had mine.

Encouragement in Action

Ibu had paid me a tremendous compliment, yet it is said that actions speak louder than words. Several months after that conversation, a local friend threw me a fantastic birthday party. Ibu shocked me by appearing with her whole family to offer her congratulations. Birthdays are not highly celebrated events in the local area, and she did not sound very interested when I called and told her about the party. She came that night, though, with her kids piled into the back of her husband's water delivery truck and gifts in hand. Since she would not know many other people at the gathering, I knew it was a stretch for someone with her shy personality to make an appearance. I was blessed that she had come, and that night we made plans to get together again soon and say our goodbyes. I would be leaving the country about four short weeks later.

I became wrapped up in the details of my impending departure, and I never made it over to Ibu's house to say goodbye. Her promise to come over to the office likewise did not materialize, and I despondently began thinking that I may not see her before leaving. Then one day Hasmah came running across the street and merrily pronounced to me: "We are planning a farewell party for you!"

"Who is?" I asked her, curious who made up the "we" she had mentioned.

"Me and Ibu Aisah," she said. "Next Saturday we are going to the beach. I only need you to pick her up on the way."

These two dear women went all out to celebrate me on that precious and bittersweet Saturday afternoon. They knew what I liked, and they had gone to no small effort to cook each of the local dishes they knew I enjoyed. A few other neighbors came along for the fun, and we all had a marvelous time jumping in the waves, floating in the surf, and sharing each other's company. I was so overwhelmed by the entire day that it is difficult to put into words, but a bigger blessing was in the revelation I had the night before the party.

Ibu Aisah had been highly traumatized by an earlier experience with the ocean in which several family members had drowned. We talked about this on several occasions, and it was apparent to me that she was still living under a great deal of fear from the ordeal. I often told her about my weekend trips to the beach with Ria and Ika or others, expressing my love for the ocean and the fun we experienced. Every time I talked about it she shuddered, immediately responding with "I will never be anywhere near the ocean again!" She was terrifyingly, deathly afraid of the water, and she had not come close to it since her traumatic experience four years prior. I had asked her several times if her children would like to go to the ocean, to which she had responded in a similar fashion. She had no intention of taking them to such a terrible place. Although she admitted the irrationality behind her fear, she was perfectly willing to let it control her.

So the night before my send off party, I awoke at about 2:00 A.M. with the shocking revelation that Ibu Aisah *was going to the beach.* She was going to the ocean, after four years of running the other way, and I knew she must be climbing the walls in anxiety. She was about to walk headlong into her greatest nightmare, and she was doing it for no other reason than to honor me. I cried there in my bed, overwhelmed with such an incredible display of love, and prayed for her peace.

Ibu was visibly shaking in the car on the way to the ocean the next day. "Ibu," I asked her from the driver seat, trying to be nonchalant in order not to highlight the problem. "You are going to the beach today. Are you scared?"

She just kept shaking, not violently so but definitely to a noticeable degree. Then she giggled in her nervous way and said, "Yes, I think so."

"Why are you doing it, then?" I inquired over the excited laughter and chattering of her kids who were sitting in the backseat. They were delighted to be going on a beach outing for the first time they could remember.

"It is important to you," she said. "I know you like it, and you are important to me."

She did not have to say anymore that day. I led her out of the car onto the soft sand, watching her body language close off into a protective posture as she came closer to the water. After a few hours I succeeded in getting her close enough to the shoreline to watch her enthralled children jump up and down in the surf, and by the time we left she had relaxed quite a bit. Still, she passed most of the time up far from the water, sitting up at the small awning where she and Hasmah had laid out the vast display of all my favorite goodies. I did not expect anything more. I did not need her to entertain me in the waves, nor did she need to enjoy building sand castles or strolling in the soft line of foam that licked the white sand where water met land. Her presence there was more than enough, for I knew what an incredible sacrifice she had made.

That night, after we arrived back home, I was reflecting on how far God had brought me in a few years' time. I recalled the first few weeks of sitting on the couch with Ibu Aisah, trying to communicate and failing miserably, and I remembered that first pivotal conversation when she found me on my bedroom floor. I let my mind wander into her village, where we had spent the second day of Idul Fitri with her family, and I laughed to think of some of the stories she had told me about growing up, her arranged marriage, and her family. I smiled to remember the times we had prayed together, both for her health and family as well as for our clinic work to be able to continue. Then I cried again as my thoughts brought me back to the present moment and how she had selflessly demonstrated her love to me that day.

I had prayed so often and so fervently, even before I boarded a plane, that God would allow me to build real friendships with people whom I knew would be vastly different from me. I had known that it would require a miracle: how else would we transcend culture, language, religion, and worldviews that clashed on many levels and were exceedingly hard to understand? Not surprisingly, I had spent time grieving relationships that I felt never moved beyond surface level.

That day, however, when she faced her fears to show me her love, Ibu Aisah showed me a miracle.

CHAPTER Fifteen:
Life-Giving Blood

Cleansing Power

I was often called upon to play "doctor" to neighbors and friends, those outside the reach of the clinic but within reach of my presence--or at least my cell phone. I was also often frustrated in these situations, knowing enough to know that I could not really help but that the person in question desperately needed something. Such was the case with Bapak Rahmat, my dear neighbor and adopted father, when his kidneys failed rather suddenly and sent him to the brink of death.

Rahmat had been suffering from mild nausea and fatigue for a day or so, during which time Hasmah had mentioned to me that he was not feeling well. She was caring for him by offering rice porridge and some other homemade remedies, and I did not think much of it on that first day. As his pain and distress increased over the following days, however, we decided to take him to the local hospital. There he was diagnosed with a large and impacted kidney stone that was blocking his urine flow, and he was told that an operation was imminent. As did many, Rahmat feared the local medical system to be less than ideal for major surgeries. So this situation prompted him to borrow a lifetime's worth of loans from friends and family to go to Malaysia for what he thought would be a curative surgery, and two days later he and Hasmah flew off for a week.

I was eager to hear the story upon their return, and they were equally eager to tell it. He showed me his lab work and ultrasound reports from the Malaysian doctors, indicating that a sizeable stone had been removed. What he failed to understand, however, was that by the time the stone was removed his kidneys had been irrevocably damaged, and the physicians had ordered for him to begin dialysis upon returning home. I tried to explain this to him and in fact tried to bring him to the hospital that day, but he said that he was feeling better and therefore saw no need to go seek further medical care. Thus, four days after returning home, Rahmat wound up in the hospital teetering on the precipice of death.

Seeing Rahmat lying there on the bed--weak, pale, unable to speak, and headed for death within twenty four hours from all evidence I could see--I experienced one of my lowest emotional moments since arriving. I deeply cared for this man and his family, and I felt completely helpless to do anything, despite Hasmah's pleas. All that would help him was dialysis, for his body was being rapidly overtaken by the toxins that his kidneys were not removing properly. His other organs were close to shutting down, yet the gravity of his condition did nothing to move him higher on the waiting list to use one of the two hospital dialysis machines. Was he really going to die from a controllable illness for lack of equipment and a waiting list?

"Surely, God," I cried in my spirit, "This cannot be Your way!" I could not create an empty dialysis machine out of thin air, so I just hugged Hasmah, tried to be encouraging, and told her that all I could offer was prayer, calling on the power of God through Jesus. I prayed with her right there in the room as I had several times earlier in the week, and God mercifully saved Rahmat's life through dialysis the next morning.

In the few weeks leading up to this critical moment, I had in fact prayed several times with Hasmah for her husband's health and restoration. Until this kidney crisis arose, all my attempts to pray with either one of the couple had been turned down, but the week's events had brought a notable shift in their spiritual receptivity. Although I would have preferred such change to come by easier circumstances, I did at least take great heart in seeing how God was working on breaking into their spirits and opening their hearts to my prayers.

After Rahmat returned from that hospital stay, admittedly weak and still quite sick, I began to ask how *specifically* my teammates and I could pray for him each day. The first day, Hasmah asked that we pray for an end to his pain. He slept through the night pain free. The next day, she asked that his nausea would subside. From the moment we prayed, the ten or more episodes of vomiting per day ceased. Every single thing we prayed for was answered clearly and directly. Each day I rejoiced in those little answers with the family, telling them all things were possible when we prayed in the name of Jesus, and for the first time I saw a small spark of recognition in their eyes that perhaps this could be true.

Nearly every day I visited Rahmat to check on the situation and see how God had answered yet another prayer. After a week or so he surprised me by saying, "Since you are praying so much, I decided that I should, too." He was praying to God, he said, to heal him so he could work and again serve his community, and I agreed to pray the same. He knew I would pray in the name of Jesus, which he was not ready to do, but we would both ask with faith for God to come touch and restore his body.

I wanted to believe for a totally miraculous healing, and so that is how I prayed. I asked God to totally restore his body, blood, kidneys, and spirit, for I did not believe the Great Physician stopped with healing halfway. Rahmat continued to follow up with the hospital and prepare for long term dialysis by having a port placed in his arm, and when I left to go on a short retreat he was scheduled to go for his first treatment the following day. He was functional-- thin and tired but improving daily--and I trusted that he would be fine during the time I was away.

I returned from the retreat to an excessively busy time, and I had too few moments to go over and visit with Hasmah and Rahmat to hear the details of what had been occurring. I did check on him, of course, immediately upon my return, just enough to see that he seemed to be continuing to improve and gain strength daily. He would be outside when I arrived at the office in the morning, reading the paper on the porch or clipping the small flowers they grew in pots outside, and he always smiled, laughed, and said he was feeling better; I breathed a quick prayer of thanks before heading on my way. I simply assumed he was taking his twice weekly dialysis treatments in the evenings after I had gone home for the day. Little did I know that during my retreat week and the weeks that followed, Rahmat had decided not to go to the hospital at all.

After about three weeks, when I saw him outside working one day, I stopped in for a while to talk. He was looking stronger and happier than I had seen him in months, and I asked him to tell me about the dialysis ward in the hospital, his medication, and how he was adjusting to life with this new chronic disease. Imagine my surprise when he informed me he had never gone to dialysis! Normally, someone with chronic kidney disease who remains off of dialysis for that period of time would be extremely ill, the unprocessed toxins having built up to a level a body can no longer tolerate. Rahmat, however, simply had not become sick again. Failed kidneys do not spontaneously heal themselves, and the only explanation for his restoration was God's hand of healing.

I think I spent the next few days alternating between shock, delight, faith, and doubt (the medical brain in me was still trying to find a logical explanation), but primarily I just rejoiced with him over his healing. It was with tears in his eyes and a beautifully restored smile that he told me he believed "our" prayers had been answered--the prayers for healing so he could work and again serve his community--and he was freely giving the credit to God. He was still not ready to confess his healing came by the name of Jesus, but agreeing that God could have worked a miracle beyond the visible medical realm was a huge step forward for him. It opened his spirit (and Hasmah's) to discussing spiritual things on many occasions, and I often reminded them of how God directly answered our prayers during his initial illness. God's Kingdom is about restoration, and He had restored my friend.

"Cuci darah" literally means to "clean blood," which was the local way to refer to dialysis. During the whole experience of Rahmat's illness, as we often discussed dialysis, I found myself thinking a lot about what that actually meant. Blood that is polluted can lead to one's death, slowly but surely overtaking a person's body until it shuts down from self-produced poison. During dialysis, the blood is removed, cleansed, and replaced, and this cleansed blood actively and quickly restores life. What a beautiful correlate this process is to the way the blood of Jesus restores us! Left on our own, our pride, greed, rebellion, and self seeking behavior become toxic to our lives, building up and overcoming any defense until we reach the point of self destruction. How mercifully, though, the blood of Christ comes in and replaces that toxic blood of self that courses through our system, immediately filling us with pure and active life that sustains and restores!

I desperately need the cleansing power of this blood, and I need it continually. Just as dialysis patients must continue treatments indefinitely, constantly battling the toxins which re-accumulate, I must continue to confess and allow the blood of Christ to purify me daily. My sin is a chronic disease. I know the final and miraculous healing will come on the day of redemption, at which point Jesus' blood will wash me clean once and for all--just as Rahmat was fully restored. Until then, however, I am grateful that God will use the machinery of the Holy Spirit and His precious blood to continually cleanse me from the inside out--no hospital waiting list required.

Giving in Sacrifice

Ria, in her mercy, was always trying to help her patients above and beyond the call of her doctoral duties. Since patients must find their own blood donors in order to have transfusions in Indonesia, no matter how ill they are, many people suffer and occasionally even pass away from the inability to have life giving blood restored. So on more than one occasion, Ria took it as her personal mission to find donors for her patients when they required a stock of extra blood before an operation could be performed. She would call everyone she knew, and then a few she didn't, until she found a match: I know of at least five occasions in which her efforts were key to having a patient actually receive a surgery that may not otherwise have been performed. Usually she did not ask me to be a donor personally, but I often heard her stories after someone was made well.

So when Ria called me late one night, sounding very disturbed and tired, I knew something was different. A hospital patient who needed a hysterectomy was apparently bleeding profusely, and she was in need of blood donors within the next forty eight hours. Ria could not find a match in the family and had tried many friends as well, but so far she had been unable to locate a donor for this woman's unusual blood type. Did I know anyone with that type, she asked, who could go give blood at the Red Crescent the next day? It was becoming critical for the woman. I did not know anyone else with that blood type, but I did know my own. I am a universal donor.

Thus, I found myself at 10:00 P.M. the following night, exhausted from a day of coordinating cataract surgeries and running on the fuel of the Holy Spirit, pulling into the Red Crescent center to be a blood donor for Ria's patient. I like to give blood and used to do it regularly at home, finding it a simple thing to do that truly helps others. Needles do not bother me, my blood flows easily, and I was never disturbed by the few hours taken out of my day. Traveling had put an end to my donating over the last few years, though, since visitors to malaria endemic areas are not allowed to donate in the West; of course in a malaria endemic area itself, this was of little importance. During the past five years I had only been able to donate one time, giving my blood to a surgical patient in Ghana. I then helped with her operation an hour later, and I watched my own blood running right back out of her as the procedure took place. It was an odd experience but one that allowed that woman to live, and I was wearily happy to know I had the same opportunity tonight.

"What do you want?" the young man behind the desk asked with a minor degree of suspicion when I entered the room. I knew it was unusual for a foreigner to enter their building, not to mention at such a late hour.

"I want to donate blood," I said. He stared, not blinking, and did not respond. "Can I do that?" I asked, "Donate blood here?"

He snapped out of his temporary shock and fumbled with papers on the desk. "Yes, yes, of course you can. Why do you want to give blood?"

"For a patient in the hospital," I responded, sitting down across from him and wondering if this was going to take a long time.

"Have you donated before?"

"Many times," I said, "In my own country. I know how it all works."

He had me fill out a short slip of paper with my address and phone number, asking me nothing about exposure to infectious diseases or any other potentially dangerous conditions. I assumed he would get to those vital points later, but he never did. However, he was quite interested in checking my iron level to make sure I was not anemic, so out came the small needle to prick my finger.

"Can you stand the pain?" he asked, again suspiciously, and I wondered silently if he really did not want to take my blood.

"No problem," I said. "It does not bother me."

Prick. I watched the drop of blood sink to the bottom of the cup, indicating by this very poor and inaccurate test that I was anemic. Almost triumphantly, he looked up and said, "You have low blood. You cannot give any more."

I argued with him, for I knew that this was a very cheap and faulty test, and I knew that I was, in fact, *not* anemic. I had just checked my blood level on our own clinic machine that day, a much more accurate measurement that assured me I had a more than sufficient level of iron for donation. After the considerable discussion required to convince him that I was a medical provider and knew what I was talking about, I signed a waiver, and he led me back to the donation room. I was glad that he was at least concerned for *my* well being, for his failure to screen me for any kind of disease made me question his concern for the blood recipients.

Since he was soon going to be sticking large needles in my arm, I thought it a good idea to befriend this now nervous young man by trying to chat to him about the donation center. While he was setting things up, I learned that a blood drive was unheard of there, and no one, in fact, donated for people outside of family and close friends. He seemed even more shocked that I had suggested it than he was distracted by the very fact of my presence. He answered my questions while pumping up the blood pressure cuff on my arm, and he also answered them while the cuff deflated.

"120/80," he pronounced as a textbook perfect blood pressure. I knew it was not correct, for it was far above the normally low blood pressure I maintain from an athletically conditioned heart. I also knew it was not correct because he had never used a stethoscope to listen to the readings. Rather, he had continued talking straight through the cuff deflating. He had not actually checked my blood pressure at all, and I tried to address this point with him with some degree of tact. Embarrassed and caught, he mumbled something in the local dialect and rushed off to go find a donation bag in a remarkable hurry. I sighed, laid my head back on the table, and wondered for the thousandth time if there was any hope to fix this medical system.

The donation, as expected, went quickly. I was glad, for I wanted more than anything to go home and go to sleep, knowing my clock was going to awaken me in less than five hours for another long day of surgeries. I was not in the mood to continue talking for long, but the young man had been slowly warming up to the novelty of talking to a foreigner and was not eager to let me go. He was piddling with the donation bag after he removed it from my arm, alternating writing a letter or two on the outside with asking me a question about my home country, and I was growing impatient.

"Do I need to tell you who the blood is for?" I finally interrupted him to ask. "The woman in the hospital? So you can label the bag somehow?"

"Oh yes, yes," he said, "Of course I need to know. Or you just take it to her."

I could not do that, for not only did I not have the time but I actually had no idea of who the woman was. I explained that to him and asked him to write Ria's name on the bag instead so she could come to pick it up. Once again he looked at me in total shock, his eyes growing wider and mouth standing ajar.

"You don't know the patient?" he asked. "This is not a foreign friend you are giving for?"

It was not, I assured him, a foreign friend. She was not a friend at all--just someone I had heard of who needed help. He did not believe me. "You are giving blood for a local person? Someone you do not know? Are you sure it is not a foreign person?"

No, I assured him again, it was just a patient in need of help. I guess the fact that blood donation for strangers was unheard of should have made me more expectant of his surprise, but I was taken aback by his particular fascination that I would give to an Indonesian. Anyway, I decided I should have Ria talk to him since

I was unconvinced the blood was going to be labeled and stored in any way where she could find it. I fished in my bag for my phone, explaining I was going to call my friend at the hospital so he could talk with her.

"No, no, I cannot!" he said with alarm. "I cannot speak English!" (We had been conversing in Indonesian). He still did not believe me that there was no foreigner involved in the equation outside of myself.

"She is an Indonesian," I said, dialing the number. "She is a medical student here."

"Does she speak the Indonesian language?" he asked nervously, pushing away the phone I was trying to hand to him. The words "she is an Indonesian" apparently had not registered in his mind.

"Yes, talk to her please!" I said, insisting he take the phone. The ensuing conversation, I was sure, involved much more explanation of who I was and what I was doing than it did details about the small bag of blood sitting on the counter. He stared with fascination at me the entire time he was talking to Ria, during which I tried to busy myself looking around at the empty walls, until eventually he handed me back the phone. Ria was still laughing and was probably more amused than I was by his reaction to me, but at least the details had been settled. She would gratefully pick up the blood an hour or so later and bring it to the patient, and in the meantime she told me to make sure I did not need to resuscitate the young attendant before I left.

He tried to make me wait a while to ensure that I was OK, and I considered it for about thirty seconds. At home they often give you Nutter Butters at a blood drive, a rare treat, and I wistfully thought perhaps this man was storing some in his closet as well.

"Ibu, you can eat an egg! I will bring you one!" he announced happily, now glad that his duties of poking me were over and he could just be sure I was OK.

My Nutter Butter dreams crumbled to dust, and the thought of eating a room temperature hardboiled egg at 11:30 at night was making me a bit nauseous. So I politely declined and excused myself, leaving behind the still shocked young man who was wondering why a foreigner would give her blood for a stranger in his community.

The woman received her transfusion and operation and thankfully went home well, but God was not quite finished. Just prior to that experience, I had been praying, actually asking God for a way in which to discuss the necessity of the blood of Christ with Ria. We had been discussing what she had read in the New Testament I had given her, and we had been discussing sacrifice in relation to the upcoming holiday of sacrifice in their community. What a perfect opportunity this was! God is creative, and I think He knows for many of us practical examples are necessary in order to illustrate His truth.

Although Ria was not nearly as surprised as the young man had been at my willingness to donate my blood, she was definitely struck with the powerful illustration of how the sacrifice of one is often necessary for the life of another. I had paid a small price of time and energy for the life of another: Jesus had paid His whole life. It was just the bridge I had been looking for in our conversation. As the woman was healed, the message of truth became clearer to Ria, and I was even offered a hardboiled egg in exchange for my time. What a beautiful experience!

CHAPTER Sixteen:
The Bible Come to Life

To Pray or Not to Pray

Have you ever felt like you were walking out the pages of the Bible? Upon opening my clinic door one day, I was greeted by quite a shocking sight. My next patient was being *carried in*, piggyback, by a friend because he could not walk. Although he chose the door as an entrance rather than the ceiling, my mind immediately flashed to the Biblical story of the friends who brought the lame man to Jesus for healing. Was I about to be a part of such a miraculous moment?

The sad history of this forty- something year old farmer was that he had fallen from a tree the year prior and broken his spine. He appeared to be crippled from the waist down. After a week in the hospital, none of the physicians had told him if there was any hope of his ever walking again; I could not tell him either without doing proper nerve studies and other advanced testing. All of these tests were well beyond the scope of the province, much less our simple clinic. So I sat there looking at the man as his hopeful eyes pleaded with me to help him, wrestling in my mind with what to do. The faith-filled side of me thought of calling the clinic staff to come pray for instant healing, while the cautious side of me made me stop, realizing we were still holding a fragile acceptance in the region. So eventually I sighed, explained some things about paralysis, gave him some vitamins, and told him I would pray in the name of Jesus for healing. I did pray--at home--for days and days and days.

I wish I had a follow-up to this story to say that the man was healed, but honestly I know nothing more. He never returned, and I do not know if his condition improved. I only know that my heart's cry was to see the name of Jesus glorified in the area, and miracles would certainly accomplish that. So I struggled over the ensuing days to imagine how the scenario could have played out. Should I have prayed for him for healing right then? Perhaps. He may have been healed and walked out the door, and the entire village would have instantly seen the miraculous hand of God. Was that God's plan, and I missed it? Had I let my fear of people's opinions and doubts that God would work block a chance for Him to do something amazing?

I knew that God certainly had the power to redeem lost opportunities if needed, and I was glad for that. There had already been many situations in which I could have prayed with more faith, spoken more boldly, or shared with more love, and there would be more to come. There had also been times when I had prayed for someone and not seen the healing occur, and I always wondered what detriment those experiences had on the faith--or potential faith--of the surrounding community. I often met people who had illnesses for which I had no capability and no resources to affect their healing, and each time I struggled with how I should best approach the situation. I saw God heal, and I also saw Him not heal (at least not at that time). In the end, I always had to settle for trying to be attentive and obedient to the Holy Spirit's leading in each particular situation. I also prayed to know when it was no longer time to be quiet.

She Spent All She Had

Another occasion arose in which I felt I was transported back to the pages of the Bible, but this time I seized the opportunity to pray. Rohana, a twenty two year old bride of one year, was carried into my tiny office lacking the strength to walk on her own. Her young husband was unusually attentive to her needs and showed concern for her that was not common amongst the males in the community. I was encouraged by his compassion and obvious desire for his wife's healing, and after a few moments I began to realize that his entire life revolved around her care. He tried to convey the long and complicated story of her illness and attempts to be treated as best he could, but the missing pieces and confusing time-line did little to help me understand what had actually transpired. Wading through the convoluted details, I learned that Rohana had first fallen ill after a miscarriage about six months prior, then she had acquired a severe pelvic infection that kept her hospitalized for weeks. Somewhere during the course of that stay she also began to go numb in her legs, have agonizing abdominal pain, and essentially became mute. The doctors eventually declared her well when her infection resolved, but they conveniently chose to ignore the fact that their patient could not physically walk out the door.

Since that time, Rohana's desperate husband had taken her to more than ten doctors and six hospitals in three regions, and he was at the end of his rope. They had received any number of diagnoses, ranging from chronic infection, evil spirits, psychological issues, and neurological viruses to being told that stomach acid had seeped down into her legs and up into her mouth. As could be expected, none of these diagnosis or their accompanying treatments had made her well. The patient herself communicated only with her eyes, and she did so only when I forced her to look at me. Occasionally she would offer a soft moan when I pushed on her abdomen or she otherwise shifted in position. Her husband spoke on her behalf, and he explained how he had heard there was a place in our tiny village where people were getting well. He was begging me to fix his wife. He also pleaded with me to do it for free, for he had lost his job from missing work so much and had since spent almost every rupiah they had in trying to find a cure.

My mind immediately flashed to the Bible and the narrative of a woman who had been bleeding for twelve years. Like Rohana, she had "spent all her living on physicians and yet she could not be healed by anyone" (Luke 8:43). I considered sharing this story immediately and praying for a similar outcome of healing, but then I decided that at least examining the patient first was in order. So I started trying to find a logical explanation for her strange affliction. I poked and prodded, tested a few things with the small equipment I had available, and finally suggested the couple get some lab tests in the city. I told them I could not figure out what was happening without some of these tests, but I could give her some pills for stomach discomfort and vitamins in the meantime. Secretly I was hoping they would leave quickly, for I simply had no clue what was going on.

The crestfallen face of Rohana's husband stopped me from ushering them out the door, and the Holy Spirit whispered into my heart: "Tell him."

"Tell him what, God?" I murmured, busying myself with writing something on a piece of paper so it would look as if I were not talking to myself.

"Tell him the story," came the gentle reply. It was clear--as clear as any directive I have ever felt from the Holy Spirit's prompting--and so I took a breath and looked straight into his eyes.

"Do you want to hear a story?" I asked.

He nodded, and I told him of the woman in the Bible who shared similar circumstances with his wife. I told him how this woman had tried and tried and tried to get better with medicine, until she had exhausted all possibilities. I told him the woman had heard of a man who could heal, and, in final desperation, risked personal safety and reputation to press through crowds of people to reach him. I told him this man was Jesus, and I told him that Jesus could still heal today. I wondered if he would consider praying to this Jesus for healing?

Rohana did not stir on the bed while I shared this story, but her husband's eyes filled with tears. He obviously empathized with this woman who had reached her end, despairing of hope, for he could relate to her misery in a very personal way. I saw a glimmer of hope in his eyes when I shared that Jesus could heal his wife as well, and I wondered at what point along the way he had lost all of his own hope. Had he ever prayed for healing, I asked?

"Sort of," he said, but without great conviction. He was not a man of devout faith, and he assumed, as he had been taught, that all in God's will would happen with or without his prayers. Prayer was an afterthought to him, but it was also a thought he was willing to try again.

The crowds outside my door grew more restless as the time passed, but I was caught in critical conversation with this couple whom I felt God wanted to touch with His presence. Rohana's husband had heard of Jesus as a prophet, but he had never been told that there was healing power in praying in His name. He was happy to hear this and willing to embrace it, and he moved swiftly out of the way for me to reach his sickly wife when I asked if we could pray at that moment. I touched her head, wiping a sweaty clump of hair from her eyes, and tried to explain to her that I was praying for her healing in the name of Jesus. I touched her stomach and asked God to heal it, followed by her legs, her head, and her mouth, asking God to restore each one in turn. I acknowledged to God on behalf of the couple that they had tried all their own natural resources and failed, and I even asked God to forgive them for not having sought His help sooner. I proclaimed her healing in the name of Jesus, believing power would flow just as it had to the bleeding woman, and then I waited.

Nothing happened. Nothing. She did not stir, nor did I, until finally the silence became unbearably awkward. Her husband cleared his throat, and I looked up at him slowly, uncertain of what I would see. Would I see anger in his eyes? Disappointment? Laughter at this silly foreign god who had not done anything? All I saw on his face was boredom, along with a politely restrained desire to go ahead and leave this room where not a lot was happening. I was crying out inside in frustration and confusion, wondering why God was not moving, but I had no answers to give. Meekly I offered to continue praying at home and suggested he do the same, and then I encouraged him to ask God for himself if Jesus was truly alive. I made a mental note to myself to ask the same thing that night, for I was feeling pretty foolish and let down.

They left, and I continued to pray. I was mad at God, honestly *mad*, for I did not understand why He had let such a seemingly brilliant moment pass by without doing anything. I wanted to see people healed and the name of Jesus glorified, but it looked to me that the name of Jesus had just become laughable and ridiculous. Where was the God of the Bible who called down fire from heaven onto the altar to prove His power? Was He not as zealous for His name today?

Rohana and her husband returned ten days later, bringing with them the lab tests I had ordered. She showed no evidence of improvement, and I remained baffled by her situation. Finally I concluded that much of her illness had begun as more psychological than physical, and in time, with disuse, her body had simply stopped trying to work. I imagine it had something to do with the miscarriage she had suffered and possibly other undisclosed emotional wounds from her past, so I decided to divert my prayers into that direction. Her husband told me that he had prayed a few times that week but not really used the name of Jesus, and in the same breath he asked me to please just give her better medicine. Try as I might, I could not enter into a good conversation with him again about God, for he was more restless and impatient this time and not overly interested in talking. So I changed her vitamins and kept praying.

Two weeks went by. The couple returned yet again, and Rohana still showed no improvement. At that point I had prayed with friends for her deliverance, wondering if she were not totally overcome by a demon, and I had stomped my feet at God hard enough to make holes in the ground. Despite this, my patient remained the same: weak, non-communicative and completely dependent on her husband for all things. He seemed to have returned to the state of sad resignation in which I initially found him. He had prayed once more, he said, but did not think it would do much good, and he noted that none of my medicines had been very good, either. No, vitamins and basic therapeutic medicines were not likely to heal this disease, I agreed. I did wonder and ask him, though, why he had returned again to see me.

"You are kind," he said shyly, shifting his weight from side to side and looking at the floor. "Other doctors do not listen to me. At least you understand how hard this is." I did *not* understand it, actually, for I had never lived watching someone I dearly loved suffer inexplicably for months on end with no hope in sight. The Spirit of Jesus in me understood, though, and thankfully His love must have been showing through my own emotional confusion.

"Jesus understands," I said to him, and the man half smiled.

We spent a short while talking before I assured them a final time that I would continue to pray. Then the young man picked up his limp wife and carried her out of the room, and I never saw them again. Maybe Rohana went home that night and was healed. I would like to think so. Maybe months later her husband prayed, really asking God to come and show him if *He* were real, and then she was healed. Maybe she never got better at all, and maybe today her husband is still taking care of her every day or has left her to find another wife. I know which ending I prefer, but I do not know which one is reality.

I will never understand many, many things about God and His ways. There are mountains of theological arguments that can be made about why Rohana was not healed, ranging from my own lack of faith to hers, demonic possession and spiritual warfare to wrong timing, and the list goes on. It all just made me tired to think about it. I had wanted to see her healed, and from all indications I could find in the Bible, so did God. Yet she had not been healed. I felt very at peace with having shared with them about Jesus healing the bleeding woman, and I felt at peace with having prayed. Her continued illness had not damaged our relationship in the community, and at the very least I had offered a compassionate ear to someone who really needed it. Speaking the name of Jesus and sharing stories of His power could never be a bad thing, I reasoned, and perhaps there would come a day when the young husband would reflect on that story and the seed would blossom into fruit. Perhaps there would not. At least I had been obedient, at that moment, to share what I felt God wanted me to share. I had to choose to rejoice in that.

This experience, along with so many others, was filed into a category in my brain that is filled with unanswered questions. One day in heaven I will ask God about them all, and I will ask Him why Rohana was not healed. In the meantime, my lack of understanding did not justify anger at the Creator of the universe for not having done something the way in which I thought He should. I had to let it rest. After all, my call to be obedient and my call to share the good news and love of Jesus with people are not conditional on seeing results; maybe God just wanted to show me that. Maybe He wanted to remind me to come to the end of myself and to be as desperate for Him as the bleeding woman was, and He had brought Rohana to actually teach me that. I don't know exactly. There will always be a lot of maybes in this life of following Jesus.

Even the Bible leaves a lot of unanswered questions for me as I study, but it never fails to confirm God's ultimate goodness. With that knowledge planted firmly in my heart, I can live with confidence in the uncertainty.

CHAPTER Seventeen:
Expectations and Hope

I cried many days in Indonesia. I cried tears of sadness for the suffering I would see, tears of humility before an amazing God, and tears of repentance over my frequent unbelief. I cried for the poor and lost, for the illnesses, hunger and despair I saw, and for the people who had little hope to see anything change. I cried that I had no doctors who wanted to really help me in the work, that God did not send more teammates, and that the job endlessly got bigger while my faith stayed the same. I cried a lot of unhappy tears.

Thankfully, I also cried tears of joy, tears of hope, and tears of expectation of what will come in the Kingdom of God.

Visiting teams did not come very often to our area, but occasionally a construction or sports team passed through and happened to have a medical provider along with them. When I was lucky, their contact person would suggest the physician or nurse work with me for a few days, knowing that I needed the help. This help excited me, for there were many distant villages I longed to visit but could not handle alone. Being the sole medical provider at a stationary clinic with a large patient load was difficult. I had learned the hard way that taking a van full of medicine to do a mobile outreach without another provider to assist me was virtual suicide.

So early in my second year, I eagerly welcomed an American physician and nurse to join me for a few days of outreach. Before they arrived our staff prayed about where to go, eventually settling on a plan to take a mobile clinic and children's program to a remote mountain village. It had been an area prone to conflict in the past, and it remained essentially closed to the outside world. The obscurity of the place was part of its appeal, but I was unsure of how eager they would be to receive foreign medical workers in their community. So as the time drew near, I had an oddly mingled sense of both anticipation and unease about the location we had chosen. My fears were assuaged by asking people to pray for protection, and I also had a sense that God was going to show up in a special way. Two days prior to going, I had a dream about people praying for a man who was lying on the ground, almost dead. They prayed, and the man rose up and walked. I had never prayed for someone that sick before and seen him restored to life, so I did not expect the dream to literally become reality. It did make me aware, though, that we needed to be alert for special spiritual opportunities in which God might move. I was watching for a divine appointment.

As are most mobile clinics, the day was hectic and busy with long lines of people waiting to see the two medical providers. Normal coughs and colds, aches and pains mingled with the occasional malaria and typhoid patient, and lots of patients with untreatable eye problems were turned away. In only a few cases did I feel there was something significantly wrong with the patient, so those few that required more attention stood out to me. One sweet woman, for example, had been experiencing difficulty breathing for three years. She turned out to have an abnormal heart rhythm. I was able to improve her symptoms by giving her medication to slow her heart rate, but it would not be curative. So I instructed her to try to get to the hospital, and then I moved on to the next patient. Baby Martunis appeared soon after, and he nearly took my breath away.

At almost fourteen months old and only about twelve pounds of skin and bones, he was the most malnourished child I had seen in the country. Many of the children were small and likely undernourished, but I had never seen anything approaching this severity in other children around the area. A swollen belly and stick thin legs supported a head marked with hollow eyes, and he was burning with fever. His mother, a young woman who seemed very easily confused and remarkably calm considering the poor health of her child, said he had kept a high fever for over three months, was not eating, and had worms coming out of his mouth. He was also continually vomiting and had persistent diarrhea. I rapidly assessed his condition, and I knew that it was grave.

"Dear God, this boy will die," I thought to myself as I examined him, rummaging through my brain to recollect any information stored there about worm diseases, extended fevers, and malnutrition. There were tidbits of knowledge there about various tropical illnesses, most of which required extensive tests for accurate diagnosis, and all of which required treatments I was not carrying in the back of our van. I knew enough about all of these conditions to know how dangerous they were but not enough about any to be certain of the diagnosis. I also knew there were at least a hundred other likely causes for his condition. Finally I threw up my hands and explained to his mother that I could give him medication for worms, but it was likely not the right one and not strong enough for his condition. I would also give him fever medication, but beyond that her only hope was to go to the hospital. I would be happy to take them back with us, help to get him admitted, and do what I could, but it was critical that he leave the village.

I had been blessed that day to have Bapak Martono, a village leader, interpreting into the local dialect for me since many of the village residents did not speak Indonesian. It turned out that he was distantly related to Baby Martunis and took a special interest in the critically ill patient who was resting on my lap. I explained *multiple* times to him and Martunis's mother that the child absolutely would die if one of two things did not happen: he was taken to the hospital, or a miracle happened as I prayed in the name of Jesus. Bapak Martono listened, repeated the information to his mother, and then said, "Ok, we will just take your medication."

"No," I countered, "you need to listen again."

Again I explained the two options, stressing the possibility that the child could die if not hospitalized or miraculously healed, and this time he seemed to pay more attention. Still their answer was the same. By the time I somewhat desperately explained my assessment for the third time, emphasizing even more that only a touch of Jesus would provide his cure, a small crowd had gathered around and was listening as well. Thirty minutes of pleading got me nowhere closer to Martunis's hospitalization. Nor were they eager for me to pray at that moment, but they did say I may do so later. I finally had to choke back my tears as I sent the child away and committed myself to pray for him every day.

At the end of the day I confess that a feeling of disappointment settled onto me. I was happy that many patients had been treated, happy for the welcoming reception we had received in the village, and happy that they had extended an open invitation for our return. It had not been a bad day at all, but neither was it very remarkable. The "big" thing I was anticipating seemed not to have happened, and I had left a dying child. That night in our prayer meeting, I wept over Baby Martunis and the village that sat in spiritual darkness, begging God to do something as only He can.

Eight days later, I was sitting in the team house talking to a visitor when my phone rang, and I answered to hear the happy voice of Bapak Martono. He rattled off a list of nine or ten patients I had treated in the village, and he reported that they were all well. I was happy to hear it, I said, and the patients themselves were apparently so happy about it that they had wanted to let me know. I could not remember all of the people he mentioned, but one of them I recognized clearly as the woman with the heart arrhythmia. She was now walking and breathing normally for the first time in years, Martono said. My own heart skipped a little beat at hearing this good news, but then it sped up to a gallop when he said: "And remember the baby, Ibu doctor?"

Of course I remembered the child, whose face had kept me awake in tearful prayer every night that week. I braced myself for the worst.

"He is well!" pronounced Bapak Martono. As I tried to keep from dropping the phone on the floor, I asked exactly what he meant by "well" and how he had convinced Martunis's mother to go to the hospital.

"He did not go to the hospital, Ibu doctor. I knew you would not believe it!" he laughed. "He just has not been sick, and his fever has been gone since the day you left."

Still hesitant to believe, I suggested that maybe the Tylenol I had given him was just keeping his fever down. It was possible that the baby was still quite ill. What else could he tell me about the baby's condition?

"Ibu doctor, he is well!" Martono laughed again, a full and

hearty chuckle filled with delight. "I would not believe it myself if I had not seen him today. I went to his house, and he has no fever. He is eating, laughing, and playing in his house, and I think he is even getting fatter!"

I teared up while trying not to scream into the phone, and I reminded him of our conversation in the clinic about healing. He said he remembered it well, how I had stated that Jesus alone could heal Martunis. Then he stunned me by remarking, "You know, I think you may be right." He definitely agreed with me that the baby's improvement was nothing short of miraculous, and he seemed to be listening more intently when I gently and simply explained that we must trust in Jesus, who is alive and present today with active power to heal.

I knew that day that the Holy Spirit was blowing His light and truth into a sheltered little village. In fact, I had known it before I ever set foot there, aware from the restlessness in my heart and pre-monitory dream that God somehow had a plan for the place. Yet I had allowed my sense of expectancy of what God wanted to do and the hope I felt to quickly be squelched because my vision was too limited. Where I had seen hopelessness, Jesus saw hope. Where I was looking at a little boy dangerously near to death , God was looking at a little boy very much full of life and an entire village coming alive to the truth of His power. I wonder if my attitude would have been different when entering that village had I known in advance--trusted and really *known*--that a miracle would take place? I wonder why I don't expect this all the time?

Seeing with Hope

The Bible promises that "hope does not disappoint us, because God's love has been poured into our hearts by the Holy Spirit" (Romans 5:5), and He certainly did not disappoint that day. I began to pray that Martunis's healing would be the beginning of many hearts turning to Jesus in that village, and I asked several others to pray the same. Over the next few months some other Jesus followers returned to the village and began building relationships, starting community development projects, and teaching the children. Every time they went in, the talk of the village was Baby Martunis and his healing, and many people seemed eager to tell the story. It was a full six months more before I allowed myself to go back, for I was very careful to distance the "foreign doctor" from the healing in order to leave the glory to God. I even wondered if perhaps this was why God, in His wisdom, healed Martunis the day *after* I left rather than in front of my eyes. When I finally did return, I was greeted face to face by a precious, delightful and yes--even fat little boy. I barely recognized the skeleton of Martunis's face under his plump cheeks, but his mother's smile provided all the recognition I needed.

I could not understand on that clinic day what God was doing in the village, but my faith in believing for a vision bigger than what I could see certainly grew. Because of that faith, I was able to pray more diligently and wait more patiently for God to move in the community. It was an entire year later before He allowed me to see a little more of His heart and His plan for that place, but He confirmed my initial feeling of expectation about something spiritually stirring in the mountains. A friend of mine, a devout Jesus follower, visited the village often to work with the men in development, and he spent a lot of time with Bapak Martono and other village leaders. During these visits, he had shared snippets of his faith as often as possible and consistently reminded them of God's power, and he often reminded them of Martunis. We shared an indescribable joy when he finally told me that the men had asked him for a New Testament, for they had decided they wanted to learn more about the Jesus who seemed to have healed Martunis and whom my friend lovingly followed. This began a weekly study and discussion group for eight men in the village, and two other similar groups that have since begun as well. Had I seen God's plan for such a Bible study in my mind's eye when I packed up the van with medication that day? Hardly.

I always retain a deep desire to see people know more about God in whatever way possible, and that desire was alive and well the day that I met Martunis. I honestly did not see God's hand at work, though, when I was wearily treating the 112th patient that day. What I saw was people being loved and cared for, certainly, and I hoped that someday they would remember we said we came in the love of Jesus. What I did *not* see was the Holy Spirit descending upon a tiny baby boy to do the miraculous. I saw a lot of people standing around me and hearing about the power of Jesus with little response. I did not see that God was gently beginning to stir in those men's hearts. My vision is so often limited to seeing only the effects of the Holy Spirit rather than His work as it begins, but He is working all the same. Knowing that, I wonder what else there remains to be seen in that village as God continues to reveal Himself there? I want the people in that village to know the love of Jesus, and personally I want to know all of the fullness of God and the marvelous mysteries of His Kingdom. Only He can open our eyes to see.

CHAPTER Eighteen:
Bringing Sight to the Blind

I do not like admitting that I cannot do something, and I like not being able to help someone else even less. Five months of saying, "I am sorry, but I am not an eye doctor and cannot help you," had just about driven me crazy; at least having learned a bit more about common eye diseases from a local ophthalmologist helped me preserve my sanity. I had been able to begin treating more tropical infections, recognizing chronic complications of infections from years past, and giving away generously donated eye glasses, but I was still immensely impatient to see many nearly blind patients have their cataracts removed. At one point there was an exciting possibility for an ophthalmologist to come and train me to operate, but that fell through. There had been two promises from other physicians to come and operate themselves, neither of which had materialized, but I was not to be deterred easily. Perseverance, a lot of phone calls, and a lot more time praying finally paid off, so it was with great anticipation and joy that I finally made plans for the arrival of an eye surgeon.

Dr. Santi and her nurse, Miriam, two wonderful women from the eastern side of Indonesia, breezed into our community with smiles that never left their faces throughout their long and tedious work days. They normally worked together in a private hospital in their hometown, which was ten hours away by plane, and they enjoyed traveling together on vacation time to volunteer their services. Our partner agency had worked with them in the past, so they contacted the two women to explain the needs in our village and see if they wanted to offer assistance. Although the two had done a considerable amount of volunteer work in the past, it had always been in a government clinic or similarly large, better equipped building. Our tiny village clinic was going to offer unique challenges. Despite this, trusting God just as we were, these kind and servant hearted women came as volunteers and operated for a salary comprised of food and a place to sleep at night. My prayers for healing for the blind were finally going to be answered!

Not long before that, a friend had sent an email that read like this: "Conventional wisdom would say the services of the clinic could not be expanded right now without more help." I smiled, knowing that God is anything but conventional, and set about planning for Dr. Santi's arrival. I had been actively screening patients for about a month, trying with my limited knowledge to differentiate cataracts from glaucoma, infections, and traumatic scarring, and I had identified around a hundred patients as tentative surgical candidates. Those chosen would undergo surgery for only 100,000 rupiah--about $10--a nominal cost compared to the $200 charged in the city hospitals. The small amount collected from each patient helped to pay for the cost of the new set of lenses they would have implanted, but it also gave them a sense of ownership in their own care. As anticipation mounted in the community leading up to the week of operations, my nervousness increased as well.

I knew God could break all conventions, but the medically trained, rational part of my brain also reminded me that bacteria can break a lot of boundaries. The staff and I spent a few hours getting a side room as clean and sterile as possible, which involved mostly sweeping, mopping, and coating the walls with formaldehyde. We covered the open slatted windows with large sheets of white paper to keep out dust, wind, insects, and other small stray animals, but bleating goats and mooing cows still roamed right outside the window. The cows even tried to poke their noses through the paper; thankfully the smell of formaldehyde eventually kept them at bay. Our makeshift operating room was functional, but it was a far cry from the sterile conditions under which surgeons generally operate. Thus we were already leaning heavily on prayer for protection before the surgeries began.

My screening skills did not turn out to be as effective as I had planned, and many of those who came hoping for surgery were sent away after Dr. Santi evaluated them. In some cases their cataracts were too old, in others too new, and in other cases their additional medical problems were too complicating. Some patients had entirely different eye diseases all together. Despite this, we easily found ten individuals who were ready for surgery and immediately began to work, certain that more would come as the week went on. Dr. Santi and Miriam worked tirelessly in the tiny room, dripping with sweat from the heat despite the fan blowing in the corner; never once did they complain about the conditions, the heat, the patients or the cows. They were a shining example of loving, joyful servants, using the skills God had given them to truly change lives, and it was a blessing and lesson for me to watch them in action.

Watching was about all I could do after coordinating the initial chaotic screening process of the mornings, but I loved every minute of it. I have never been squeamish about much of anything (a good thing in the medical field), but I must confess that watching a large needle poke into an eyeball made my stomach turn a few flips. I soon grew used to it, though, and I tried to stay in the room as much as possible to see the surgical proceedings. Secretly I was still hoping that one day I would learn to do them on my own.

Although it is unlikely that I will ever actually be trained to do surgery, someone else was being trained that week. Nuri, Laila's older sister, had been interpreting the local provincial dialect for me in the clinic for several months. Initially she had volunteered her assistance. Since her family could not afford to allow her to finish her two remaining years of high school, she frequently wandered around the clinic out of boredom and curiosity. One day I stumbled on the idea to hire her for a small salary, with the condition that the money would be saved for her to return to school the following year. She had been a fantastic help to me, and she really seemed to enjoy the work. So she was the obvious choice to provide interpretation for the surgeries as well. Dr. Santi spoke the national language of Indonesian, but most of the surgical patients were older and spoke only the local dialect. So, undaunted by the strong smells, heat, and squishy eyeballs, Nuri bravely volunteered to stand by her side and interpret what was happening to the patients. She also quickly began to help handing off instruments and lenses to the surgeon, and she watched with rapt attention every detail of what was occurring. Dr. Santi treated her as if she was a surgical nurse, and Nuri was brimming over with pride at her important position. A few months prior, with her hopes for school long since gone, her only aspirations had included finding a husband and washing clothes all day. Now she was dreaming again, and by the end of the week she had committed herself to seek nursing training after finishing school.

Remember Bapak Abu, the blind man who cried when he saw his son? Thirty two patients received their sight back in that first week of surgeries, just as he had, and thirty two times my heart turned over in praise. Bapak Abu's was the most dramatic story of the surgical week, but each of the patients had been limited in their lives to some degree by their cloudy vision. Most of them were older adults, but we operated on a few younger ones who had congenital defects as well. There was a mixture of women and men, and they came from several different surrounding communities. Some were quiet, and some were loud; some were nervous, and others were calm; some were appreciative, and others were resiliently silent. What they all had in common, though, were the smiles that would cross their faces when the bandages were removed from their eyes and they could see clearly for the first time in years. Some of them laughed, and several of them cried. All of us rejoiced together. I told many of them that their sight had been restored by Jesus, and I shared with several the Biblical stories of how He healed the blind.

Under the best of surgical conditions, there is invariably a small complication and infection rate. In our case, though--in our humble, small, impractical, and ill equipped clinic--there were no major complications. Patients returned for several days to follow-up with Dr. Santi and then for a few weeks afterward with me, and we dealt with very few problems--even minor ones. God had truly protected us all and worked through us in unlikely conditions to prove His sufficiency and glory. For the following weeks, long after things had settled back to normal, I still remembered the broad grins of the patients when their gauze first came free and wanted to jump for joy. I marveled that God allowed me to be a part of such amazing things, and it made me hunger to see more of how He is moving in the world. After all, He says in the Bible that Jesus came to give sight to the blind, and He had done it! What other Biblical promises did He have for us for which I had thus far been too fearful or ignorant to pray?

My prayer following surgery became that each of the patients who received their sight would begin to see the truth of *who* had actually healed them: not a foreign doctor, not Dr. Santi, but Jesus. I knew we had scattered seeds of this truth far and wide, and I prayed for those seeds to bear fruit. In the Bible, God reminds me that it is He who grows the seed we scatter (Mark 4:26-27), so I prayed for those seeds to blossom into a whole field for His glory. I prayed that the patients and their families would clearly see the Light of Truth of Jesus just as they could now clearly see in the physical realm. I deeply desired to see people's spiritual eyes opening, so I prayed more in earnest for that to happen as I moved into my second year of ministry.

Round 2

As the word spread in local communities about the surgeries that had taken place, people who needed an operation continued to trickle in to the clinic. I tried to work with some of these patients to help them obtain a reduced fee for surgeries in the city, but it was not easy. So I kept a running list of the needy patients, continued to pray, and hoped to repeat the surgeries the following year. Doing so involved some interesting trials, including stolen money, disappearing lenses, doctor swapping, and a web of lies, but eventually Dr. Santi and Miriam returned. Almost one year to the date of when the pair had departed, we were ready to operate again.

The second surgical week bore many similarities to the first. As we had the year prior, we again cleaned the makeshift operating room as best as possible and papered the windows. We screened the patients (a little more effectively this time), but we also planned an entire half day for the doctor to do her own initial assessment. During that morning she was able to offer a lot of advice and medication for different eye disorders, and over two hundred people walked away satisfied and well on the way to healing without surgery. This was a major improvement. The patients who were chosen this time for surgery had similar stories to those the first year. Some were old, and some were young; some had congenital disease, and others had been slowly growing the shadowy lesions that blinded their eyes. All were eager and hopeful to have their sight fully restored. Two patients were even repeat customers: they had received an operation on one eye the first year and now needed the second one done as well. Once again, I heard not the slightest complaint from Dr. Santi and Miriam, despite some fairly difficult circumstances which arose during the week's work. God provided His incredible covering of protection just as He had the first year, and there were very few minor post surgical complications. Close to sixty patients had their sight restored that week, and once again our praises reached to the heavens.

Seeing the Light

Although each healing that year was praiseworthy, certain ones just knocked me to my knees in gratitude. Three years of sightless life had kept one elderly gentleman confined to his small village house, and his face was somber as he entered the clinic for eye screening. "He does not get out, and he is very sad," said his daughter, looking as if she shared a heavy load of his sorrow herself. This previously capable man struggled under the burden of being dependent on others to take him anywhere, and the emotional strain, combined with his sightlessness, had robbed him of much joy and hope. Bapak Hakim was thus chosen to receive an eye operation on the first day of surgeries, and forty minutes later his life had been changed.

At his first check up the following day, Hakim's two daughters and son all led him into the room and helped him to find a chair. His right eye was still sightless, and his left eye was bandaged. So his world was still dark when Dr. Santi approached him to remove the surgical gauze, and he seemed a bit startled when she started asking how many fingers she was holding up. Quickly, however, his surprise gave way to enthusiastic cries of "two, one, four!" and his daughters both started to cry. Of course, I began to cry as well. So did a few other people in the room, and a broad smile soon spread across this dear man's face. By the end of the week, new lenses had been placed in both of his eyes, and two weeks later the now ever-smiling Bapak Hakim came into my room for his final follow up. That time he was able to come alone.

Another young patient had bilateral cataracts induced from trauma in a motorbike accident. Only twenty two years of age, he had lived with blindness for six years. Although one eye was irreparably damaged, this young man regained his life, independence, and hope after receiving surgery in the other eye. I was not sure who was happier, the patient himself or his brother who had been caring for him. Another patient thanked me so profusely and so many times that I was not sure I had any more "You're welcomes" left to say, and he announced that it was absolutely the best week of his life. I really enjoyed getting to share with this man, who had a beautifully humble and open spirit, that his sight was restored by the power and name of Jesus. I enjoyed it even more when he said, "Well, then, I will start to thank Him, too!" Yes, I pray that this may be so!

Interesting Trials and Provision

God's protection and provision were apparent throughout all the weeks of surgeries. One day, I was sitting outside talking to waiting patients when I heard a cry from the surgical nurse saying, "Mati lampu! Mati lampu!" (dead lights)--meaning the power had gone out. My teammate and I scrambled around to find and borrow a few flashlights, then we ran into the room to hold them over the patient's eye for the next twenty minutes so his stitches could be placed. Thankfully the more difficult part of the operation was already over at that point, so it was able to be completed with relatively little difficulty. Still, operating on tiny eyes with barely visible needles under flashlights is not something I would recommend trying again.

We waited for a few minutes, hoping the power would be restored quickly, and we began to pray. When we finally grew tired of waiting and decided something had to be done, I walked over to discuss the situation with the village leader, Bapak Umar. He ran off to use someone's cell phone and returned in five minutes saying, "Just wait."

"Wait? " I thought. "Sometimes the power is out for hours here! How long do we wait?"

Ten minutes later the power returned. Bapak Umar cheerfully explained that he had called Pak Budi, a former political party leader who was well known, well respected, and often slightly feared in the community, and sent him to have a short discussion with the power company. Since Pak Budi's own mother had successfully received eye surgery the previous year, he had been very happy to oblige. I don't know exactly what took place in his conversation with the power company, but I was suddenly glad to know men who can be feared. God can use all people for His purposes.

Two days later the power went out again. I was on my way down to call for help from Bapak Umar when a young man sitting outside the clinic yelled at me to stop. He had noticed that only our building, not the whole community, had lost electricity this time; this meant that perhaps there was a problem in the wiring rather than a cut from the power company. The man proceeded to set his cigarette down (on the wooden windowsill, by the way), and begin yanking wires around on the fuse boxes. He pulled off some pieces that looked fairly important to my non- electrical mind, and then he disappeared.

"Ibu doctor," said one of the patients waiting outside, "He just told me he is an electrical worker, so don't worry."

"Is he from the village?" I asked. Personally I had not recognized his face.

"No, I have never seen him before," the man replied.

Five minutes later the young man returned and fiddled around a bit more, and the lights popped on again. "Are you waiting with someone for surgery?" I asked him. He was not a registered patient for surgery, so there really was no other explanation for his being there. "A family member maybe?"

"No," he replied, "I'm not."

Then he simply turned and walked down the street. No one in the waiting crowd had any idea who he was, which was very unusual in an area where virtually everyone is related to everyone else. I do not know that I have ever been in the presence of an angel before, but I think I may have been that day. I did not even care if he smoked.

In the weeks following the surgeries, I again loved seeing the patients and hearing their happy comments about how great it was to see light. I reveled in their excitement about seeing things clearly, for many of these people had not been able to see for a long time. I had been praying that spiritual as well as physical eyes would open, and God was also busy answering those prayers. One follow-up visit with a surgical patient led into a half hour conversation about Jesus, and I explained to many others that it was in His name that they could now see. The two surgical weeks were highlights of my whole time overseas, and I still get chill bumps thinking of those days.

Jesus said he came to give sight to the blind, to make the lame walk, to make the deaf hear, and to preach good news to the poor (Matthew 11:5). So if we have the Spirit of Christ inside of us, can we not trust Him and operate on these promises? My mind tells me it is not possible, and my field of vision sees the limitations. God, however, sees things differently. As I saw Jesus fulfilling His promises during our surgeries, I was challenged to continue to pray for bigger things. Perhaps it was never wise to pray for eye operations to happen in a tiny, nondescript clinic in the middle of a rice field, but it was certainly good. May God help me to trust that He will always provide what is needed, and may He give me eyes to see what to pray for next.

CHAPTER Nineteen:
Perfect Provision

Time and again God provided for our outreach work, for individuals, and for complicated situations in remarkable ways. He is, after all, Jehovah Jirah, the Great Provider. I have always known that He cares for me by His provision of food and shelter and relationships, and I have even come to understand how He provides by granting the desires of my heart to see His Kingdom grow. The Bible tells me that my Father in heaven "gives good gifts to His children" (Matthew 7:11), and I have learned that sometimes those gifts also come in unexpected packages.

Take, for example, the gift of a broken down car. Most people would not consider this much of a gift if it were just handed over, nor would I. The day our agency's car broke down *again* didn't seem like a gift to me at all, for it involved time and hassle in order to get it repaired. I was grateful to have a vehicle for transporting people to the clinic, and I was continually aware of God's protection as I drove it in crazy traffic, dodging motorbikes and cows. However, I was learning enough from the constant repairs of this car to earn a license in auto mechanics, and another breakdown was not a welcome interruption in my busy life.

It was a Sunday morning, and I was actually looking forward to some rest. We had been going full steam ahead in the village and had several visitors, and I was exhausted. I planned to go to the market for vegetables then hibernate in the house for the rest of the day to spend some overdue time with God--and with sleep. I had also recently moved into a new community, and that morning I had been praying and asking God to allow me to meet some new neighbors. I knew that our foreign faces were being watched with a degree of suspicion, and my level of activity had prevented me from speaking to many of the neighbors beyond short greetings. The few times I had tried, I had not met with much success, and I was disappointed that my home was not yet beginning to feel like any sort of community.

A few rupiah in hand, I sat in the car and dreamed of the papaya I would soon be eating after a quick jaunt to the market. I turned the engine over. Silence. I tried again. Silence. Again--silence. I banged on a few things on the dash, which would occasionally shock the car into submission, but not this time. It was dead. I was tired, and this is not what I wanted. I also did not want the man sitting on the corner watching me to yell, "Your lights were on all night," but he did.

"Thanks a lot for noticing and coming to tell me," I grumbled under my breath. I had to overcome my irritation quickly, though, because I needed his help.

Within ten minutes, a handful of neighborhood men were out in the street pushing the car back and forth and trying to get it started. While they worked on it, I had a chance to talk to some of their wives, who had become curious bystanders as well. A somewhat entertaining display of chivalry ensued when each new man arrived on the scene, came up in turn to ask about the problem, and proceeded to proclaim that he could fix it. They all peered at the dash, pushed and pulled on various parts of the vehicle, leaned on the car deep in thought, then pushed and pulled some more. The car did not start.

Eventually the battery disappeared with Bapak Amir, my next door neighbor. While he was getting it charged, I was left with the women of the street who had gathered to watch the morning's events unfold. We were able to talk for several more hours, more than fulfilling my request of God to have some good conversations with them! It is amazing what can happen when I am forced to be still for a while, and that gloriously slow Sunday afternoon I probably met over twenty people who lived in the community. The barrier of lack of familiarity had been shattered, and I was on my way to developing friendships with my neighbors. Gifts of provision don't always come in pretty packages!

Not long before the car incident, as I had been praying one day for relationships in that new community, God answered almost immediately. Again it was a Sunday morning, and I specifically asked God to allow me to converse with one lady who lived on my street sometime later during that week. That afternoon I would be attending a birthday party for some of my Filipino friends on the other side of town, a drive of a good twenty minutes away, so I naturally assumed the conversation I desired would need to be on a different day. As expected, almost all of the guests at the party were foreign workers (most of whom I knew), with the exception of one local woman. I had never seen her before and did not pay her much attention as I chatted merrily with my friends. She recognized me, though, as the newcomer in her neighborhood, and she came over to introduce herself. Yes, she just *happened* to be *my* neighbor and lived three houses away, and she immediately invited me to her home. Thus Ibu Sabeen became a dear friend over the following year, and I passed many happy hours in her home sharing recipes, telling stories, preparing for her son's wedding, and laughing at the world around us. Sometimes God delays in answering prayers, but sometimes He doesn't. He always provides what we need exactly when we need it. That day I needed a local friend, and the sun did not set before God provided one.

God regularly provided for me in gifts of relationships, but other times He provided in protection or by offering favor in unlikely places. After several months of operating the clinic, I had begun to notice that the village leader, Bapak Umar, came around every day that the building was opened. I knew that he was not an incredibly busy person, but I did assume that being the village leader presented him with a level of responsibility that required some time. I became quite curious as to why he spent so much time just loitering around the clinic, despite never being sick himself, so finally I asked him. His response shocked me. I found out that day that some local men in the community were very hostile to our presence and work and were continually threatening to shut us down; Bapak Umar, by his presence, was offering his affirmation of us as a protection to our staff. Until that moment I was completely unaware that we were being opposed, and I certainly had no idea that God had been providing a protector for us!

Another time, when I was away for a month, an issue arose involving a local midwife who wanted to move into the clinic. There was tension about the decision; the newly elected village leader was unhappy with a lot of things, and the situation was becoming heated in the village. I was not there to try to manage the issue, and no one else on the clinic staff was bold enough to tackle it. Immediately my friend Edward, the leader of another organization, stepped in and met with the village chief and a few others to diffuse the situation. This was unbeknownst to me as I prayed and worried from across the ocean, miserably and naively thinking that I could actually work things out better than God. Even had I been there, my standing with the village leaders as a woman would have been questionable at best. God knew this, and His provision was perfect in sending this man in my place. Edward was very well liked and trusted in the community, and with his recommendation and explanation, things quickly settled back down to normal with all relationships intact.

After six months of watching patient after patient stumble out the door, semi or completely blinded by cataracts and other eye conditions, I embarked on a mission to bring better eye care to the community. This had not been a strong point in my training, and I had been praying in earnest for an eye doctor to come and run a clinic for a week or two. When I grew tired of waiting, I eventually decided to explore the options actually available in the local medical community. There were several city hospitals, at least three of which I knew had ophthalmologists, so off I went one morning in the hopes of finding information about how they could help my patients.

The first two facilities were not at all helpful, as I found it difficult to get past the registration staff who seemed to know the answers to exactly zero of my questions. I left frustrated. I knew that surgery could be performed for cataracts, but I could not get anyone to explain how much it would cost or how that cost could be subsidized for the poor. Luckily I knew that information can virtually always eventually be obtained with due diligence, so I threw on my best "important doctor" look and entered the third hospital.

Finding the eye clinic was easy after asking several curious people sitting in the hallways to direct me there. In these hospitals, clinic visits take place behind firmly shut doors, and the only opportunity to register or let a nurse or other helper know of your presence is to sit by the door and wait for the flash of a momentary opening. Doors were virtually never opened in response to knocking, but I decided to take a gamble and try anyway. To my surprise, the door swung open immediately, guarded by an equally surprised nurse who stumbled through asking me what I wanted. After I quickly explained who I was and that I wanted to talk to the doctor, I was instantly ushered into the room. The door slammed shut behind me.

Dr. Nita sat bright eyed and attentive to the patient in front of her, her young appearance belying the fact that she was old enough to be a physician. I sat and watched her finish with the patient, not wanting to disturb, and was pleased to see her providing thorough care with considerable kindness. We talked cordially for a few moments, during which time she entertained my simple questions about how to access services for my patients, when surgeries were scheduled, and other details which I thought may later prove helpful. She in turn asked me two questions: why was I helping the village people, and did I know anything about eyes?

I told her I had come to provide medical services for those in need because I considered my medical skills a blessing from God to be shared. I then explained that I knew very little about eyes beyond how to treat basic infections, and I was desperate for someone to help in the village. Although she did not jump at the chance to come out and see the patients herself, neither did she tersely answer my questions and send me away. Rather, she asked me to stay with her all day long and learn. She then proceeded to spend six hours educating me about eye illnesses, showing me individual patient diseases, discussing the common problems in the region, and introducing me to staff at two other hospitals. She took me to her home, chatting happily all the way about her career and her life, and she loaned me a book to help me learn more about the most prevalent eye conditions I was seeing every day. I had gone into the hospital that day looking and hoping for information, but God had given me so much more. He taught me volumes through this sweet spirited young doctor, for He knew I needed much more knowledge than I was asking for that day. As a result, I was later able to handle many of the eye disorders I was seeing without outside help, and I gained a friend. Dr. Nita and I spent time together on several occasions after that initial encounter, developing mutual respect and friendship, and I even went to her house on Idul Fitri. The Bible says, "Knock and the door will be opened unto you." (Matthew 7:7) Sometimes that knocking, quite literally, can have wonderful results.

Personal Provision

God is ever concerned with the details of our lives, not only those of our ministries. He is busy working all things out according to His plan, and although I often fail to comprehend it, that plan weaves together every aspect of life. In order to keep my legal status as a medical provider in the US, I need to complete a licensing exam every six years. My second year overseas just happened to be year number six. I pleaded and made multiple requests to the board for extensions, all of which went unheeded, and so I turned my energies towards complaining to God about it instead. I was indignant about having to return just for the exam, for I felt it would be interrupting outreach and costing way too much money for something so, well--*personal*. I think that sometimes God must just smile at my grumbling and complaining, knowing the future as He does. Ever faithful, in time He showed His perfect provision to me for even this--something so *personal*.

My sending organization's headquarters just happened to be based in my home city, and it just happened to be having a candidate week as well as a pastor and donor event during the same weeks in which I needed to take my exam. The trip, which had seemed annoyingly personal and "business" oriented, taking me out of ministry, suddenly became a ministry in itself. I was able to be the representative for my agency's work for the poor in Southeast Asia at both of these events. I spoke with passion about capturing God's heart for justice and the poor and encouraged others to be involved. What had been an annoyance suddenly became a joy, as God provided both for my personal needs in the exam (and helping me to pass it!) as well as for the needs of the ministry. I wonder if the national medical board would be interested in knowing how they were a part of moving people into third world nations to show God's love.

Across the Oceans

Two days before I left the country for that exam, we ran out of malaria test kits. Our previous supply had been donated by a large agency that had since left the country, and my hurried attempts to find other donations or a place to purchase them came up empty. I sighed and thought, "That's one more thing to figure out when I return," adding to the growing list of things I was afraid would get too far behind in my upcoming absence. No matter how many times God had showed his sufficiency and my complete insignificance for His work, I was continually forgetting that and thinking a bit too highly of myself.

On the first week of visiting my sending organization's office for the conference, I had a quick meeting with their medical director. We were discussing the work in Indonesia and what other medical work was going on around the world, when suddenly he stopped mid-sentence and looked at me. "By the way," he said, "this may be a strange question, but you don't happen to need malaria tests, do you?" The two large boxes of new testing kits sitting behind him on the floor had been left from a short term medical team, and he was eager to clear them out of his office. I left the office with several hundred malaria testing kits that day, humbled by how God continually and graciously provides, even across the oceans.

More Supplies

Someone donated some used eye glasses to the clinic, and they were very well received. Many patients in the villages suffered from near and far sighted vision, problems which were easily correctable but could also greatly debilitate an individual. I allowed patients to sort through the glasses on their own, and then I smiled watching them walk out the door with the often oversized frames adorning their weather worn faces. They were happy.

When those glasses ran out, I was very disturbed to think I may again have to turn patients away when they asked for help with their sight. I never enjoyed doing that. In fact, on the Wednesday afternoon that I looked down into the newly empty box, I was downright depressed. On Thursday, a friend called whom I had not spoken to in about four months, saying that she had cleaned out their agency garage and found several boxes of medical supplies which she wanted to give to me. I drove to pick them up without question (we were always happy for donations of any kind) and happily found a hundred sets of glasses included! God's timing is perfect indeed. The glasses came again in an array of all sizes and shapes and measurements, producing some funny matches between elderly women and men and glasses twice the size of their faces. My smile grew wide as I marveled at God's provision, and I smiled a bit more at my friends' funny appearances. They did not seem to mind, though, and their own smiles grew twice as wide when they realized they could suddenly see.

Safety on Vacation

Eleanor and I decided to celebrate New Year's with a short vacation, and our Indonesian friends recommended that we visit a well known and beautiful lake on the island. The eight hour journey it took us to get there was admittedly arduous, but the scenery that greeted us upon arrival more than made up for the trouble. We passed a few glorious days sitting by the water, praying together and resting from our labors, reflecting on the goodness of God during the year, and entering the blissful state of not being worried about much of anything for a few days. On New Year's Day, we decided to rent a motorbike and go explore the area, circling the windy mountain roads around the lake and stopping for breathtakingly photographic scenes. Then, always in the mood for adventure, we went for a long, long ride away from the lake in search of a hot spring.

The back tire of the motorbike busted out when we had reached a town almost two hours away from where we were staying. Everyone we saw along the street was friendly and kind, but they offered us no help for our predicament. They merely smiled and told us that no shops were open on the holiday, nor were buses and other transportation running, and we began to wonder how we were going to get home. Not knowing what else to do, we stopped in the middle of the street and prayed for God to send us someone to help us in this unfamiliar place.

Five minutes later we pushed the bike up in front of a store that said motorbike accessories. It looked closed. The doors were tightly shut with no one in sight, but we thought perhaps someone would take pity on us if we knocked loudly and looked desperate enough.

"Eleanor!" called out a voice from the next door over, much to our surprise. This is not an Indonesian name, so we could not be mistaken in hearing it.

"Eleanor!" came the voice again, and we turned to see the smiling face of David, an Indonesian friend who worked in our province. He was home visiting his family for the holiday, and his family lived right there on that street. They happened to live directly next door to the bike repair shop, in fact, and the shop owner was one of David's good friends. Fifteen minutes and a phone call later, the sealed doors swung open, and the bike was repaired. Soon we were on our way, rejoicing in our great and protecting God!

Hemoglobin Machine

One of my patients' frequently self-proclaimed diagnoses was "kurang darah," which means "low blood." Not only was this a popular idea in the community for anyone who felt tired or generally sick, but unfortunately it was a diagnosis often given by doctors as well. At times there would be absolutely no proof of the patient being anemic, yet he would walk out with vitamins to "raise his blood" and persist in thinking he had this malady. Among other things, the desire to correct this frequent misdiagnosis was one reason I wanted a Hemoglobin machine in the clinic. I wanted to be able to show people that they were *not*, in fact, anemic; in the meantime I tended to generally write off most people's suggestions that they had "low blood."

I had been looking for a way to purchase a machine for a while when a generous friend in the US surprised me with a donation. He worked for a medical supply company and said he was able to donate the machine free of charge, and so I happily awaited its' slow journey across the oceans. It was almost six weeks before the machine actually arrived, during which time I almost forgot that it would be coming. Thus I was pleasantly surprised one Thursday afternoon to find the it finally sitting in our post office box, and it came along with me to the clinic on Friday morning.

Three people that morning told me that they had low blood, but I had, as usual, brushed their complaints off and gone on to other things. The fourth patient to complain, however, an older woman, caught my attention, for she actually looked fairly pale and tired and had some signs and symptoms consistent with true anemia. She told me that three months prior she had completed three blood transfusions, after which she was told she must add blood every month in the future. Unfortunately, she had not done so, and she also had absolutely no idea why she required such large volumes of replacement blood. Her only guess was that perhaps she had worms. Not being a tropical disease specialist, I chose not to argue the point, but I seriously doubted that worms were the root of her problem.

This frail woman, appearing to be in her mid fifties but claiming to be around forty, was complaining of fatigue and slight difficulty breathing. Her eyes were also as white as sheets, and I decided it was a good time to break in the newly arrived Hemoglobin machine. Her blood count registered at 4.0. Since 12.0 or above is normal, I had to check twice to make sure I was not seeing things. While trying to get over my shock that she could still actually walk, I called in the patient's son and had her promptly taken into the city to get a transfusion. This woman truly had "kurang darah," and dangerously so; we caught it at a critical time when she was likely on the brink of heart failure. I had wanted that machine primarily to prove to people they were *not* anemic, but in this case it may have saved a patient's life by showing us how anemic she truly was. Had the woman come one day sooner, when the machine had not yet arrived, I would have been likely to underestimate the severity of her condition. God's provision and His timing are perfect indeed!

CHAPTER Twenty: Good Things Come to Those Who Wait

Picture Germany in 2004, at Christmastime. A group of laughing, singing, jubilant children and their parents are busy making shoebox gifts for other kids around the world. They lovingly and happily place each item into the shoebox, trying to imagine as they work what the kids will think of their presents from overseas. In goes a pencil or two, then a small stuffed toy, followed by a nice oversized bar of chocolate. What child does not like chocolate, no matter where he lives? A toothbrush is a nice addition after that chocolate, topped off by a nice warm pair of socks. The sides of the box are lined with some stationary and paper that can be used for school or maybe just for drawing, and another small toy may just fit into the corner. There. What a beautiful gift to give to the needy children of the world this Christmas!

Hundreds of these boxes disappear out of churches that year and are sent to a large nonprofit donation agency, leaving the givers with feelings of goodwill in having done something for those less privileged. Along with the boxes, mountains of clothes, winter hats, and jackets are collected because the kind donors believe that the shipment is going to be sent off to Russia. "Some mittens and extra sweatshirts will be nice as well for the winter chill in the air," the donors think, "and perhaps when the recipients wear the youth camp T-shirt underneath they will know something about God's love."

The scenario is not just in your imagination. It is real, and all those donations did pour into a German warehouse over the holiday season. Workers packed all the shoeboxes into a forty by forty foot container, along with the boxes and bags of clothing, but there

247

was still a sizeable hole remaining in the container. A rehabilitation facility in Russia was in need of orthopedic and physical therapy equipment, they were told, so piles upon piles of medical supplies went into the giant crate as well: mountains of crutches, wheelchairs and toilet chairs by the hundreds, bathtub seats, trolleys for patients with muscle disorders, tables, stretching equipment, and assorted other things.

Packed to the brim, the container set sail across the seas, headed for snow covered Russia. Then, for reasons I have never discovered, it suddenly turned around and changed course, arriving back at the port in Germany. Perhaps Russian law had changed to no longer allow donations, or any number of other forces could have been at play. Regardless of the exact reason, the ship did an about face. When it did so, this container and its contents were positioned to become one of my biggest (quite literally!) teachers.

Empty Rooms

After a year in Indonesia, I had begun to fancy myself a more patient person. Life has a way of knocking such silly ideas out of me. Somewhere during that first year, a volunteer with my agency mentioned to me that he had had arranged for the German goods container to be redirected to us. He let me know that it would be arriving sometime in the port (which was located in a bigger city eight hours down the coast), at which point I would be contacted to sign some paperwork and arrange for trucks to bring the supplies to our area. Then we could have a delightful time of giving all the donations away. I heard that the container was full of medical supplies which I could use for our clinic along with a few other things, and I filed the information away mentally until I was contacted.

I forgot about the promised shipment for a while, until a visit to a remote mountain hospital jogged my memory. Winding roads, breakneck speeds, and a loudly singing driver had made the two hour drive to the facility pass quickly, and breathtaking views had dominated my thinking as lush green mountains, rolling rivers, and the occasional monkey passed by the window on the way. This beautiful village was nestled far in the mountains and very unfamiliar with foreigners, but it was actually the seat of government for that particular province. Jason and I had traveled there to finalize our government approval for the clinic, and on the way back we thought it may be good to stop in and visit the hospital. We hoped to perhaps work in partnership with them in the future. A volunteer surgeon had used the hospital for surgery in the past, we had been told, so we were expecting to find, at a minimum, a functional operating room, decent wards, and equipment available to assist in surgery.

High expectations melted into sadness when we discovered the dire lack of supplies in the facility, which was intended to provide care for a very large province of people. The empty feeling inside me matched the emptiness of the rooms I wandered through as I thought of the thousands of people nearby without medical care. My disappointment was only appeased by the presence of the staff, for at least they obviously had very kind hearts. The large, expansive buildings that had been built by nonprofit donations were still under construction but held little to no equipment in each room; the equipment and beds I did see were broken, rusty and out of date. It turns out that the volunteer surgeon had brought his own supplies and only done minor surgery, and the operating room contained only one bed (half of which was broken), an anesthesia machine that no one knew how to operate, and a tray of small cutting tools. There were no machines with which to monitor heart rate or breathing, no stands for tools or containers for supplies, no respiratory equipment, and no one who seemed to know what to do about any of this. There were only two beds in the recovery room, and they were both missing mattresses. The newly built radiology room was awaiting both an actual X-ray machine and someone who knew how to use it, while the newly built rehabilitation ward contained nothing but paint and sawdust.

Disturbed at seeing what appeared to be yet another example of kind hearted but misplaced generosity, I wondered how new buildings without adequate supplies or the staff knowing how to use them would help patients. "Why does the government not give you needed supplies, since this is a government hospital?" I ignorantly asked the kind director of the hospital while sitting in her office that day. After touring the hospital's empty rooms, meeting the staff in every location, and explaining for the umpteenth time where I was from and how I loved the province, I had settled into her office. After having refused the tea that was offered several times, I drank thirstily from the small plastic water container I was given and focused carefully on her explanation. This was the first time I had been exposed to the bureaucratic workings of the local health care system, and I was eager to learn when the people would actually be able to help themselves so that the hospital could become a viable hub of healthcare for many surrounding villages. Ibu Cut smiled shyly at me and indulged my ignorance, explaining that the government had promised equipment to the hospital for over a year, but there had been no further word on when it may arrive. I noticed the frustration in her eyes as she described what the hospital needed and how she desired to better serve the people who came to the sprawling campus for help. A dentist by training, she had inadvertently found herself in this position of hospital director, but she seemed to cherish the role with the hopes of actually making things better. I felt instant compassion for this kind woman who was trying patiently to wait for long promised aid, and I decided in that moment that I wanted to help her hospital.

The attitude of many local people I had met at that point was very fatalistic and apathetic, traits which generally made me want to climb the wall. Ibu Cut, in contrast, had an obvious desire to make a difference for her people and an interest in doing whatever was necessary to make that happen; these traits instantly appealed to me. Her attitude seemed to have infected most of the staff as well. The thought came to me during our visit that the mysterious German shipment I had been promised held some hospital supplies, so I offered the suggestion that perhaps at some point our agency could provide them with equipment. As far as I was aware, after all, the container held beds, wheelchairs, useful diagnostic machines and basic hospital supplies that would not be useful to our clinic but could be life saving in this location. In addition to waiting for that shipment, I determined that I would try to locate donations of used but functional equipment in order to outfit the operating room quickly.

We briefly discussed volunteer surgeons being able to use the facility, and I happily received Ibu Cut's assurances that she was eager for this to happen. This was a refreshingly positive response compared to those I had received by querying the city hospitals. Not long before this visit, I had been trying to find a suitable location for a group of specialty surgeons who wanted to perform free operations for a week. Each hospital I approached, though, had demanded several thousand US dollars as compensation for use of their operating room--for providing free surgery for their people! This sweet woman's opposite response instantly doubled my motivation to help her.

Over the course of the next few months, I researched methods to obtain used monitors and machines, priced new equipment in several countries, and inquired of some nonprofit agencies whether they could potentially send equipment our way. I did not have a great degree of success, and admittedly the project soon slipped into the periphery of my focus as our own clinic steadily grew. I could not devote a great deal of time to stocking the facility as I desired, but the thought remained in the back of my mind that at least, at some point, the large container would arrive, and the donations could be used to bless the hospital.

Releasing the Container

In early December, an envelope arrived at the office with notification that a large container from Germany had just arrived in the port down the coast. Fantastic! Uli and I eagerly discussed how we would contact the port authorities, get the supplies sent up to our region, and possibly even send them to the mountain hospital before I went home for Christmas at the end of the month. I asked her to make the necessary calls to see what exactly needed to be done, and we intended to work on it right away.

A few days later Uli brought me a list of fourteen documents that needed to be obtained before we could take possession of what had already been designated to us. Because the goods were donations, we were required to have a letter of certification from the sender noting that they would not be sold or used for illegal purposes. We needed a similar notification from the local agency that coordinated foreign aid efforts, and we must also obtain letters from this agency stating that we were in good standing in the community. Inventory lists, lists of approximate price and condition of the goods, notification of intent on where they would be distributed, and letters certifying that the donor was a not for profit agency were requested, as was approval from both the local social department and the local health department. The paperwork seemed a slight bit overblown to me at that point, but we sighed and got to work at getting it done anyway. We naively persisted in thinking that we could make short order of the task and soon be spreading donation cheer.

The agency from which we most needed help—the one that coordinated foreign aid--was a haven for confusion and bureaucracy. It only seemed logical to me that a place which existed to help process donations would have a system devised for quickly obtaining the kind of paperwork we now needed: I was certain other aid agencies had received donations from the same port. So I was quite surprised when Bapak Marsoni, the man whose job it was to process these papers, appeared to be looking at the whole thing for the first time. Mystified, he seemed eager to help and yet completely unsure of how to do so. Over the next few months this poor man would become the recipient of my appreciation, compassion, anger, frustration, impatience, patience, and eventual joy.

I stopped counting the trips Uli and I took to government offices after seventeen. There may have actually been twice that many, and they all tended to follow a similar pattern. First, we would head out to an office in need of one or two letters and signatures, hoping to finalize something on our to-do list for that day. Upon entering that office, we would search for ten minutes or more to find anyone working there; usually that first person directed us to walk down a dark hallway to a smoke filled room where the workers were sitting at their desks and looking very official. I began to think, over time, that some of these men had made the task of consciously doing nothing an art form, and one which they seemed to relish displaying to us at that.

Uli or I would then walk to the closest desk of a man who, after waiting to finish the newspaper article he was reading, would look up indignantly at us for disturbing his peace and ask what we wanted. Then he would say he was not the person to help and point to an empty desk across the room. *That* person was the one we needed to talk to.

"Uli, do you see a person?" I would whisper as we walked over in the general direction of his pointed finger and ignored the stares of the men around us and the smoke being blown in our faces. She would ignore my rhetorical question, walk over to someone else and ask again for the needed help.

The person we apparently needed to talk to, the owner of the empty desk, was frequently off at prayers, taking an extended lunch from eleven until maybe three o'clock or so, in a meeting from which he could not be disturbed, or had flown off to Jakarta for important business and would not be back for several days. Never mind, another worker would tell us, just leave what we needed, and he would pass it along.

Obtaining one document in this manner frequently required a week of turnaround time, and very often we would return for the requested approval only to find that we needed three more documents before that one could be completed. Notarized letters from our international office which defined the exact nature of our work, financial status, intentions in the country, staff lists, and description of other projects were demanded. Countless days I left one of these offices and screamed in frustration (or broke down to cry), wondering how and why anything could *possibly* be that difficult. My excitement about potentially receiving all the donations diminished as time went by, fading into a far off and seemingly unobtainable dream. The project was beginning to annoy me, as well, for it seemed to hold no relevance to the other daily concerns of my life with patients, neighbors and friends. Besides, I had never asked for it in the first place.

For a while Uli and I approached the whole debacle with a degree of determination, for neither of us was likely to back down from a challenge. However, after entire days fruitlessly spent in government offices, dropped phone calls, and endless emails sent to our international office, Germany, the port, Germany, back to the port and so on and so on, our determination eventually gave way to weariness. Frequently we prayed together and with others that we would be patient and would love those we were dealing with despite the misery they were causing. God graciously answered and revived our spirits at their lowest points, and each of us encouraged the other from time to time that something good would come of all this. We wanted to believe that God was indeed capable of finishing what seemed like an impossible task, and we wanted Him to refine our character and faith in the process. I have prayed for much of my life to develop patience, but this situation seemed to move beyond patience into the realm of sheer perseverance and faith in the unseen. My faith wavered more than I liked to admit.

About seven months into the process, having just arrived at a point when we could see potential for the container to actually be released, we were notified of the exorbitant storage costs for which we were being charged. The fact that it was the port authorities who were demanding unreasonable documentation and actually causing the delay in the container's release was of no concern to the billing agent. We also discovered that the company which owned the actual container, which was based in France, was demanding retribution for having held onto their steel box for so many months. The fees all totaled together equaled thousands of US dollars, the payment of which would have wiped out a good portion of our clinic budget for the year.

At certain moments in life, God will take us to the end of ourselves. Then when we are personally just about to break, *He* breaks through instead with His power and provision enough to keep us going for the continual battle ahead. This was such a moment. I was beside myself with frustration over the whole process, and I had neither the energy nor the creativity left with which to figure out how to get these debts released. So it was truly miraculous when, after much prayer, we were able to succeed in getting the French company not only to reduce, but graciously drop all of their fees. As an added blessing, a donation came in unexpectedly that covered the cost of the storage. Having prayed for and received overwhelming provision every step of the way, we never truly doubted God and His desire to give abundantly. Yet the donation was a perfectly timed encouragement in the midst of a daunting process, and it was welcomed with much rejoicing.

By that point, the container's release had become a battle on multiple levels. Personally and spiritually, my human nature constantly warred with the Holy Spirit in me for control of my mind and emotions about the whole situation. This process resulted in alternating moments of aggravation and joy, boldness and faith, sadness, anger, love, and a slew of other emotions that I ran through on a weekly basis. Everything related to obtaining the shipment's actual release--the ability to obtain the requested documents, favor needed with certain officials, and wisdom to handle delicate situations such as requested bribes—involved an obvious battle as well. It occurred to me that God must have a pretty big plan for those hospital beds if it was requiring such a war to get them, and I derived an odd sense of comfort from that thought. After He helped us to release all the debt we had owed for storage, I moved forward into the following few months with renewed energy and a timid sense of hope.

Four more months passed, during which time I tried to hang onto that hope. Then suddenly, with no notice or explanation, the port authorities decided to inspect the donated goods. They did so, declared the items in good condition, and then pronounced that used clothes and toys of *any* condition were not allowed to enter our province. This obscure and yet seemingly vital piece of information had not yet been given to us by anyone involved in the whole process, and it launched a new wave of office visits, letters, phone calls, and calling upon those we knew in positions of authority to try and make an exception to the rule. We even appealed to the mayor about the inane regulation which withheld aid from needy people, but with no results. After exhausting all avenues of appeal, we finally settled on figuring out how to separate the contents of the container--extracting the usable medical supplies and shipping the other donations back out of the country. I was honestly not very concerned with the clothes and toys that had been donated. They would be nice to have, but they were not worth a continual fight if we could just get the valuable supplies to the hospital.

God's Mysterious Ways

God truly does work in mysterious ways, and always according to His timing. So it happened that in the third week of November of 2007, *eleven months* after starting the process of trying to release the container from the port and *three years* after the shipment had been packed, Uli answered an unexpected and shocking phone call. Bapak Ali, a conscientious and kind mover who had been trying to help us in the port for several months, matter of factly informed her that he needed money wired over in order to hire a truck and get our container on the road. It had been released.

"That is fantastic! Send him the money for the medical supplies to come as soon as possible." I instructed Uli somewhat quickly, for I was answering her call in between treating patients. "And what about the toys and clothes, by the way? What will we do with those?"

Inexplicably, according to Bapak Ali, those goods were to be coming as well. He had faced no resistance at all from the office at the port when he simply and clearly stated that he was taking the whole container. The regulation against used goods that had held up the process for the last few weeks had mysteriously vanished, as had the bribery charges demanded from the storage facility. I did not in any way understand what had happened, but I certainly was not interested in arguing the point. The container was on its way!

The semi- tractor trailer that arrived two days later had a hard time maneuvering into the narrow street outside the office, but neither that nor the torrential rain that was falling could dampen our spirits as we began to unload. Out came box after box filled with clothing and shoes. Out came bags and bags overflowing with stuffed animals and toys. Out came large boxes filled with the smaller Christmas shoe boxes, each of which contained various trinkets and toys. These boxes and bags filled the two story home that functioned as our office nearly to overflowing, consuming two bedrooms and the entirety of the living room, and we tried not to think too much that day about the upcoming work of sorting and actually distributing these things. That task, while large, seemed slightly less monumental--and decidedly much happier--than the work we had gone through to have the container delivered.

I was eager to see the hospital goods and watched with interest as the movers began unloading the supplies. They brought down a few wheelchairs, toilet chairs, and a pile of crutches, then quite a few large boxes of equipment with German labels I could not read. Desks, tables, and various other items of furniture unexpectedly appeared from the recesses of the truck, followed by ten hospital beds, mattresses, and hospital tables. I noticed with disappointment that there seemed to be no diagnostic equipment at all and little equipment of use for general hospital care. The majority of the supplies, it seemed, were designed for rehabilitation, logically so since they had been donated from an orthopedic hospital. At the time I did not know that, though, and I was confused. My heart sank as I considered how little I could offer that would practically help the mountain hospital, and I also wondered how I would get rid of all those other supplies. Their designs and functions were too specialized for most of my own patients, and suddenly I saw looming in front of me another exhausting process for which I had little excitement.

I brushed aside this thought in order to celebrate the container's delivery with my teammates, stopping for a while to pray in thanksgiving and later rejoicing over a meal out at a nicer restaurant in town. This was cause for a feast! Later that evening we prayed and worshipped together again, and I wept in acknowledgement that God had finally completed *through* us, the task He had entrusted *to* us. It was truly miraculous.

Giving with Joy

The following day we began sorting. We decided to start with the boxes and bags which filled the living room, wanting at least to clear a path to the kitchen, and we invited some other friends over to help. Clothing moved into piles designated for women, men and children. A pile was also created for unusable clothing that said things like "Jesus is Lord," or had printed Bible verses on the front. Those who repacked the container after it was redirected had apparently not been educated about cultural sensitivity to an Islamic region, and we eventually had to discard quite a few shirts and stuffed animals that voiced Christian messages. The repacking efforts had also not succeeded in supplying what I considered weather appropriate clothing, and we found bag after bag of sweatshirts, sweaters, and long sleeved shirts amongst the donations. I could not imagine a use for any of them in the tropical heat.

The shoeboxes that had been lovingly packed by the German kids at Christmas posed a challenge. Each one had to be opened individually and the few things that were still in good condition taken out for distribution. The remainder had to be discarded because much of it had been destroyed by chocolate which had melted all over the boxes' contents. When someone read out an expiration date of 2005 on one of the unmelted chocolate bars, our group of cheerful volunteers erupted into laughter. Should we give away candy that had passed its prime years ago while floating on the open seas? The outdated chocolate, as amusing as it was, also brought food for thought in considering how long ago the whole journey had begun.

"*Why*, God," I wondered that evening, "would You have kind hearted kids and adults in a foreign country pack their things for donation four years ago, only to have much of it later destroyed? Was it just human error that has brought us to this point, or are You doing something I still don't see? And *what*, God, am I supposed to do with all that orthopedic junk in the garage? I don't need something else on my to-do list, and I cannot begin to figure out how to get rid of it!" I did not hear any answers.

I have often thought it would be fun to be a millionaire and have lots of money to give away. In a small way, this container allowed me to live that dream. Many of the donations were different than what I had expected to receive, but it was still great fun to begin to give them away to various people. A large percentage of the useful clothes and toys were given to our clinic village, and they were distributed judiciously to those most in need by several respected women in the community. Many toys went to different orphan programs, and some went to the city hospital to stock a children's entertainment cart which Ria had designed. Remarkably, even the cold weather clothing found good homes. During harvest time in the villages, the men stayed out all night to guard their crops and fruit from invading animals; high up in the mountains they could get chilly during these vigils. Friends who visited one such remote location told us that the men had eagerly accepted bagful after bagful of sweatshirts and coats and even asked if more could be brought back later. I certainly never would have thought to pack a container headed for the tropics with coats and hats, but thankfully God thinks differently than I do!

The larger household furniture pieces were distributed to several friends in need: a newly married young couple with no income and a baby on the way, a street kid ministry that was trying to start a library and had no shelves for books, and a small clinic down the coast that needed tables and chairs. We gave odd pieces here and there to other local friends as well. All of this giving was delightful, and I felt blessed to be operating out of God's abundance. I wonder what would happen if I operated in such a spirit of freedom and giving at all times? What would happen if I let my love simply overflow out of His continual abundance? It would be amazing.

The problem of what to do with the medical supplies still remained. I was completely baffled about the orthopedic supplies, but at least there were some beds, tables, and a few other things I was eager to take to the mountain hospital. Eventually we filled up two small moving trucks with a variety of furniture and small equipment which I thought that they may appreciate, and we followed the winding road back up to the tiny community. I was happy to be bringing them some small amount of aid, but the thought of how empty the entire hospital had been checked my enthusiasm. Our donations would barely make a dent in the list of what they needed.

We were very pleasantly surprised to see that a year's passing had brought great improvements to the facility, and some of the equipment the government promised had finally arrived. Still, however, the operating room sat empty, as did the rehabilitation wing. Wait a minute--*rehabilitation wing*? I had forgotten about this unit entirely, but I was suddenly excited to see how the small amount of orthopedic supplies we had brought along could actually be useful. The general beds and tables easily found purposeful places, and all of the donations were accepted with gratitude and smiles. Although I never did accomplish my goal of outfitting their operating room,

I left that day feeling that our efforts had resulted in great good for the place. I also felt confident that God was at work there and would continue to provide for their needs in other ways.

So what was to be done with all the other orthopedic supplies? We still had a garage full of simple wheelchairs, wheelchairs with toilet buckets under them, crutches, walkers, and pieces of equipment I could not even recognize. I personally had no idea what to do with these things, but it occurred to me that I knew someone who did. Several months prior, a volunteer physical therapist had arrived in our area, and he had been coming out to our clinic every week. Steven treated patients who had generalized aches and pains from backbreaking labor in the rice fields, and he also did his best with limited resources to provide rehabilitation therapy for stroke patients. As I looked again at the walkers, I suddenly thought, "That lady whom Steven just treated for her stroke—the one who lives in the second hut past the well—she needs that! Oh, and that wheelchair, actually, could go to the man with the bum leg whom Steven has treated several times."

I was instantly excited to recognize that at least a handful of these things could go to specific patients. Some of them I knew personally after having made hut calls to them with Steven, and others I just remembered that he had treated. The clinic actually had quite a few post-stroke patients suffering from varying degrees of disability, and their faces crossed my mind as I sent off a quick text message asking Steven to come take a look in our garage. Curiously, just before he arrived, Hasmah came bounding across the street to ask if she could have a wheelchair for her distant relative who was staying with them. He had just suffered a stroke two days prior. The wheelchair her relative received was the first of many, many providential donations we would make to individuals in what proceeded to be a very joyful giving process.

If I was excited, Steven was ecstatic. He was like a kid in a toy closet combing through our garage, for he knew far better than I did what each of the odd trolleys and strangely shaped walkers were designed to do. Better yet, he was already considering many patients for whom he thought they would be beneficial. On days he was not in our clinic, Steven spent a lot of time traveling to visit people in their homes in very distant villages; in the process, he had come across several homebound patients whose lives could be dramatically improved with one of these pieces of equipment.

In the next month Steven did a fairly good job of clearing out our garage. I was able to be with him a few times when he gave a walker to someone with whom he was working, and it was sheer delight to watch as he or she took shaky and yet hopeful first steps across the room. On one occasion, Steven showed me pictures of a lady who, due to being both incontinent and unable to walk on her own, had not left her house in two years. For her, a wheelchair with a built in toilet (a concept I had previously found rather odd) was a perfect fit, and we had many of them. The smiles of the entire village that came out to see her receive the gift were priceless. In another case, a man was in the hospital, severely burned and unable to walk. His immobility had prevented him from visiting his child, who was also burned and staying in the pediatric ward. The wheelchair we gave him helped him to reconnect to family and give his daughter the support she needed to heal from her own wounds. Crutches and braces and small appliances of many kinds went into many eager and thankful hands and lives. As they did, the frustration of getting the container delivered faded behind the smiles of the recipients.

A Perfectly Planned Gift

A nine year old girl who lived three hours into the mountains had cerebral palsy, and she had grown up with progressively weakening limbs from atrophied muscles. Eventually she had become totally immobile. The situation was difficult for her family, for they were simple rice farmers with neither a way to transport her to medical care nor the money to pay for it if they could. On one of his recent journeys Steven had discovered this beautiful little girl, and he explained to her family how she needed physical therapy to slow the course of the progressively debilitating disease. The girl was basically never taken outside, he told me later, since she would have to be carried, and he expressed frustration that if only she had a certain kind of trolley--one designed to hold her arms and legs in the right position to help her muscles develop--he felt that she could be much more functional. He knew of no place in the province that would have such a resource, however, so on that day all he could do was offer the family advice and a kind word. He prayed for her briefly and left.

One day I was looking with curiosity at a purple pushcart that sat in the garage, a strange contraption which resembled to me an overgrown baby stroller with a lot of straps hanging in illogical places. There was only one of these carts in the shipment, and I simply could not figure out what it was intended to do. It did not look quite like a wheelchair, and it was too small for an adult anyway. It was also not a baby stroller, I determined, and I was stumped. So I called Steven over to ask him what it was. "God at work is what that is!" he practically shouted. Then he explained with disbelief that this contraption was the very trolley he wanted— the one designed to be used in therapy for kids with cerebral palsy.

I did not get to go give that little girl her trolley, but Steven took a picture of her and her family for me. That picture remains permanently etched in my mind as a reminder of God's provision, faithfulness, and incredibly intricate concern for the details of the lives of His children. Consider the number of things that could have stopped the miracle from happening for that little girl. To start with, if the donation container had gone to Russia as it was planned to do, the trolley would not have come to Indonesia. If the container had been released easily, when I wanted it to, Steven would not yet have been in the city to tell me what to do with all the supplies. Had the container been delivered more than three weeks prior, Steven would not yet have met that precious little soul. At just the right time, however, several days after Steven had actually met the girl in the mountains, that container had been mysteriously and miraculously released into our care.

Heaven and earth touched each other that day, and a dear little girl and her family learned not that medicine can fix everything, but that there is a God in heaven who cares deeply about the details of their lives. I learned the same lesson as well, certainly not for the first time but in a surprisingly new way. I realized that God is not only concerned with the smallest details of my daily life, but He is also concerned with the smallest details of my character. He may stop a freight ship in order to bring a tangible gift, but He will not stop difficulty in my life if it will bring me closer to Him. His allowing me to come to the absolute end of myself during the container ordeal had forced me to develop desperate dependence on His grace. The Holy Spirit is ever working to make me more like Jesus, but there are still a lot of details to be worked out.

Things are not often what they appear to be on the surface, I thought to myself as I reflected on the whole experience of obtaining the container and distributing its contents. So many times I had fallen prey to discouragement, and many times I had been tempted to give up on our efforts entirely. Not having laid eyes on any of the donations made it hard to be enthusiastic about their arrival, and I began to question whether I would ever actually see them at all. Most days all I could see was more and more paperwork being thrown my way, and the situation appeared almost hopeless. I felt God kept prompting me for some reason, though, to keep going, so I did. Then, when the shipment arrived, my eyes saw a pile of nice but mostly impractical donations. I was discouraged once again, for I was not looking through lenses of hope.

What God saw was quite different. I now know that when I feel God leading me to do something (as I had with that shipment), I must persevere in faith. That faith must believe that He who called me to the task is faithful to complete it, and I must believe that He is ultimately working out something for good. Giving diagnostic machines and operating equipment to the hospital would have been nice, but it was not His perfect plan. Not having to visit all those offices and complete all those documents would have saved a lot of my time, energy, and tears; such simplicity would not have often brought me to my knees. The entire process could have been much easier, faster, and more reasonable in my opinion, and I still cannot quite grasp why expired chocolate bars are part of God's great yet mysterious logic. I smile, though, as I look at the picture of the little girl sitting in her trolley, and I know I cannot question the God who ordains all things. My plan had been to create happiness. His was to create glory.

CHAPTER Twenty-One:
Inward Illumination

Surprise Positions

If I were to make a list of things I did not think would ever appear on my resume, "Clinic Director" for a clinic in a third world country, in a region where few foreigners have ever left their footprints, would probably top the list. So when I found myself in charge of this startup clinic in the middle of a beautiful, traumatized, and somewhat mysterious mountain region on an island in Indonesia, I had only one thought: no one can ever say that life following God is boring.

That position topped my "resume curiosities" list for a while. That is, until one day "Power of Attorney for a fish farm in a third world country," came along. Yes, indeed, right in the midst of the lively but mostly happy chaos of the day to day operations of the clinic, I was instructed by our headquarters office that Uli and I would need to be involved with paperwork to finalize the purchase and operation of a fish farm. Money had been given for the project and initial plans laid, but the individuals who were to come and work with the project had decided at some point that their lives would be better lived in another location. So when the attorney called to say that all of the previously filed documentation was expiring, I was required to take over.

I never saw any fish. Actually I never even saw the land that was eventually purchased for the fish, but I did see a lot of paperwork and a lot of our attorney. I signed my name onto all kinds of legal documentation in order to keep our "company" registered, and I learned about taxes and justice fees, legal standing and registration, visas and worker rights--and the list goes on. I did not ask for this job, nor was I happy about taking it, but I tried to be patient and understanding of the potential the project had for good. If it were to get off the ground eventually, it would generate income for local people, with a target focus towards widows. This thought was the only thing that kept me in the realm of sanity when I was faxing forms, calling our headquarters, visiting government offices, and spending countless hours with the lawyer. He was a perfectly nice man, but his office was a dark, musty room with no fans or air conditioning. Files were stacked up to the ceiling, and I never could decide if I was more amazed by his ability to find things there or his uncanny ability not to sweat through his shirt and tie. By the time I left his office, I was always a puddle.

So I somehow found myself (in paperwork anyway) on the Board of Commissioners for this non-existent fish farm and holding power of attorney over all of its operations. Since we had yet to find someone to actually construct and operate the farm, that job itself did not require any of my attention. Once the paperwork was under control I began to be quite amused by the whole thing, for it was a great example to me of the way God calls us into all kinds of positions which we never expected. I think He does it just to keep us humble. It was also a good reminder that I needed to be able to look for what God may be teaching me in those situations. In this instance, two lessons were evident: I needed to develop patience, and I needed to be willing to submit to authority.

If left to my own devices, I would have been very happy to never look beyond the world of our village and medical work. My international leaders, however, needed someone on the ground to help keep a vision and plan alive for future fulfillment. I honestly did not want anything to do with the fish farm, and I resented it greatly in the beginning. I grumbled and complained every time something came up that needed my attention, irritated that it was distracting me from what I saw as my real work. Over time, though, I began to understand that serving my leaders by being obedient to their desires was a critical step in my slow and inching crawl toward holiness. God calls us to serve each other, especially those in the body of Christ, and He distinctly calls us to serve and honor those He has put into authority over us. It was remarkable how much relief and happiness my help brought to those desiring to keep the fish farm alive; I learned to delight in that rather than to look at the time and energy I was expending in the process. I realized that my time spent in serving them--my brothers and sisters in Christ--was no less significant than the time I spent with patients, and this was a lesson I would learn again and again.

Lessons in Leadership

"Clinic Director, Public Health Educator, First Aid Teacher, Auto Mechanic, Director of a Country Branch of a Nonprofit Agency, and Power of Attorney over a Fish Farm." My resume was growing as I adopted each of these unexpected roles, and each of them caused me to grow and to adapt, to learn and to be stretched. None of these experiences, however, matched the learning curve I assumed when I became a ministry team leader. I had joined a team when I arrived, and that team had subsequently left. I had struggled through the early dark and anxious times of being alone, and I had forged ahead by involving myself with the local people God had placed around me for support. Although I prayed often for new teammates to come, I had eventually become quite comfortable with the time I spent with local friends and other aid workers and felt happy in that routine. Uli and I worked closely together on most things related to ministry, and I enjoyed a depth of relationships with local people that I would not have achieved had I been more invested with foreign workers.

So I had mixed feelings when I received the news that two new teammates were planning to join me in our outreach--excitement to have others with a similar love for the local people, but also concern about how they would fit into the work and the structure of my life. In addition, I would now become the official leader of our work from the perspective of our larger ministry. This meant that not only was I responsible for helping my new friends through the acclimation process, but I would also be responsible for helping them make decisions about their outreach, encouraging their strengths and working with their weaknesses, and trying to spiritually shepherd them. It was not a responsibility I took lightly, for I personally grieved never having had a strong leader and mentor for the time I had been in the ministry thus far.

In the beginning I threw myself wholeheartedly into this new role, believing that if they were able to adjust well in the first few months then my new friends would require less attention from me later on. I did everything in my power to make their transition as easy as possible: practically I provided a comprehensive orientation, and personally I spent long hours listening to them share their dreams and fears about this new season in their lives. I loved this time with each of them, and God blessed me greatly with these two wonderful women. I saw His hand at work in both of their hearts, and I saw how He could use their gifts and talents for His glory there in Indonesia. They both became my friends, and we mutually encouraged each other while enjoying many times of shared laughter and fun. The heavy investment of time upfront, I thought, would be well worth it if they could become settled and more independent. Slowly, though, I realized that this investment was not going to reach an end.

Leading is not easy. Anyone who has ever led a group of people and tells you that it is easy is lying. I thrive on challenges, though, and I had assumed many leadership roles in my life prior to this point. In fact, I was already actively leading a hired staff of seven people in the clinic when my teammates arrived. I did not find it difficult to plan logistics or meetings, cast vision, or maintain momentum for a project I was leading, but this was different. Now I was to lead a community of believers in not only a project--aka "work"--but I was to lead a small group of women who needed discipleship and who needed to learn to experience life together. Their needs became my needs, their fears and concerns my fears and concerns, their joys my joys. I needed to pray for them, often and well, and I needed to ask them how they were doing on a regular basis. More importantly, I needed to be prepared for their answers to that question. I had to provide encouragement when necessary and to be willing to lay down my own agenda to spend whatever time with them that was required to do so. In short, in order to lead them in community life, I needed to love them more than I loved myself. This timeless teaching from Jesus was not new to me, but never before had I been called to walk it out in such an intense way.

Projects require time and energy; people require a lot more. Although I loved my teammates, it was not long before I almost began to resent the time investment I felt I needed to make in them. Each group meeting with them had a purpose: we discussed goals that could be accomplished, and that was something I could enjoy. The times of just sitting and talking, though, seemed unproductive to me after awhile, and they were taking my time away from the local people. I had expected that the women would find their own outlets for socialization and outreach after a month or so of orientation, after which I would be able to return to my established routines of clinic duties mixed with visiting local friends. In my head I had inadvertently assigned levels of importance to the people God had placed in my life: the local people came first, and my new teammates came second. After all, I reasoned, I had come to show the Indonesian people the love of Jesus, and spending too much time with people who were already believers seemed contrary to that purpose. The scarce amount of time I had just to spend in everyday life with local people was already sacred to me, and I did not appreciate my teammates' presence taking that away.

I never did manage to regain the schedule I had with my local friends, and if anything, time with my team increased rather than decreased over the ensuing months. Their emotional needs, while by no means excessive, were very real, and living in community simply requires a lot of time. Throughout that entire next year, God had to chip away at my self-defined categories of what constituted the best use of my time. Just as He had taught me that my fish farm duties were an outpouring of service and submission to my leaders, He showed me that the time I spent with these sweet sisters in Christ was a daily demonstration of His love. He pointed me to passage after passage in the Bible that instructed me to serve the church--the body of believers--and I saw how my reactions to them were a reflection of how deeply I was allowing the Holy Spirit to work in my heart.

Many leadership teachers talk about the investment you make in those you are leading as being a wise use of time, for eventually one of those people may blossom into a far more effective and widespread resource than you could ever be on your own. They talk about your time and energy being multiplied in the end, and they boil it all down to an equation. When I was first struggling with the amount of time I was spending with my new team, I liked this formula: it had an end result which was greater than the initial investment. I do not think that math works the same way in God's Kingdom, though. Using such a formula to evaluate my investment of time and energy and hoping for a return of seeing the women be fruitful in ministry devalued them as individuals. It also never allowed me to truly love.

Deep Lessons of the Heart

As I was complaining to God one morning about all of this, asking Him why I had to lead people anyway, I started to reflect on Jesus. What if He had looked on His disciples only as projects to be poured into so they could later produce results? If He were looking for a return on His investment of time with them, He was going to be looking for a while. Peter would eventually deny him, Thomas would later doubt him, and Judas would finally betray him. He *knew* that, and yet He never stopped loving them. He modeled constant, unconditional love for those outside the community of twelve disciples at all times, but He continued to pour into the lives of this close little group with great passion. Never once did he indicate that He was waiting to "get on with the real ministry" of sharing the truth with those outside. The disciples *were* his ministry--the objects of His love and affection simply because they existed--and my teammates were to be mine as well.

God taught me more about the selfishness, pride, and sin in my heart through leading that team than I ever thought possible. My reactions to my teammates often highlighted the depth of my self-interest, even after I was convicted that loving them was of ultimate worth. I confess that I often found myself wishing that they would ask *me* how I was doing, and I often wished I did not have to listen to them so much. Many times I found myself listening merely out of a sense of obligation and the selfish desire to appear to be a devoted leader; then I would take prideful pleasure in their noticing that I was so lovingly concerned. I knew that in order to be a servant leader I must listen to their opinions, validate their concerns, and honor their ideas, and I had absolutely no problem doing this--as long as in the end I could be right. I too often caught myself enjoying the control I had over a lot of our circumstances, and I had great difficulty delegating tasks to others. It was never that I thought they could not handle a job. I simply thought I could do it better.

I wondered sometimes why my teammates did not take more initiative, until God showed me that I often dominated to such a degree that they did not feel affirmed to do so. I wondered why they would rarely state their opinions until I noticed that I was often too quick to share my own. When I felt that God was calling me to encourage and re-envision our little group to the task before us, I was quick to do so and delighted to see the response. Then I went home and secretly patted myself on the back for having heard from God so well. I sometimes marvel that He does not allow me to drown in my own pride.

An entire book could be written about the refining process that God took me through in leadership, and the things I learned about myself would probably appall any reader. The incredible thing about it all, though, is that I think few outside observers would ever notice. For God, in His mercy, worked in our team despite my faults, and we were blessed to have a close group of women who loved each other, loved Jesus, and loved our neighbors. We were able to minister together, to share a passion for people to enter the kingdom of God, and to live life together with minimal conflict, and every bit of that is a testimony to God's grace. I never asked for the job of being a team leader, and I think God certainly could have chosen someone better equipped for the job. (I also think He could have picked someone who actually knew about fish to be involved with a fish farm, but I try not to question His sovereignty). As I watched my teammates grow in their walks with God and in their ministry gifts despite my shaky and fledgling leadership, I was reminded of His ability to show His strength in our weakness.

The more I was faced with the ugly dragons that arose from my heart, the more desperate I became to have the Holy Spirit weed them out and refine me. Every time I would identify something as the sin that it was, sighing relief that I had conquered that particular woe, God would highlight another level of darkness in my spirit that would drive me to my knees once again. I wanted to love these girls well, but I had no power to do that on my own. Only Jesus could love them well; in order for Him to do that through me, my heart must be pure and focused on Him.

Through this leadership experience, God taught me the most powerful lesson of my time overseas: He is far more interested in refining my character, forcing me to my knees in pursuit of His holiness and His working in me, than He is about any ministry, projects, outreaches, or results. I could have been more effective, in my own judgment, by being used to treat more patients, run more mobile clinics, and teach more health classes. I could have been more effective by administrating additional projects like the fish farm, for, like it or not, administration is one of my gifts. I could have been far more effective in outreach, I thought, by having more time to sit on the ground and chat with my neighbors; after all, I loved these times and thrived in them, unbothered by difficulties of communication and circumstance. Yet in each of these things, I judged that I could have been more effective in *my* strengths.

While I would have acknowledged these strengths as gifts endowed by God, I would have had little motivation for seeking growth in dependence on the Holy Spirit and in personal holiness. So instead of allowing me more time operating in these strengths, God walked me straight into my areas of weakness. Successfully working out of my strengths, I could have floated easily above the dark clouds that filled my heart and never noticed they were there; God thought it better to send me plunging straight through them instead. While it was not always fun, I can say that it was always good.

I desire the "holiness without which no one will see God" (Hebrews 12:14), but I am not going to attain it by always living life according to my plan. If personal growth requires placing me in unknown, uncharted waters, God will put me there. He will help me to sail, but only so long as I acknowledge the wind comes from Him. If refining my character requires placing me in positions I never dreamed of, God will place me in those, too. He will lead and direct and grant me wisdom, but only so long as I acknowledge that guidance comes from Him. If I am ever tempted to stray from that acknowledgement, He will not hesitate to let me fall, straight back on my knees, in order to bring me back on course.

The Spirit Gives Life but the Flesh Is Useless

John 6:63 says, "The Spirit gives life but the flesh is useless." My initial foray into a foreign land with no language skills was more than adequate to show me the uselessness of my flesh, and I spent more time in prayer during those first few months of living overseas than perhaps ever before in my life. I knew that since I was incapable of communicating with anyone verbally, only the Holy Spirit operating through me in prayer could bring any form of life to the people around me. So I committed myself to extended times of daily prayer for my neighbors, our village, and others I passed along the road in the course of my day, and I committed to pray for them fervently.

At first, I found that being more attentive to prayer was remarkably difficult. My spirit battled with my mind, which told me that the real work was outside rather than on my knees. Yet as I let my own thoughts settle, I heard more from the Holy Spirit during those months, felt a deeper burden for people and leading on how to pray for them, and experienced more of God's heart for people than I ever had before. I am grateful for those times (before my human capabilities again took control of my schedule), for I honestly looked with total dependence to the Spirit of the Living God to be my life and life for those around me.

As time went on and I adapted, I also became more self sufficient. Things I used to ask for in prayer became matters of everyday routine, and I often forgot to thank God for the gifts and provision He was giving to me each day. I became comfortable in my activities of daily living: treating patients, talking to friends, and taking care of the general necessities of life. There were always experiences that stretched me, and each day brought something new to learn. For the most part, though, I could cope fairly well. At some point during these times, when I realized I was being tempted to rely on my own strength and no longer recognized the life-giving Holy Spirit at work, I made the mistake of praying that God would keep me humble. He found a number of creative ways to do that.

To start with, the positions I held were a challenge. Each carried a certain degree of confusion, multitudes of questions, and endless decisions to make, and each required that I learn to cope with people and operate projects under a radically different social and marketplace structure than that I knew. Each of these unexpected positions--Director of the Clinic, Director of our Nonprofit Agency, Fish Farm Executor, Team Leader--brought me to my knees regularly, for I did not feel trained, equipped, or adequate for any one of them. For example, I knew nothing about legal issues, and so God had to guide me through the process of creating a fishing company that involved three different nations and their government processes, as well as hundreds of thousands of dollars. Did my flesh accomplish that? Hardly. The Holy Spirit had to guide me each and every day as I asked for direction in whom to talk to and how to navigate the right channels, and it was the Holy Spirit's working that miraculously delivered needed documentation right on time and brought uncanny favor with high level authorities. Similarly, my training in how to practice Western medicine and treat disease with readily accessible tests and therapies was not very helpful when faced with tropical diseases and minimal resources. The Holy Spirit had to guide my medical decisions and teach me how to manage a clinic, as well as renew my strength every day to take on a patient load four times greater than I was accustomed to handling. Then when I wanted help, I prayed for teammates and asked God for a good team leader. He challenged my self-confidence and pride by making me a team leader instead. "Humility 101" was well underway.

My taking care of patients was a definite miracle in its own right, and I prayed often for more doctors to come and help in the clinic. In fact, I asked God every day for twenty months for other medical providers to come and help, and yet He never brought one. Instead, He brought more patients than I could possibly handle alone from a worldly viewpoint--and then He proceeded to heal them one by one. I cried out to God, saying "Help me! I cannot do this alone!" and He asked me: "Do you believe I am sufficient for this task?"

I asked God to give me wisdom before every patient I treated, especially since there was much I did not know about the diseases endemic to the area and little diagnostic equipment to help. I also asked God to strengthen me on the days when there were more than a hundred patients waiting to be seen, giving me love and encouragement for the last one as well as the first. If He had provided another doctor, it would have been very easy to shift my dependence toward that individual and offer him/her the thanks for treating more patients and helping me to diagnose difficult illnesses. On my own, however, I clearly saw that it was only the Holy Spirit who gave life to each of those under my care, as well as to me as I cared for them.

Aside from the major roles I assumed, each of which forced me into deeper dependence upon God, there were many individual, entirely overwhelming days that reminded me of my sheer inability to do anything on my own. One day I was on the way to clinic, driving our rickety old car down pothole speckled roads and listening to our nurse and maintenance manager argue with each other. These two were not only good at arguing, but they also both originated from an ethnic group well known for its loud and opinionated people. I was developing a headache after half an hour of listening to their bickering. Perhaps it was the noise of their arguing that kept me from noticing any abnormal sounds coming from the vehicle, or perhaps I was so used to the car clanking and clanging that I had learned to tune it out. In either case, I was unaware of anything unusual and tried to focus my thoughts on the day ahead.

I was eager to arrive at the clinic because I was expecting a surgeon to join us that day. Dr. Johanes had promised on three separate occasions to come out to the village, perform minor operations, and screen for larger surgical needs, and I had spread the news widely in the community. I had advertised his coming on each occasion, but unfortunately he had cancelled each time. He had assured me repeatedly that this day would be different, and I had offered my apologies and promises to the community once again that the surgeon would indeed be coming. Many of them, I knew, would schedule their time around bringing sick relatives to be evaluated, so I was anxious to see how the day would go.

We pulled up outside of the clinic and were greeted by seventy or more patients waiting at the door. This was not unusual, but looking at the sea of waiting faces that day for some reason already had me slightly tired. Thus, my nurse's sudden and rather forceful announcement that she was quitting (as a result of the argument she had been having) was not well received. I could handle treating the patients alone, but it would be extremely difficult without her managing the crowds up front and helping to dispense medication. I would certainly not be able to do it in less than twelve hours. So before I hopped out of the car, I turned to her and suggested that she sit for a minute and collect herself. I asked her to pray for strength and to please consider quitting *after* our clinic day was over.

Stepping down into knee deep mud, I was immediately met by the scowling face of an impatient and unhappy man who was inquiring after Dr. Johanes. I had already noticed that the surgeon's vehicle was not outside, but I was hoping that he was merely running late as usual. The man told me that he had carried his daughter there from three kilometers away for the third time, and he demanded to see the surgeon immediately. Behind him a small posse of other patients also awaiting Dr. Johanes was forming, and each agreed with nods and verbal grunts that it was past time for the specialist to make his appearance. I asked them to wait a moment while I called to see when he may be coming and tried to skirt around the edge of the agitated crowd. Then, while reaching into my bag and scouring for my cell phone, I noticed from the corner of my eye that splashes of red were decorating the white ceramic tile in front of the clinic door. I also noticed that new splashes were forming every five seconds, originating from the macerated hand of a man who stood there dripping with blood. He would need to be the first patient.

"Come on, Dr. Johanes, answer the phone," I thought to myself, listening to the ringing on the other end of the line while unlocking the clinic doors.

"Hello?" I heard a gruff voice say when it was finally answered.

"I am in the hospital. What do you want?"

"Are you on your way here soon?" I asked with feigned cheerfulness, my spirit sinking as I braced for the answer coming my way.

"Of course not, I am busy," Dr. Johanes said.

No amount of pleading, bribing or reminding him of his promise was going to alter his decision, but I desperately tried anyway as my eyes wandered back to the disgruntled crowd waiting by the car. Somewhere in the middle of this conversation, the bleeding man (who was remarkably calm considering his situation) wandered over to me and pointed at his hand with a questioning look in his eyes. I nodded and smiled, slipped inside the clinic and threw him a piece of gauze, and thought that dragging my nurse out of the car may soon become necessary. It did not seem likely that she was going to appear on her own.

I hung up the phone, tried to smile, and braced myself to bear the disappointment and ire of the patients who had once again been promised something that would not come true. They would be upset about the time they had spent waiting; I was personally more concerned that I appeared untruthful to them and was losing the trust I had been building in the community. Having no choice, I took a deep breath and announced as calmly as I could that Dr. Johanes would not be coming today but would come the following week instead. Then I pushed through the crowd, tried to ignore the angry words I heard and fingers shaking in my face, and approached the car to beg my nurse to come out. Right at that moment, just before I reached the door, a man who had been circling the car with interest for the last five minutes yelled out above the crowd: "Hey Ibu doctor! Your wheel just fell off!"

Had I been in a better mood, or owned a better car, I may have laughed and not believed him. However, since this car had already thrown a wheel off once before and trouble seemed to be the theme of the morning, I absorbed the news with resignation. I promptly turned on my heels, marched back through the crowd, walked right past the poor man at the door who was sweetly sitting in a pool of his own blood, and entered my office. Then I sat on the floor and cried.

My attitude at that point will not go into the archives of holiness.

I was somewhat angry with God for allowing me to be there alone to handle all this craziness, and I wasted no time in telling Him so. Beyond anger, though, what I felt was a deep and aching desperation for Him to *do* something, for I knew that absolutely nothing in my own power could handle any of the four major disasters occurring right outside the door. I was desperate for His grace to handle our nurse, who seemed to me to be behaving entirely selfishly, and I was desperate for His forgiveness for Dr. Johanes to flow through me instead of the outrage I felt inside. I was desperate for God's wisdom and authority to take over and show the people I could be trusted again, and I was desperate for Him to heal the man's hand that was oozing blood onto the front steps. I needed God to provide someone to repair a broken car wheel, and I needed help to take care of the crowd of people, as I did every day. I longed for someone stronger, smarter, wiser, more courageous, gentler and more spiritual than I to take over the whole big mess. Was my flesh useless that day? Absolutely. In every way possible, my own capabilities landed flat.

The Holy Spirit gave life, though, in every way possible, and each of the problems was handled in turn. The patients were eventually all cared for, most of the angry ones were appeased, and the man's bleeding stopped. My nurse returned, the car was repaired, and I went home still in one piece. God even helped me--although later--to forgive Dr. Johanes for his string of consistently broken promises. God delights to show His strength in our weakness, and I am always happy for His strength to be shown. I sometimes wish, though, that He could find a less painful way of revealing my weaknesses!

More Character Definition

The forgiveness I had to uncover for Dr. Johanes (who eventually did come weeks later and graciously arranged free surgeries for over fifty patients) was new to me. I had always considered myself a fairly forgiving person. In fact, rarely did I feel bothered enough by things that I needed to forgive someone anyway, and so I had little experience doing so. The exception to this had been the time

I spent living in India some years prior, when on a daily basis I found myself faced with the decision of whether or not to forgive the men who groped and hollered at me everywhere I went. At that time, I truly had to allow God to love through me, for I honestly felt something much more akin to hate than love for those lustful men who were violating my dignity. My instinct told me that they were simply walking in the ways of a godless world, but it took many months before God was able to completely instill His forgiveness and love in my heart for the men. The lesson was memorable to me. During that same time, I found myself having to concentrate on actively forgiving those who ignored the people dying in the streets around them. Many local people were more interested in where I came from than they were with the human beings starving at their feet, and I was livid. Eventually God was able to work His forgiveness into my heart for those people as well, and that season of my life passed by.

Since that time in India, I had not often considered the call to forgiveness--not until I found myself, anyway, answering to disappointed and frustrated people for the unfaithfulness and apathy of another. I was angry with Dr. Johanes for lying to me, lying to the patients, and living according to his own timeline. I was angry with him that patients who paid him in the city took precedence over those in the village who could not pay, and I was angry with him because he behaved this way while actively professing belief in Jesus. At that point the majority of the village knew that all of our staff believed in Jesus, and we had gone out of our way to work well--with love and compassion and diligence--to set an example of work done to the glory of God. Dr. Johanes' actions did not send a good message to the village, and I was worried that he was ruining our rapport in the community and the reputation we had all worked hard to establish.

I went home that evening and asked God to help me to forgive him. Then I asked again, and I asked again. Each time I asked, I expected some wave of love and joy to wash over me, after which I would get up, go eat my rice, and go to bed content in my holiness. Yet each time I heard silence, and I felt resentment and anger sitting like an elephant on my heart. Then finally, after arguing this out with God for quite some time, I felt Him telling me I needed to honor Dr. Johanes.

Honor him? I wanted to kill him! How could I honor him?

Several days of taking this issue before God passed before I was truly able to forgive him, for in the beginning my heart was simply not sincere in the asking. On a theological level I knew that I was supposed to forgive, and I had wanted a quick fix to my distress. Saying a brief prayer had seemed sufficient, but it had done nothing to remove the bitterness in my heart. I began to see that forgiveness was going to have to translate into more than just words: thus God began urging me to actually honor the one who had offended me. Actively forgiving Dr. Johanes would require placing his best interests at heart and allowing God to love him through me, just as God continually offers me His mercy with my best interests at heart as well.

I needed to honor the man as my Christian brother, and I felt I needed to do so verbally to other people. So, begrudgingly at first, I began to speak to people of his good heart in wanting to come to the village, the job he had given up in the capital city to come to the tiny province, and his fine abilities as a surgeon. The more I did so--the more I verbally spoke affirmation about his life to others--the more I found myself able to focus on those things instead of the offense he had committed. Although I had never spoken badly about him in front of others, my choice to actively honor him in front of others melted away the anger in my heart.

Leadership had shown me that God was more interested in my holiness than my work for Him; learning to forgive was a baby step towards that holiness. God's strange answers to my prayers about Dr. Johanes proved to be tools for showing me I could not operate out of my own desires, and He graciously and patiently taught me several times over how important it is to forgive and love those in the body of Christ. This was a good lesson for me in the early days, and it was also one that I found repeated several times.

A Path of Forgiveness

I had prayed for a good group of people who loved Jesus to work together in the clinic. My own teammates had left, but the staff I hired was made up of Indonesian believers who had each moved to the province, as I had, to share the love of God with the people there. With this common purpose, I did not anticipate that there would be a lot of conflict amongst us. I was wrong. While each person who came to work with us had a genuinely loving and willing heart to serve, some of them were also genuinely difficult to deal with. Of course the same can often be said of me. They could be lazy, complaining, argumentative, impatient, unkind, unreliable, and uncooperative, and so can I. Some of them argued incessantly with each other, and I am apt to be argumentative as well. Conflicts will naturally arise when people are dealing with each other, for all of us are imperfect. I had longed for a stable and loyal staff that would show a consistent face of love to the village, but many of them came and went on a whim, sometimes leaving me with vacancies in critical positions. There were broken promises which had to be forgiven, behavior which had to be overlooked, and poor attitudes which had to be endured, and I regularly found myself thinking perhaps it would be easier to work with those outside the church rather than those within it. Yet all along, God pointed me toward multiple Biblical passages which speak of actively loving our brothers and sisters in Christ. It was not enough to simply forgive my staff members when conflict and uncomfortable situations arose: if I wanted to be like Jesus, I must also love them well.

I love to remain at peace with people in my life, and thankfully I cannot recall a lot of experiences in which I felt I was actively wronged, at odds with someone, or disliked. So my surprise and hurt were almost unbearable when an Indonesian physician who had come to help for a few months announced that he would soon be leaving, and he made it quite clear to others that it was because of me. He told them that I was arrogant, unhelpful, and not treating "real" patients anyway. To make matters worse, he never came directly to me with any of these issues, but instead spoke about them to other staff and to my teammates. I was crushed. At first I was angry with him for quickly abandoning our dear little village and for spreading malicious criticism of me to my friends, but sadness quickly overcame that anger. Later, after much soul searching and contemplation, I came to believe his problems actually had a lot more to do with jealousy over the favor I had as a foreign medical provider than with our relationship. His biting words, though, drove me to search my heart to try and see what was hidden inside.

I want to *be* holy, and I tell God that regularly. I could do without the process of *becoming* holy, however, for it is often painful when He shows me my sin. At that time, however, I willingly examined my heart, my words, and my actions towards this man who was a fellow believer in Jesus, for I was anxious to see how I may have wronged him, offended him, treated him poorly, or hurt him. I felt as if I had actually bent over backwards to help him adjust to the clinic and the village and to help the community accept him, so his apparent disdain for me cut even more deeply. The situations about which he criticized me had to do with my correcting his medical care, disciplining him for showing up late to work (or not at all) and other necessary management issues. So despite much reflection, I never did identify behavior that I feel was uncalled for or unreasonable. What I did find in my heart, though, surprised me: I uncovered thoughts and resentments towards him and his behavior that I had conveniently chosen to ignore and none of which were holy. God used this man's words to others to force me to look at the sin inside my own heart, and I was glad.

As He had with Dr. Johanes, I felt God encouraged me to seek active reconciliation with this doctor. It was far from easy. Thankfully I can say that I did it, though, obedient for once in plodding along the difficult path towards holiness, and we were able to talk through some of the issues between us before his departure. He still desired to return to the big city, breaking the agreement we had made for his work, but at least he eventually left on good terms. I was simultaneously disappointed and relieved: disappointed by knowing that I would be treating patients alone again after having had six weeks of greatly appreciated help, but relieved that the tension of the last few weeks was over. Through this process, in the midst of my hurt, God revealed Himself to me in His mercy, and He allowed me to show mercy to another. As I released him, I saw clearly that the ability to forgive another person brings incredible freedom.

Testing My Heart

After the experiences with Dr. Johanes, the staff, and the physician who left, I thought I had learned a lot about forgiveness. My greatest test, though, was yet to come, when money disappeared under the table at the hands of a fellow Christian. Our second year of cataract surgery had arrived, and we were all excited to see how God was again going to heal and bring sight to the blind in our communities. The prior year we had set aside a good amount of money--around $3000 US—to use for another surgical week, and it had been entrusted to the care of a partner agency's leader. All of the staff of this agency professed to follow Jesus, and it never occurred to us that our money would not be safely stored for the year. After all, we all had the same vision to show the love of Jesus in this region.

That may have been so, but certain people had other ministry visions which required money as well. We discovered that the money which had been set aside for our surgeries had mysteriously been diverted in other directions, not all of which were ever completely explained, and we were told that we would have to raise the money again in order to fund the operations. I had already had money stolen several times from my house and handbag--minor offenses that were annoying but easy enough to forgive--but this was shocking. Using our ministry money for other purposes, however good they may have been, amounted to major theft in my mind, and it was happening through people who served God. To add insult to injury, the month of conversations that ensued over the money's whereabouts involved multiple attempts to cover up the transgression and blame it on other people. Each offense added to the hurt I felt inside, and when my anger finally subsided, I felt a sense of sadness and defeat. How could I love people who appeared to be taking money from poor people in the villages? How could I forgive them if they never even admitted their fault?

God does work things out according to His plan, and He wanted the surgeries to happen. He provided in other ways for the finances (as I should have expected He would), and the second glorious week of free operations restored sight to many people. My own process of gaining clearer vision, though, was not as instantaneous as that of my surgical patients. I wanted to see God's providence, or at least redemption, in the events of the previous weeks, but I was still looking at the situation through a haze of frustration, resentment and judgment. Then again God whispered into my heart that I needed to actively honor those who had hurt me.

"Really, God?" I thought. "This *again*?"

God had encouraged a work of forgiveness in me in the smaller issues I had already faced, but this seemed much bigger and more difficult. It was not going to be easy to let go of the resentment I felt toward the leaders who had taken our money and never admitted it.

God does not love us only when we are loveable, nor does He forgive us only when we ask for forgiveness. Even with His dying breath, Jesus asked God to forgive those who had wronged Him, although they had not admitted their wrong. Every day I know that I, too, personally walk in a multitude of sins, some of which I notice and confess but many of which I don't. Through this time of struggling with the issue of stolen money, God (who judges not only actions but thoughts and intentions in my heart) gently showed me how deeply my offenses run yet how rarely I ask forgiveness for many of them. Despite that, His mercies continue to be new to me every morning, and He faithfully forgives. I am so, so grateful for that! If I were forgiven only of the things for which I ask forgiveness, I would long ago have been condemned to an eternity of darkness. So if His mercies are truly so sweeping and broad, must not mine be the same for those who wrong me?

I never repeated any grades in school, but in God's academy I have repeated several. So I walked this forgiveness lesson out yet again, choosing to actively honor my offenders with words and love, and freedom again came to my spirit. Then an amazing thing happened. About two months after everything had taken place, I was called to a meeting with the head of the agency. I was a bit worried, for I was not quite sure that the forgiveness I had offered verbally had yet taken root in my heart. During those two months I had spoken on several occasions to others about the good character and service of the leaders who had been involved, and I had asked God to help me to love them. Seeing them face to face would test the sincerity of those prayers.

To my surprise, when I entered the meeting and sat down, I found that I *did* love them. I felt freedom. Gone was any desire for rebuke or harsh words: I did not even feel a need for them to express apologies. The incident was not spoken of at all, in fact. Instead, we passed a pleasant hour discussing other ministry plans and inquiring after one another's well being. I found that I honestly cared about their interests and desired God's best plan for them. Judging their actions was God's responsibility, so I chose to let it belong to Him. My responsibility was to love and serve these men as fellow Christians, and that was enough. It is amazing what freedom comes when we do what God calls us to do and let Him do what He alone is able to do!

Outside of the work God was doing in my heart as a result of forgiving, there was a greater good in all of these circumstances. The world is always going to have a difficult time believing in a loving God if His followers cannot get along with each other, and the Bible points out that "the world will know you by your love for each other" (John 13:35). When I made a choice to start speaking words of affirmation over my fellow believers, both to those in the church and those outside, it was noticed. I overheard patients discussing how our clinic staff and the two agencies worked so well together, and they noticed that several different nationalities were cooperating without a conflict. It was so nice to see, they said, and they thought that we all must love each other very much. I almost laughed out loud one day when a patient asked me how big our house was, for she thought we all lived together somewhere in the city. She assumed the Indonesian staff members were all related to each other and all the foreigners must be family, too, and maybe we were all related somehow by marriage. Otherwise, she asked, how could we all like each other so much?

The image that woman saw is that of the family of God--a unified group of people who love each other because they love their heavenly Father--and it is an image I want to see reflected around the world. If I am to be a part of that reflection, I know I will be faced with many more circumstances in which I have to actively choose to forgive, overlook, and love those who make up this large family, for each of us is a highly flawed individual. God is showing me my own flaws each day and graciously, patiently, and faithfully rubbing them out of my character. I trust He is doing the same with other people. In the future, I hope I will remain content to step away and allow Him do His work in their hearts and to step forward and let Him do miracles in mine.

CHAPTER Twenty-Two:
Waiting

I am not good at waiting. I don't like to wait in lines, I don't like to wait for people to call me back, and I most definitely do not like to wait for people to get out of my way on the interstate. I am not exactly sure why I am so impatient; perhaps I think that something important is just going to pass me by someday. Although God has gradually been trying to teach me patience, it has never been one of my stronger character traits.

Habakkuk 2:3 says, "If the vision tarries you must wait for it." My inherently impatient nature makes carrying a long term vision very difficult, for I want to set a goal, accomplish it, and see results *now*. Yet sometimes God wants me to wait, and such was the case in the entire process of my moving overseas. The day I set foot in Indonesia was actually the fulfillment of a ten year vision --ten years of working, praying, dreaming, and planning which required a phenomenally abnormal degree of patience for me. The journey had been long, but in every step of the way God had showed Himself faithful. He knows, I think, how difficult long term trust can be for me, and He allowed me to see smaller goals met and visions fulfilled along the way so that the wait did not seem so long.

From the time the dream in my heart to serve the world through medical practice was born, I had to wait a year and a half to begin my training. During this time, I enjoyed pouring myself into the lives of high school students while teaching, so that first waiting period passed fairly quickly. The next season of my life, the time waiting to get through medical training, really never felt much like a wait at all. Rather, the two and a half years of intensive study felt more like a course in daily survival. This season passed extremely quickly, except for the occasional day I'd spend waiting on lab results at a government hospital. Those days individually each felt like a thousand years.

After my medical training was completed, waiting to move overseas while paying off my loans became a bit more difficult. Changing jobs every few years in order to obtain a different skill set provided enough variety to prevent my becoming too bored, and God was very faithful to continually remind me why I was going through this season of life. My eyes never really left the third world, despite living very much in the first, and annual trips overseas helped to refine and encourage the vision He had placed in my heart enough to keep me going. I counted down the years, then the months, then the days of paying off the loans that had financed my education, and I eagerly ripped open the statement every month and immediately slipped a check back in the mail. Waiting thirty days for the next loan statement and knowing that each one brought me a step closer to my goal of leaving the country was a lot easier than waiting for something to happen in four more years. Patience is encouraged by celebrating small victories.

One of my life's goals is to be able to rest daily in God's deep and abiding peace while waiting for His purposes to unfold. I wish I could say that playing this waiting game had developed a high level of patience in me by the time I actually arrived overseas, but I cannot. Although I may have inched toward that goal, I was still far from achieving it. God still had plenty of work to do in my spirit in this area, and day to day waiting was still hard for me.

However, the ten year process of God bringing me to Indonesia *had* succeeded in making me very aware of how perfect His timing is for a long term vision. The journey would not have been complete--my skills not sharpened enough, my heart not ready enough, my vision not refined enough, my knowledge not deep enough--without each step I had taken in that long waiting process. I was astounded by how the puzzle pieces fit together so perfectly. So I was becoming more willing to trust God's plan for the unseen by the time I arrived, for I saw how He had guided my steps so intricately at each point along the way. Each moment had a purpose in leading me to fulfill the vision He had laid before me, and understanding that made my faith in His providence soar. Then, as if that were not enough, God taught me to trust His dreams by fulfilling another vision I had forgotten He had ever given to me.

The Timing of Dreams

Reel back the film of my life ten years to the first time I traveled overseas for ministry. As an eager young college graduate with the world at my fingertips, I boarded a plane for Bangkok, Thailand, along with a nervous and excited group of twenty four middle and high school students whose parents were silly enough to entrust them into my care. Talk about a leap of faith! We were to spend the next five weeks ministering in the streets and schools of Bangkok, performing drama presentations about God's love and trying to meet felt needs wherever possible. That entire trip was pivotal in helping to define my path and life vision, for there I was brought face to face for the first time with people who had absolutely no knowledge of Jesus. Immediately I knew my life would be marked by trying to change that. God instilled many dreams into my heart throughout that trip that would last for years to come, starting with a powerful one the night before we even left the US.

At that point in my life, having truly sought after God for only a few short years, I was not entirely sold on the idea of miraculous healing, supernatural deliverance, prophecy, or other seemingly strange tenets of the faith. It wasn't that I *didn't* believe them; I just rarely had been exposed to them. Admittedly, I was not entirely tuned in when the speaker at our commissioning service referenced praying for people for healing, trusting God for the supernatural, or anything of the sort. I was much more intently focused on praying that God would allow me to survive this crazy thing I had gotten myself into, as well as not letting any of my young charges be injured in the process.

The Holy Spirit whispers softly sometimes and at other times shouts very loudly. I honestly don't remember how it was that He spoke to me that evening, but I do know that sometime during worship a thought was impressed strongly enough upon me that I was inclined to write in my journal: that I would make blind eyes see.

"Excuse me? I will make blind eyes see, God?" I pondered this from my seat as the worship time continued. "What is that about, God? I just want to go to Thailand and do some drama presentations, hang out with some teenagers and disciple them into knowing Jesus better, and let the Thai people know that they are loved. Making blind eyes see? Hmm."

At this point in my life I had never entertained thoughts of practicing medicine. In fact, I held a fairly strong conviction that I did *not* want to practice medicine. The training seemed too long, too intense, and possibly too boring, and it was not in my plans for the future. So bringing sight to the blind, as nice as it sounded, had never been one of my basic life goals. Since I was not yet well versed in the supernatural ways God works, I was not sure about praying for people to receive their sight, either. However, I never wanted to argue with something that I thought God may be speaking to me, and the impression sat strongly enough on my heart to make me write it down in my journal. I prayed about it for a few days afterwards, then I filed it away in the recesses of my memory. Once in Bangkok, I actually prayed for a few blind people on the street, half- heartedly and without effect, but mostly I focused my mind on other things. The note in my journal was dated June of 1997.

Throughout the next few years, God taught me a lot about healing, and I began to pray for people more actively and with increasing faith. Brief notes in my journals during those years show that God occasionally reminded me of the strong impression that I would make blind eyes see. Well, *He* would be the One to make them see, of course--but there was an idea that somehow I would be involved with it. The vision never consumed much of my daily thinking, but when it recurred I would try to pray about it for a little while. Then I quickly moved on to the next thing in life. At one point I journaled that I was not sure why I kept having this crazy thought about blind people. After all, aside from those few people on the streets of Thailand, I had never even met anyone who was blind! I finally decided that the whole thing must be a metaphor for God wanting me to help people see past their spiritual blindness, for nothing was happening in the physical realm. The whole idea seemed a bit outrageous to me anyway, even after I ventured into the world of medicine.

The next part of Habakkuk 2:3 speaks of the vision having an "appointed time." I am so glad that God's appointed times are better planned than mine, but I definitely wish I was more patient in waiting for them. He will fulfill His purposes regardless of my faith--or lack thereof--but I miss a lot of joy in watching Him work when I become too impatient. God is busy orchestrating events in the world in order to redeem and restore all people to Himself through Jesus, and He is not particularly interested in my timelines. He is, however, very interested in reminding me that He is in control.

By the time I set foot on Indonesian soil, it was ten years since I had first felt the Holy Spirit's promptings about sight. Yet when Bapak Abu took off his eye bandage after his first surgery, my vision--which was really *God's* vision--found its appointed time. It had tarried for ten long years, and I had, somewhat unknowingly, waited that long for it. The tears I cried that day were certainly tears of joy for this precious man and the many others who received their sight. I could not imagine what greater gift could have been given to them, and I was overwhelmingly grateful to participate in this life changing experience. Yet the tears I cried were ones of joyful repentance, as well.

"You will make blind eyes see. Remember?" I heard the Holy Spirit's gentle whisper that very instant. I had not remembered. In fact, I had all but forgotten, until that moment, the deeply buried dream.

"I told you that you would make blind eyes see. And look what I did through you!" These startling words resonated in the core of my heart.

Where oh where had my faith been to believe this? Why had it not withstood the tests of passing time and unfulfilled desires? As I stood there and watched Bapak Abu look around the room, seeing things for the first time, I was stunned into humble silence. God's plan all along had been to make *this* man--Bapak Abu--see. I could barely wrap my mind around the idea. I had not been crazy, after all, when I first thought God spoke to me that night long ago, but I had allowed time's passage and my waxing and waning faith to rub the edges off of the vision. How incredible was it, I thought, that the appointed time for that vision was *now*, ten years after it had been revealed, and I had been forced to wait for it. What a glorious fulfillment it was! Never in my wildest dreams could I have imagined that the vision of making blind eyes see would be fulfilled through my hands orchestrating surgery for, not just one, but over one hundred patients, in a tiny village clinic in the middle of nowhere on an island in Indonesia.

God's plans for us are so much bigger and better than we imagine. As I asked forgiveness for my lack of faith that day, He sweetly reminded me that it brings Him joy to redeem the hurts of the world through His servants. We can trust that the dreams He gives to us, however outrageous they may seem, will be fulfilled in order to heal, restore, and reconcile people to the God who loves them. The vision God gave to me in 1997 was about Bapak Abu receiving his sight, for He loves that man and the others who were healed with a depth I cannot ever comprehend. The vision was also about my learning to trust, to be patient, and to believe that my God will fulfill all things in their appointed time. This powerful illustration of a loving God at work continues to challenge and encourage me, and He reminds me of it quite often. For I have other dreams that God has given me which are yet to be fulfilled, and I am still woefully impatient to see them come to pass. Each time I look at Bapak Abu's smiling picture, however, I am learning to trust a little bit more and find the waiting is not quite so hard.

Still Waiting

When a ladies sewing class was first formed in the village, I was delighted. The twelve participants, chosen by the village leader's wife as responsible and dedicated community members, began to gather weekly to receive sewing lessons from one of my friends. Her intention was to eventually market the goods they learned to sew and to help them start small businesses. I was very excited and curious about the whole venture, so I would often pop my head into their gatherings to see what was happening. Sadly I never learned to sew a stitch, but it did not take long before going to the classes became one of the highlights of my week.

These ladies were lively, fun, loving, chatty, friendly, and patient with the foreigner among them, and they were always full of joy. Even to this day I don't know all of their names, for half of them I called by the all encompassing feminine address of "Ibu." Despite not knowing this personal detail (which is not nearly as important in Indonesian culture as it is in the West), I quickly began to truly love and value these women. They were intelligent, creative, loving individuals who had distinctly different personalities; as I watched them and talked with them I noticed how they were already gifted and molded to be leaders in their community. Some of them maintained a status of influence by virtue of their marriage, but most of them had earned their standing as community leaders by their genteel natures, selfless attitudes, and integrity. In the group was Amina, who could charm a snake with her sweet smile, and Miriam, who had a gift of giving that was unparalleled. Rohana could keep us in stitches for hours with her jokes and teasing: she did so one memorable day by explaining in great detail why I should not marry someone with a moustache because of how itchy it would be to kiss him. Karina, the ornery, older single woman who had initially declared me a "stupid doctor" for my failure to give her enough pills, always asked me to give her things: my scarf, watch, bracelet, or anything else her keen eye saw that I was wearing that day. I never gave any of them to her, but she smiled and let me sit with her anyway. The leader's wife Fauziah was gentle and kind, and she always patiently listened to the concerns of others and tried to offer wise counsel. Each lady was gifted in her own unique ways.

The Bible teaches that we, as God's workmanship, are created by Him for good works which He prepared in advance for us to do (Ephesians 2:10). I often thought that God was preparing these women to be amongst those who were building His Kingdom, for each of them had an influential voice and a generous heart that desired to see life renewed in her village. These twelve ladies (a suspiciously familiar number for possible disciples) already sat uniquely poised to change their community, and I prayed it would one day be change stemming from the influence of Jesus.

Since I spent a lot of time with the women and knew them better than I did most other villagers, I was not surprised when I had a dream about them. I awoke that night with a song in my heart, and the memory of the dream was strong and vividly clear in my mind. As I quickly wrote it down in order to not forget, I could not keep from smiling at the scene that repeated in my head. In the dream, the ladies were sitting in their circle, sewing and chatting as they always did, while their laughter interspersed with gossip about who was struggling with certain things in the village. This scene was played out nearly every day in real life, so it was not unique in itself. After some time, however, the atmosphere in the room changed, and what happened next was different than anything I had ever seen. While their hands flew nimbly over fabric that passed beneath their scissors and needles, the women began listening to a story. The story was about a wonderful man--a man so wonderful, in fact, that He provided healing for all the sick, raised the dead, delivered people from oppression, and placed needy people on thrones with princes. The story was about Jesus, and they were enraptured with it. When it was over, they spoke about how this story, like the others they had heard about Jesus, added to their love for Him, and they talked about the good news of salvation He brought. They happily exclaimed how the prayers they prayed were being answered in ways they never had before. They spoke about how glad they were to have become followers of this Jesus, how He had transformed their lives, and how glad they were that they could share His good news with many of the other village women.

"Ibu Miriam prayed the other day to become a follower of Jesus," smiled Halima, stitching as she talked. "She is filled now with so much joy."

"Yes," said Rohana, "And isn't it great how Bapak Iskandar's son was healed when we prayed in the name of Jesus for him? He is so good to us."

The dream went on for some time more, but the essence of it remained the same: these beautiful women had met Jesus, been filled with the Holy Spirit of God, and were rejoicing in Him. The scene was so vivid in my mind that I could almost tangibly feel the sense of joy and anticipation in the room when I awoke. It gave me chills.

I have not seen that dream come true. In fact, I saw very little response at all from most of these ladies any time an issue of faith was brought up. Yet I believe, as surely as I believe that I am breathing, that this dream came from God. I would love to have seen it played out while I lived amongst the women: to take part in their conversations, to hear the excitement in their voices, and to watch them enjoying the glorious discovery process of learning who God truly is. The dream belongs to God, however, not to me, and He must bring it to pass when His appointed time has come.

Since I left the country, I have heard reports from friends that two of the ladies have actually begun to ask questions about Jesus. That news brings me hope. Even greater hope comes from the fact that I know God loves each of these women, and He alone is able to draw them into a relationship with Himself. Perhaps someday I will return and be able to sit and tell Jesus stories with them, and I can tell them at that time about the dream that I once had. I would simply love to do that. In the meantime, I will continue to pray for the dream to be fulfilled, asking God to increase my faith and vision along the way. After all, I learned to be patient and to wait on God while waiting for blind eyes to see. Thankfully He is ever patient in waiting on me.

Still Waiting for Ria

Ria's lack of healing, and actually her whole situation, are still somewhat of a mystery to me. I cannot rationally explain why God has not yet healed her knee. I have prayed and cried, and I have asked for increased faith. I have proclaimed Bible passages over her and claimed healing in Jesus' name, and I have fasted, wept and stood with many others around the world in asking for this to be accomplished. Yet still she limps. As dumbfounded as I am by the physical healing I do not see, I am even more confused about why Ria's spiritual growth seems to have reached a plateau. I had wanted to leave the country having made a disciple--someone who was following Jesus, trusting His promises, and learning to walk by faith. I expected this disciple to be physically walking as well. In actuality, though, I left a dear friend who is still crippled, struggling to walk with braces and special shoes, and dealing with daily pain as she moves through the halls of the hospital. I left a genuine woman of faith who is seeking in the best way she knows to follow the God she believes is true; I also left a friend who is missing the integral piece of knowing God through Jesus.

I believe Ria will be healed. Call it naiveté, call it silliness or call it wishful thinking. Call it what you will, but I believe it. I believe that the Biblical story of the lame man who dances (Acts 3) is her story, and I have told her so. I read and re-read that story prior to moving to Indonesia, and I told many people that it was the dream in my heart: to see the lame person who had been healed walking and leaping and praising God. That is still my dream, only now I think it is also Ria's dream. She just does not know it yet.

Why else would this young woman dive eagerly across the bed and reach to see the Word of God? Why else would she later want to sit and study the Bible with me, placing post-it notes filled with well thought out questions all over it in a genuine search for truth? Why would this lady, unlike most of the local doctors who tried to leave the province for bigger cities and more money, have a passionate desire to return to her village and serve the poor in medicine, if it was not placed in her by the Spirit of God? Why would we have crossed paths with each other at all, and why indeed would she have been ministered to through the years by not just me, but no less than eight others who follow Jesus? I no longer believe in coincidences, but thankfully I do believe more in the faith building process of waiting.

Leaving Ria without seeing her healed or truly knowing Jesus was one of the hardest emotional experiences I have ever had. Yet I must be willing to entrust her to the hands of the God who loves her a thousand times more than I do. How was I ever going to be the one to heal her, anyway? All of my best efforts, despite how generous and eager they had been, had failed. Likewise, how could anything I said regarding Jesus ever convince her of His truth more than the Holy Spirit working on her heart could? The vision tarries, and yet I must wait for it. God, who is ultimately good and infinitely patient, helps me to do so.

CHAPTER Twenty-Three:
To See Clearly

It is the Holy Spirit who draws people to God. I know this, but all too often I am tempted to believe that I have something to do with it. Then God decides to remind me otherwise, in a humbling but often delightful way. Such was the case with Ika.

Ika and I spent a lot of time together in social settings. She declared herself my personal tour guide around the city, and we frequently took day trips to the beach. She taught me to cook local food (or at least tried to!), and we also visited every roadside food stall in a ten kilometer radius. She threw me an incredible birthday party, and we celebrated most national holidays together. She was remarkably easy to be around, and we always enjoyed talking, laughing and simply enjoying life together. Ninety percent of the time these outings included Ria or another friend, too, so it was rare that Ika and I were alone. As a result, our conversations never went very deep.

I tried periodically to engage Ika in conversation about God, but most of the time her one or two word responses did little to encourage me to probe further. Whereas Ria jumped at opportunities to talk about matters of faith, Ika seemed to live behind an unidentifiable spiritual barrier that I could not quite penetrate. I never felt I was sharing my love for God with her in a significant way, and she, to my perceptions, did not seem to care. On the few occasions when we did talk about the basic differences in our respective faiths, she responded with the surprising declaration that all religions are basically the same. I think this was her way of trying politely to end the conversation, for I knew good and well that she did not really believe it. Despite the appearance of disinterest in discussing her faith, her lifestyle showed me she was fairly devout in its practice. Perhaps saying that many paths could lead to heaven was an easier response than her trying to change my mind.

As I was preparing to leave the country, I was busy packing and saying too many goodbyes. I was also busy feeling discouraged that Ria seemed to have backtracked spiritually, and I certainly had never felt encouraged about Ika's spiritual growth in any way. God really loves to surprise me, I think, and He startled me out of this sadness in a completely unexpected way. I sometimes marvel at my own foolishness, wondering if I will ever cease being surprised by God when He simply acts according to His good and faithful character. Then again, a sense of normalcy would take some of the fun out of His surprises.

It is considered rude to not give people gifts when you leave Indonesia. In contrast to the West, where the traveler is given a souvenir or parting gift from friends, in Indonesia the person who leaves is the gift giver. That individual is fully expected and often even asked to leave behind mementos for those with whom she is close--and sometimes even for those with whom she is not. When my roommate was preparing to leave the country, a neighbor actually came over and started walking out the door with one of her lamps. The woman stated very matter of factly that the lamp *would* be her parting gift from my friend! In my case I was happy to leave things behind for those whose friendship I cherished, and I tried to carefully choose things that would be significant for each person. Ika's interests were so simple and immaterial, though, that I was having difficulty thinking of a gift that would be special for her. Finally I settled on a few pretty head scarves, thinking that at least I could give her something she needed. I planned to give them to her on our upcoming beach outing when I said my goodbyes.

The night before our trip, I awoke with the distinct impression that I should give Ika a New Testament. I was not at all sure that this was a very good idea, so I began to argue with God about it.

"God, Ika has never shown any interest *at all* in Jesus or much of anything spiritual when we talk. Why would I give her that?"

He nudged me again to give her His Word.

"God, she is going to think I am crazy! Isn't it bad timing and a bad idea just to give her part of the Bible and leave her with no one to follow up? Besides, she seriously does not care. I know that she won't read it!"

The Holy Spirit nudged me again, and the thought would not go away. I could not sleep well for the rest of the night, so I resigned myself to wrap up the New Testament and give it to Ika the next day. I had little hope of her ever reading it since I had never seen more than a flicker of spiritual concern in her eyes, but I could not ignore the persistent voice in my head that told me to do it anyway. I sighed, prayed, and wrote her a note explaining that the Book I was giving her told stories of Jesus.

Gift giving, although expected, was not usually done with a lot of fanfare. So I waited to give Ika her gifts until she exited the car, and she accepted a small bag holding the scarves, New Testament, and my note through the window. We had already exchanged a few tears and hugs at the beach, and it seemed easiest to let the final goodbye be brief. I handed her the bag, took a long last look at my friend, and drove off with mist-filled eyes. I did not expect to ever hear from her again, and three days later I would be on a plane out of the country.

The following morning I was awakened by a beep on my phone telling me that I had a text message. Loosely translated, the message from Ika said this: "Hadik (little sister), thank you for the wonderful gift. The Book is the best gift anyone has ever given to me, and I stayed up half the night reading it." I bolted upright, suddenly very awake.

I returned a text to her: "Ika, I am glad you like the Book. It is precious to me, and I hope you read it all. The stories about Jesus are wonderful."

Immediately her reply came through: "Yes, I know they are. For a very long time I have wanted to see this Book, and I am so happy now that you gave it to me. It is definitely the best gift I have ever received, and I will try to finish reading it all very soon."

Messages flew back and forth in a similar fashion for some time, culminating in her asking me for a copy of the entire Bible in her language. As it turns out, Ika had previously been friends with a girl from another island who was a follower of Jesus. This friend had visited her once and brought her a Bible, but two days later it had been washed away in a flood. Ever since then Ika had been very curious and wanted a Bible of her own: she was spiritually hungry to know the truth. *Why* she had never mentioned this to me or asked me for a copy I have no idea, for she had certainly known for almost two years that I followed Jesus as well. I was suddenly horribly ashamed of both my pride and my lack of faith. While I had been busy berating myself for not doing a good enough "job" with her to make her interested in Jesus, the Holy Spirit had been busy preparing her heart.

We talked on the phone for a little while later that day, and I left the complete Bible with Uli to give to Ika a few days later. I was awed at the powerful and yet mysterious leading of the Holy Spirit, and I was overjoyed that my perceptions about her lack of receptivity had been wrong. That day I began to pray in earnest that the Word of God would convict and lead her. Although I still did not expect to hear from her again, I left with a deep peace in my heart that Ika was on the path to finding truth.

A month later, she sent me an email. When I left she had told me that she did not use email, but something had changed her mind. Her message asked me how I was doing back home and told me that nothing much was new there. Then "oh by the way," it said, she was spending all her free time reading the Bible.

What?

Once again, for some reason I was surprised by God simply doing what He does. He had been continually leading Ika on a quest for truth, and she asked a lot of difficult and thoughtful questions in that email and in several that followed. Her genuine desire for understanding established once and for all in my mind that God had her in His grip. She was well on the way to seeing and believing His grace.

As Ika and I continued to communicate a few more times, it dawned on me how little of reality I ever truly see. I had spent so much time pouring spiritually into Ria, thinking I was seeing interest and hope in her eyes, and I had let Ika fall by the wayside. I had operated with more direction, more energy, and more conviction around someone for whom I thought I may be making a difference while forgetting that it is only God who can really make a difference for anyone. When Ika had appeared hopelessly out of my range of influence, I had little faith to believe. Had I looked through the eyes of faith, I could have seen God working all along.

I am delighted for Ika and the journey she is on. I was encouraged to be able to leave my beloved second home on such a hopeful note, and I was reminded on those final days of my journey that my sight is still far from perfect. I thought that I had developed eyes of faith during the time I spent overseas--eyes that saw God purely, and eyes that saw into the spiritual realm beyond the world around me. This was true, to an extent, but God reminded me ever so gently through the experience with Ika that He is not finished with me yet. He certainly had already done much to strip the self-imposed blinders off of my eyes, and He had allowed me to see His character more distinctly day by day. He had focused my vision on His glory with a much greater degree of clarity, allowing me to look past much of what I saw in the circumstances around me. He had given me lenses of trust that magnified His goodness and faithfulness, and I chose to wear them more often than I had before. Yet, despite all that God had done to improve my vision, I still had failed to see what was right in front of me in Ika. I hold onto hope, though, in knowing that He has much more in store for me in the days ahead.

I know my sight is not yet perfect, nor will it ever be this side of heaven. God has promised, however, that the path of the righteous will shine brighter and brighter until the light of full day (Proverbs 4:18), so I trust that He will continue to adjust my vision incrementally in accordance with His perfect plan. He tells me in His Word that although I see but dimly now, one day I will see clearly and see Him face to face (1 Corinthians 13:12). In the meantime, I try to be patient and enjoy the journey.

For every adjustment God has made to my sight thus far, however small, has allowed me to see more of His beautiful truth and more of His glory. Already full and complete, this glory has no need to change or grow. The degree of it which I can see, however, grows day by day. Every time my eyes have been opened further or my vision made clearer by the Holy Spirit, the effect has been stunning.

I simply cannot wait to see what is next.

To order more copies of "Degrees of Sight," or
to email the author, visit
www.degreesofsight.blogspot.com